AT THE HEART OF DARKNESS
WITCHCRAFT, BLACK MAGIC AND SATANISM TODAY

D1561698

AT THE HEART
— OF —
DARKNESS

*Witchcraft, Black Magic
and Satanism Today*

JOHN PARKER

A CITADEL PRESS BOOK
Published by Carol Publishing Group

CONTENTS

CONTENTS

PART THREE
SATANISM
235

INTRODUCTION

As you read this, a witch coven or secret society in your town or village is perhaps engaged in ritual practice. They may be naked, or in sinister robes. They may be white witches or black magicians. They may even be your friends. They will be alert to strangers and will maintain utmost secrecy. And with very good reason . . .

The deeply emotive allegations of satanic ritual abuse became the in-topic of the late eighties, especially among social workers and child-care organizations. Dark and evil practices were thought to be rife in suburban and rural Britain, just as they were alleged to be in the United States on a much greater scale. A series of high-level conferences was arranged under the auspices of various Christian and medical organizations who brought out one speaker after another, from home and abroad, to give confirmation of the atrocities committed in the name of the devil, giving rise to such tabloid headlines as 'Rape Hell in Satan's Coven'; 'I Skinned My Baby For Satan' and 'Satan Pervs Eat Babies'. This sort of press reaction was not in the least unjustified *if* the speakers were to be believed. But alarming figures and statements were being reported in the newspapers without qualification because the stories emanated from 'experts'. No evidence was offered and it all took on the hue and cry of a witch-hunt of the kind not seen since the eighteenth century.

One of the speakers at a conference on Incest and Related Problems, co-organized by a Harley Street psychotherapist, was billed as a 'survivor' of satanic abuse, now engaged in counselling others. She said she received ten helpline calls each week from fellow survivors and stated that fifty cases she had dealt with involved cannibalism. She said human foetuses were being killed and eaten by satanic sex rings; that children were hung up by their feet and suspended over electric saws; that they suffered all kinds of sexual depravity including rape, buggery and bestiality.

The conference, attended by therapists, psychiatrists, social workers and others, ran for three days and naturally achieved a great deal of publicity. A psychotherapist said there were an estimated 10,000 human sacrifices in America each year, most of them of foetuses bred especially for the purpose. It was happening in Britain on a smaller scale.

By then, the hue and cry was in full flow, boosted by publicity, aided by evangelical groups and American anti-satanic lobbyists who dismissed suggestions of gross exaggeration and myth, arguing that lack of evidence merely showed the cleverness of the perpetrators. Such outrages, even on a small scale, would naturally be sufficient to arouse public indignation and attention from the authorities.

But there is a stark statistic which emerged from these allegations. In Britain and America between 1985 and 1991, well over 10,000 cases of such alleged ritual abuse were investigated. Thousands of man hours involving police and social workers were expended, thousands of children largely under the age of eight were subjected to the trauma of being questioned about devils and ghosts and snakes and horrible things. But at the end of the day only *four* known cases where ritual abuse was specifically on the charge sheet were brought to court – and two of those failed.

One case in America involving a hundred children took seven years to bring to court, cost £8 million to prosecute and one of the defendants who was refused bail spent five years in prison. At the end of the day, the case was withdrawn. Meanwhile, in Britain dozens of children were taken from their homes while social workers investigated all kinds of horrific allegations which, had the laws of the sixteenth century still prevailed, would have meant the mass execution of parents on charges of witchcraft. It was Salem, *The Crucible* and the witch-hunt all over again, except that no charges were laid, no arrests were made – except in one case where the police refused to include any reference to satanic abuse in their evidence. On the face of it the whole business was so inconclusive in terms of actual evidence of devilish goings-on that it was natural to suppose such things did not really exist.

There remained, however, a lingering doubt about the claims of dastardly deeds on black altars in shrouded, incense-filled rooms, that the devil was still about, that witches were up to no good, that black magicians were still messing around in graveyards and defiling the dead.

So this is a journey of discovery, to try to find out some answers to some pressing questions about the occult. Fact, fiction, fallacy, rumour and mythology appear to have been merged into a new witch-hunt, and for once the word would be taken literally. The public at large was being asked to believe that all involved had but one aim – to corrupt and deprave all who came within their sphere as part of a menacing international conspiracy to promote the forces of darkness against Christian society.

In attempting to cut a path through what was once described as the marshes, forests and badlands of magic and superstition, I have separated this book into three sections in order to try to simplify the route towards understanding and reason, especially for the lay reader. This was necessary not least because of the great morass of beliefs and activities which persist today in the spectrum of interrelated occult subjects, but also for the reason that pagans and witches shudder at the prospect of being mentioned in the same breath as satanists.

Similarly, occultists who are members of the serious and often complicated cults and lodges of ritual magic and mysticism, or who embrace a voluminous number of secret societies made up of academics and students of esoteric teachings, would feel insulted to be attached in any way to either of these movements. Therefore, I will look first at witchcraft, revealing current trends and its leading participants; secondly, I will examine a selection of other occult groups and beliefs; thirdly, I report on my investigations into satanism. Lastly, as an appendix, I will list the worldwide organizations and occult media which now exist in what is a very, very big industry.

What links them all, for good or evil, is the exploration of the paranormal abilities of the human mind, the belief that the mystique and magic into which serious occultists immerse them-selves is a natural human faculty and can be developed like any other faculty. It is as controversial as it sounds, especially since Christianity has attempted to impose the view that all magic is black magic, and that the power source is the devil himself, aided by the demons he dispatches to the side of all those who call down these powers. Meanwhile, most satanic worshippers have other views which are largely committed to a total reversion of Christian values. What I now set out is the result of many months of research and more than 120 interviews with occultists at all levels.

I have also included intermittent excursions into the past to discover the original settings, because it is a crucial element in understanding what transpired in the twentieth century and how ancient beliefs have been researched and repackaged as the rule of law for activities that are without question practised in abundance today.

John Parker,
March 1992.

PART ONE

THE CRAFT
OF THE WISE

Witchcraft is described by its elders as a religion and is officially recognized as such in America. British witches who support this school of thought prefer to call themselves pagans. They claim that their roots are in the old religions of pre-Christian times and are derived basically from the ancient nature and fertility rites of the original pagan mystery religions which were outlawed and went underground in the third century AD under pressure from Christianity. In spite of purges and persecution through the ages, knowledge of the 'old ways' is said by its supporters to have been retained through oral tradition, handed down within families, and confirmed by the salvage of written evidence. This historic justification is in fact a rather romantic notion. Modern witchcraft as practised in most-covens is basically the creation of one man, who called heavily on the researched practices, legends and superstitions of the past.

Witches, men and women, meet at the new and full moon and at festival times. They aim to put themselves in tune with natural forces and thus often work naked or naked within a robe. They believe it is within everyone's capacity, with teaching, to reach out and experience the Mystery; they believe it is possible for each individual to make contact with the deity they worship and invoke the spirit of that deity into their own bodies. Today pagans or white witches are not apprehensive about magic, because they do not connect it with the devil; they regard it as part of their religion. Their faith encompasses the teachings which encourage the development of second sight, extrasensory powers, clairvoyance, spirit communication and the like. They meet in small groups called covens and participate in creative experimentation within the agreed group structure.

Witchcraft cannot be a mass religion. The worship is conducted before an altar from within a sacred circle in which two main activities occur: the celebration of the Witches' Sabbats, involving ritual dancing and chanting, and the practice of magic. Their magic is not about pulling rabbits from a hat. It has been broadly defined as the art and science of using little-known natural powers to achieve changes in consciousness and in the physical environment, enabling contact with non-human entities. There are good witches and bad witches, black and white. There are also hereditary witches who operate alone.

CHAPTER ONE

THE POND

'To understand witchcraft', wrote Jeffrey Burton Russell in his acclaimed *Witchcraft in the Middle Ages*, 'we must descend into the darkness of the deepest oceans of the human mind.' It is a descent that is wrapped in mystery and the inexplicable, and what cannot be explained is feared. Fear may lead to hysteria and because of what has gone before in the persecution of their predecessors, this fear can become the nightmare of modern witches, if not of modern society. Not long ago, there was sufficient hysteria to inspire the fear that a twentieth-century witch-hunt was about to begin, encouraged by the claims of anti-occult groups, such as those I have discussed in the introduction, and supported by the Conservative MP and lay preacher Mr Geoffrey Dickens who sought in the House of Commons to reactivate the Witchcraft Act of 1735 – an act that had finally been laid to rest in 1951. He tabled an amendment to the Criminal Justices Bill, seeking to make it illegal for any person under eighteen to join or participate in any secret occult ceremonies or groups.

His attempt, branded by occultists as repressive, was not admitted on the grounds that it was beyond the scope of the new Bill. But by raising the issue at the highest level in the land Mr Dickens gave credence to the view of the witches themselves, that witchcraft is not the bizarre and unimportant hobby of a mere handful of cranks – a claim to which I can now testify. It clearly is not. Mr Christopher Bray, one of the country's largest purveyors of equipment to the occult world – whom I will discuss later – stated that he has 40,000 customers recorded on his computerized records, to whom he can supply everything from two grams of bat's blood to a complete altar set for the most complicated of occult rituals.

Stewart Farrar, one of the most famous of British practising witches, a former Fleet Street journalist and prolific author and lecturer on both sides of the Atlantic, says, 'Modern witchcraft in Europe and America is a fact. It is no longer an underground relic of which the scale and even the existence is hotly disputed by anthropologists. It is an active religious practice of a substantial number of people. Just how large a number is not certain because Wicca, beyond the individual coven, is not a hierarchically organized religion. But the numbers are sufficient to support a variety of lively periodicals and the publication of an ever-growing body of literature. All the evidence suggests it is growing steadily.'

Best estimates put the number of practising witches in Britain at a figure in excess of 250,000. This does not include practitioners in other fields of the occult nor the many thousands of pagans who do not pursue witchcraft but use the basic study of the old religions as their spiritual base.

In trying to assess this claimed importance of witchcraft and the official line of the Wiccan elders that theirs is a definite religion, I was struck by another problem. Because of the lack of any formal structure, the whole movement appears so fragmented and loose in its form of worship, that I could not see how it could be pulled together and arranged under the one heading by which they now wish to be known, that of Pagans with a capital 'P'.

Another difficulty in forming an understandable perception of this 'religion' is that while at the centre of the pagan movement there is a strong body – a majority in fact – of witches who abide by the written laws and oral traditions of their craft, there are also many dangerous dabblers and renegade covens on the periphery. These witches are beholden only to themselves, and certainly do not necessarily conform to the rules of harming no one. They deal in black magic, and some deliberately label themselves as Satanic Witches, not to mention a few groups who veer towards purely sexual and sadistic excitement and use witchcraft and the occult as shelter.

Contemplating this thought, I stood one day, as I was about

to embark upon the writing of this book, gazing into the old pond at the bottom of my garden. I idly tossed in a stone and as I watched it disappear into murky waters, it occured to me that this was a perfect analogy for a summary of witchcraft, and even the occult as a whole: the stone hits the water and causes outward ripples, strong and vibrant at the centre and becoming weaker at the farthest circle, the stone itself sinking down and down into the darkening gloom as the brightness of the moon's light slowly fades, until it hits bottom and is lost into black and mysterious depths. The analogy will, I think, become obvious as this book proceeds.

My pond was eminently suited to inspire this thought, since it is an ancient waterhole; village records show that it existed when, as a child, Catherine Parr, the last wife of Henry VIII, used to wander the estate of her uncle, on an acre of which my house is built.

As far as I know, there is nothing to confirm in parish records that the pond may, at one time or another, have been used for the traditional East Anglian practice of floating or dunking local witches but one can imagine it probable. Hundreds of similar village ponds and streams became the recipients of alleged 'whores of the devil' in the terrible era of persecution that was being launched throughout Europe as Henry VIII came to the throne in 1509. By the time Catherine Parr came to his side, the persecution was in full flow, made official by an Act of Parliament pushed through by Henry himself. And before we go any further, it is as well to remind ourselves of what exactly has gone before.

The witch-hunts that came to the fore during Henry VIII's reign and continued well into Georgian times, began the 1486 publication of the shocking work on demonology, the *Malleus Maleficarum*, or *The Hammer of Witchcraft*, written by two German inquisitors and inspired by Pope Innocent VIII as a textbook for the suppression of underground movement against the structure of a Catholic society. All Christian religions took up the call, though many Church leaders later had second thoughts as the hysteria ran riot and left thousands of murdered witches, so-called, and alleged heretics in its wake.

Witchcraft and sorcery and secret societies had been around for centuries, though in an altered form, but some historians are dubious that today's witchcraft has much to do with early times. Dr Hugh Trevor-Roper, for example, is one of several writers on the subject who insist that witchcraft was the invention of the Inquisition and it did not exist until the Middle Ages. So it has become important to witches to argue otherwise and prove that their ceremonies and ritual have existed far longer than Christianity.

In fact, it became something of an obsession among the leaders of modern witchcraft to prove their religion predates Christianity and Judaism by many thousands of years. There are two reasons for this, as it was explained to me. Firstly witches of recent times were often alone and needed a sense of belonging and spiritual involvement with the old gods and goddesses who they believe are the true inspiration of their religion, i.e. the pre-Christian pagan gods worshipped around the world in remarkably similar but unconnected rituals, stretching from ancient Greece, Egypt, Celtic Europe, the Nordic lands to pre-colonial America. Secondly, they wanted to go back in time to reach out to these origins and make contact with the old gods to get away from the stigma of the Inquisition years and the witch craze which followed, when their persecutors and numerous historians purported to show that all witches were 'bounden slaves of the devil'.

There is a third reason which is not generally spoken of and which lies in the explanation of certain magical powers witches are said to possess, that come to them either through learning or by inheritance. Those who claim they were lucky enough to be born with the powers are known today as hereditary witches. The magic is as much esoteric as it is practical, covering their talent for clairvoyance, astral planing, telepathy and in general the use of the extrasensory powers of the human brain. To all this has been added the training of sorcery and alchemy, which involves the systematic use of spells, potions, rituals and so on for a specific purpose.

Belief in these extrasensory powers is quite easily traced back to primitive man, who possessed the instincts of animals – a kind of supersensory intuition, or sixth sense, which would alert him to danger and guide him to good hunting. When, through the process of man's evolution, many of those powers slipped away witches and sorcerers found a way of retaining them by discovering the path to higher levels of consciousness than are normally used. My reservations towards this theory are noted as we proceed with the examination of these aspects of witchcraft, and the occult.

The word Wicca itself came from the Saxon word witega – meaning prophet or sorcerer – and there seem to be plenty of pointers to show that the rituals practised by witches and occultists today have been copied from known practices of prehistoric man, the hunter whose life was ruled by the elements of nature which he consequently worshipped – the sun, the moon, the earth, the wind, fire and all the elements that affected daily life.

The concept of Wicca worship can be tenuously identified with the cave drawings of these primitive communities, in which the women were seen as the vessel through which contact with the Gods was made. They were depicted as the source of life, naked and pregnant. Today, women are still revered in witchcraft, as priestesses, maidens, high priestesses and, finally, witch queens.

In the primitive civilizations, two main godheads evolved, and they became modified and established over the decades to provide a female goddess of the skies, usually symbolized by the moon. Sometimes she was called the Great Earth Mother – the names varied according to country and language but they all linked her conclusively with nature and fertility. Eventually she was more universally known by the Roman title of the moon goddess Diana, representing the feminine side of witches' theology.

Their male God of the Earth can be linked to early cave drawings of a Horned God, symbolically a stag or a goat, used to ward off danger. The Horned God became the phallic god, representing the strong and masculine side of nature.

One of the earliest signs of the horned creature was to be discovered in the Stone Age relics of the Caverne de Trois Frères, Ariège, France, which showed a dancing figure, half beast and half man, with the sprouting antlers of a stag. These drawings are the earliest source of connection with today's witchcraft, which worships the naked goddess of life and the Horned God.

Around these images, the early communities built their rites and prayers to encourage the gods to bring them safety and good fortune. The gods were especially linked to fertility, so necessary to man's survival, through crops, animals and their own children. And so, long before Christianity introduced the image of the devil, the horned god with tail and hooves could be found in cave art. The horned god was also linked with early human sacrifice.

Primitive cults believed that in order to sustain him and to prevent him from dying, his living representative, the Divine King and Incarnate God nominated by the community, had to be sacrificed on their altar so that his young blood would be taken to give continued life to the true god. Later, as the faith became more widely based and extended on tribal lines, the kings began to insist upon their divine right to rule, and rejected the need for sacrifice and so animals largely replaced humans for sacrificial purposes.

It has been argued that these ancient gods and rites have actually nothing to do with witchcraft, that they were simply a part of the evolution of man's wisdom, and that witches merely adopted the old pre-Christian gods of paganism and assumed the ritual and magic as their own heritage. It can certainly be shown that many of the witch practices performed today are almost perfect replicas of primitive ceremonies, as this description given to me of a ritual acted out by a recent gathering of modern witches shows:

> Those taking part formed a circle around a large unlit bonfire, at the side of which there was a large oblong box. To begin the ritual, the circle of people joined hands . . . they began to dance to a hypnotic drumming and suddenly the Grain God appeared in the middle of the circle, dressed in skins and with white make-up from the chest up. He wore antlers on his head so skilfully applied that they looked as if they were his own. He began his Dance of Death, moving around the circle stopping before each person and showing them his Mystery – the perfect ears of corn he held in each hand. When each had experienced him, the drumming and the chanting increased in tempo and volume until, at its peak, the High Priestess appeared in the middle of the circle and, letting out a bone-chilling scream, she stabbed the Grain God with her Athame (the witch's knife) and blood spurted from the wound as he fell forward into the oblong box, which was now revealed as a coffin. To the cries and gasps of the

assembled witches, the coffin was solemnly carried to the bonfire which was lit and blazed high, accompanied by the cries and chants and the furious drumming. By the light of the funeral pyre, a virile young man appeared among them and was proclaimed the new Grain God and the blessed wine was shared amongst his subjects who danced and chanted until the fire faded . . .

This, the witches believe, is a carbon copy of the ceremony of pre-Christian times, the only difference being that the old God would truly have been sacrificed to make way for the new.

In this case, it was acted out like a play. The athame, the witches' black-handled knife, had a retractable blade, the blood came from a bottle and the 'dead' man escaped from the coffin through a false bottom before it was thrown on to the bonfire.

Are today's witches justified in claiming this heritage as their own? Who is to know what happened in those far-off centuries? It is certainly an unprovable claim but no worse than Christianity. At best it provides pagans and witches with a traceable history of gods whom they can worship, a tradition of ritual they can copy and an example of primitive magic which they can develop as their own.

Though the Bible provided no evidence that witchcraft was considered to be an organized religion, it certainly acknowledged the existence of witches, as in 1 Samuel Chapter 28 of the Old Testament, where we are given a dramatic account of Saul's visit to a witch at Endor because he believed God had deserted him. He went in disguise and pleaded with her to 'bring up Samuel' who was dead. The witch performed her ritual and . . . 'The woman said to Saul, I saw gods ascending out of the earth. And he said unto her what form is he of? And she said, An old man cometh up and he is covered with a mantle. And Saul perceived it was Samuel and he stopped his face to the ground and bowed himself.' This was one of the earliest published examples of necromancy, the revival of the dead or the contact with the spirits of the deceased, which is now practised by many witches and black magicians and is one of the pursuits which is largely responsible for graveyard defilement.

Yet if Saul had found comfort in his visit to a witch, other

11

biblical passages could be drawn upon to provide evidence in Christian belief that witches should not be tolerated, as in one of the more notorious passages used in the sixteenth century as total justification for their persecution, 20 Leviticus 27, which reads: 'A man also a woman that hath a familiar spirit or that is a wizard shall surely be put to death.'

The familiar spirit is one of the earliest keys to the identification of witches. They were said to be capable of summoning an assisting force which was a spirit of a dead person residing in the body of a small animal such as a cat or a dog, or a toad. These animals required the sustenance of witches' blood, obtained by pricking her own skin, and thus when the witch-hunters came, they often first examined the witch's body for marks – any mole would do. Alternatively, the spirits were said to be capable of existence in an inanimate object. The infamous occultist of the Renaissance, Paracelsus, was said to have had a familiar spirit which dwelt in a crystal.

The Roman Church was especially sensitive to all forms of magic and sorcery, because the practice had been rife through Roman society, as was the belief that to encourage constant renewal of power young men, women and animals were required to be systematically sacrificed. These practices remained until the official repression of the old pagan religion in the Roman Empire. In AD 313, the Emperor Constantine issued an edict of toleration legalizing Christianity throughout the empire after he saw two visions which caused him to adopt Christ as his patron.

Just to be on the safe side, however, Constantine never fully abandoned his earlier patron, Apollo, in spite of the pressure from priests and bishops to eliminate pagan practices entirely by threat of death. Christians were not content with merely being the favoured cult; they wanted to establish one true faith for the whole of mankind and all other forms of loyalty to past gods should be abolished. Neither was it the instant 'conversion' that Sunday school teachers would have us believe. It took another two centuries before this progression was confirmed, when the rights of pagans were gradually reduced by imperial decree.

Sacrifices were forbidden in 391 and all pagan holidays and festivals were banned. Pagans were ejected from public office and lost the right to own property or defend themselves in court. Their temples were destroyed by Christian troops or crusading monks and finally, in AD 529, all citizens were ordered to convert to Christianity. Parents were told to bring all children to Christian churches for baptism. Paganism, in the heart of Europe, was reduced to scattered and secret worship, driven underground until, as the years went by, only scraps of folklore, song and dance and superstition remained.

It took longer to disappear elsewhere, as the influence of the Roman Empire diminished and in Britain paganism actually went through a revivalist period as the hordes of barbarian raiders replaced the Romans. The Angles, the Saxons, the Picts and later the Vikings battled to forge powerful new regional kingdoms, enforcing worship of their own gods and attempting to force their own order on society. One of the most enduring legends from the time of the eclipse of the Roman Empire is that of Arthur, who fought the Anglo-Saxons and who is a hero of present day occultists. The Arthurian legends, with Guinevere, Camelot, Excalibur, the Round Table and the wizard Merlin are all debatable creations, but it is of special significance to all who follow the dark arts to recall that there were twelve knights to the Round Table, thirteen including Arthur – the number of witches who make up a coven.

The Anglo-Saxon regional kings were eventually won over to Christianity but the new religion lost ground again in the face of the marauding Vikings, whose pagan rites were said to include human sacrifice when the victims's lungs were cut from the body. The tide began to turn against the Vikings when King Alfred of Wessex, then aged twenty-two, defeated them at the Battle of Ashdown in 871. The young king of Wessex was from a close-knit, pious Christian family and was a devout follower of the Roman Church, having been taken to be blessed personally by the Pope by his father King Aethelwulf at the age of four. Alfred began the task of uniting England under the Christian king which his descendents were finally to achieve. During his life, Alfred taught himself Latin, the international language of western Christendom and began translating Latin pastorals [by Pope Gregory the Great] into English and sent copies to every bishop in his kingdom. His grandson, King Athelstan, brought in the first legislation against witchcraft [and the banning of Sunday trade, incidentally] in AD 930.

There, out of the decimation of paganism as a religion, is the more likely setting for the birth of today's witchcraft and it is to these roots that witches turn for their inspiration.

As Christianity prospered, the imagery of the primitive cultures and the sacrificial rites which had been used to maintain idolatrous worship were taken as an example personifying some of the elements of evil; thus the horned god of pantheistic beliefs became the accepted form of the Christian devil and was used by Christians in their denouncement of all pagan worship. Gradually, the devil became drawn into every facet of medieval life. He and his demons were blamed for every mishap, whether a destructive storm or disease among the farm animals. The vivid image of this horned and hoofed invader, ruler of the dark forces, was blamed by the teachings of the Church for virtually all ills.

The legacy of this confusion – which still exists – is the belief that the devil is an essential part of pagan worship or witchcraft. In fact, with the exception of a group known as the Satanic Witch Cult, neither mainstream witches nor pagans now recognize the existence of the devil or Satan.

CHAPTER TWO

THE BURNING TIMES

As the horned god became the Christian symbol of the devil, some witches did come to believe in and worship that Christian entity as their own and by the Middle Ages, witchcraft and devil worship were being treated as one and the same. Even Lewis Spence's *Encyclopaedia of the Occult*, published in 1920, opens its entry on witchcraft with this quotation:

> The cult of persons who, by means of satanic assistance or the aid of evil spirits or familiars are enabled to practise minor black magic. But the difference between the sorcerer and the witch is that the former has sold his soul to Satan for complete dominion over him for a stated period, whereas the witch usually appears as the devoted and often badly treated servant of the diabolic power . . .

There was a surprisingly benign attitude to witchcraft for several centuries and a number of early medieval writers dismissed witches as a delusion, in spite of the fact that witch-dunking was recorded in seventh-century Russia. One early debunking of witches was contained in a Canon Episcopi in 906, which described them as 'certain abandoned women, perverted by the devil, seduced by illusion and phantasms of demons, believe and openly profess that in the dead of night they ride upon certain beasts with Diana . . . fly over vast tracts of the country and obey her commands . . . the priests throughout their churches should preach with all insistence to the people that they may know this to be in every way false.'

The inclusion of the name Diana, a pre-Christian goddess, was important, and as we shall see, figured strongly in later attempts to flush out the origins of witchcraft.

Christianity often denied the existence of witchcraft until the arrival of the Inquistion, introduced in 1163 by the Council of Tours to bolster the Church and drive out the rising tide of immorality and heresy. It heralded the first witch trials and some spectacular accusations of devil worship at the highest level.

Until the latter stages of the Middle Ages, witchcraft, sorcery and wizardry were a rather confused package that generally went under the label of heresy – i.e. 'Any belief that is contrary to the established view of the Church' and many of these accused of it were actually priests and members of the Church. This heading was also used as a damning indictment against those in dispute with authority. It was easy to brand opponents as heretics, or witches, because there was no need to find proof. However, though there appeared to be no organized structure of witchcraft or pagan worship, there was undoubtedly an aspect of community celebration which could be classed as pagan.

The Maypole, that symbol of old English springtime tradition, was the phallic symbol of pagan worship. In local communities, the village wise woman who knew herbal medicines and could treat all manner of family ailments, foretell the future and be the guide and comforter of tormented women, was to be seen by religious authorities as a witch and the Church wanted rid of them, and their kind. An early example of what has become the stuff of Christian legend used to propagate the fear of liaison with the devil is a story which dates to the twelfth century, but became the subject of a country ballad much later.

It was alleged by William of Malmesbury, who claimed the authority of an actual eye-witness for the story, that an old witch woman who had confessed to making a pact with the devil became worried when the expiry of her contract approached. She decided she must repent of her sins before her death and summoned some neighbouring monks to her home and told them that she was worried that the devil would secure her body as well as her soul. She gave directions that her body should be taken to the monastery, sewn in a stag's hide, placed inside a stone coffin and fastened down with three strong iron chains. She directed that fifty psalms should be sung by night and fifty hymns should be sung by day to confuse the demons and if her body was still secure after three days, she might be buried safely.

All these precautions, wrote William, were of no avail. For two nights the monks bravely resisted the demons, but on the third night amid terrific uproar and the clatter of thunder, an immense demon burst into the monastery, snapped the iron chains like threads, pushed the stone lid aside and commanded the dead witch to rise. He grasped her around the waist, carried her to his huge black stallion and galloped off into the night with her shrieks resounding through the air. Such legends impressed and scared the peasant communities and were inspirational in the first stirrings of the movement against witches.

More sinister and believable stories were becoming known. Often the subject was neither an abandoned woman nor an old village crone. One of the first recorded witch trials involved the Lady Alice Kyteler, said to be the wealthiest woman in Kilkenny, who was accused by a bishop of being a witch, of parodying religious cermonies, sacrificing animals, creating powders and ointments containing 'horrible' ingredients which included parts of dead men and unborn babies – and most terrible of all, engaging in sexual relations with a man who appeared in the form of a black, shaggy dog, i.e. the devil himself.

Lady Alice was undoubtedly up to something, and fled Ireland to seek refuge in England. She left behind her maid, Petronilla, who was tortured until she confessed that her mistress was a witch of considerable talent and had arranged spectacular night-time orgies in which Petronilla had taken part. The result was that on 3 November 1324, Petronilla was taken to a place in the centre of town, tied to a stake around which dry branches had been piled and ceremoniously burned alive.

By the time of the accession of Pope Innocent VIII (1484–1492) something of a milestone was reached in the general disposition among local rulers against any form of witchcraft. It had been gathering momentum across Europe as the aristocracy, the Christian Church and the Papacy fought to rid themselves of the rebellious factions who dealt in the mysterious and the malevolent and who could be conveniently packaged together as being in league with Satan. The devil, his attendants and courtiers were important ingredients in the whole persecution period when the Church was fragmenting and losing its power, especially in England where Henry VIII would soon break with Rome after passing a law enabling him to divorce.

Pope Innocent VIII brought the whole matter to a head with his accusation that witches 'by their incantations and spells, conjurations and other accursed crimes and crafts, enormities and horrid offences, have slain infants yet in the mother's womb, as also the offspring of cattle, have blasted the produce of the earth, the grapes of the vine, the fruits of the trees . . .' The inquisitors were 'empowered without let or hindrance to proceed to just correction, imprisonment and punishment.'

The two authors of *Malleus Maleficarum* were Dominican friars named Jacob Sprenger, dean of Cologne University, and Heinrich Kramer, prior of a monastery. They had been operating as inquisitors in Austria and appear to have begun their writings as a justification for the brutality against those suspected of being witches and servants of Satan. In their opening statement, they set out the dictum which still stands in the Roman Catholic Church and is propagated by Christian fundamentalists to this day: 'Whether the belief that there are such beings as witches is so essential a part of the Catholic faith that obstinately to maintain the contrary opinion manifestly savours of heresy.'

And so began the absolute purge of witches and devil worshippers which proceeded with bloody passion for the next three hundred years.

According to Sprenger and Kramer, demons filled the air waiting to be called down by the witches, preying on the simple peasants, plodding through their dull, daily lives with only marginally more comfort and pleasure than the animals they tended for sustenance. Wars, plagues and poverty made peasant populations throughout Europe easy targets for both the perpetrators and the persecutors of witchcraft and, with copies of the Bible now to hand in the communities, the witch stories of the Jews

18

could easily be applied to people with unusual powers in their own midst.

In the early 1500s, the scenario of the witch-hunt was one where local bureaucracy ruled, where prince-bishops and barons could employ many helpers to root out the unnatural and unwanted in their midst. Torture and tyranny provided the basis for the hysteria and *Malleus* quickly became the handbook of witch-hunters and inquisitors, of sheriffs and judges.

The publication of *Malleus* also coincided with the introduction of printing techniques, and in the following two centuries more than forty editions of the work are known to have been published, at least six in English. At the same time more and more witches were being tortured, burned, hanged and drowned, literally by the thousand, as each year passed. Wholesale trials of witches spread terror and fear through Europe. The first Act of Parliament against witchcraft in England came early in Henry VIII's reign but it was not until 1562 that it became a capital offence; by then, witch burnings were already rife in many parts of the continent of Europe.

There are no overall figures that can be accurately drawn upon as a total for any country, but there are individual tallies which give an idea of the scale of the eradication. In Strasbourg, during a twenty-year period, 5000 witches are known to have been burned. A figure of 4400 were killed in Scotland during the witch-hunt era and 900 in just eight years at Würzberg. All over Europe, the witch-hunts were pursued with vigour and one estimate puts the total number of alleged witches killed at over 300,000, 80 per cent of them being women.

Sometimes, whole villages were deemed to have been infected and were wiped out or forcibly split up, and moved to other areas. The system of torture encouraged the victims to name names; in one study examining the case-histories of 300 witches, each was alleged to have 'named' an average of twenty others – producing a list of more than 6000 who might pass through a single court during a five-year period.

Historian Trevor-Roper has said, '[*Malleus*] forms a reservoir of monstrous theory from which successive persecutions were fed, persecutions which did not diminish but intensified over the next two hundred years.'

Malleus laid down the guidelines for assessing supposed witches who, the inquisitors wrote, were servants of Satan and his demons and possessed great powers which enabled them to inflict disease, tempests and death by imagery. They could bewitch their opposers and judges with their evil eye and thus it was necessary to extract confessions by torture, to ensure that the truth was revealed. It was designed entirely to obtain forced confessions – resulting in statements which bore a remarkable similarity in description to witch trials across Europe, and later in America.

The quotation in *Malleus* that began the witch-hunts reads:

> She [the witch] may be promised her life . . . provided that she supply evidence which will lead to the conviction of other witches . . . let her often and frequently be exposed to torture. If after being fittingly tortured she refuses to tell the truth, the judge should have other engines of torture brought before her and tell her that she will have to endure these if she does not confess. If she is not induced by terror to confess, the torture must continue on the second and the third day.

Hundreds of towns and villages across Europe were, at one time or another, racked by the drama of the witch-hunt – the screams of tortured women, sometimes men and children too, and the smell of burning flesh. The most notorious were carried out by the prince-bishops of Würzburg and Bamberg who perpetrated brutal and sadistic tortures. Whether it could be proved that the victims were witches or not often went unchallenged; who could dispute the claims without bringing suspicion upon themselves?

Those who did challenge were often arrested and similarly accused. The list of inducements for a confession included hanging the witches by their thumbs and sticking them with needles; immersing them in baths of boiling water or oil; crushing their bodies under heavy weights or presses; forcibly feeding them on salted herrings and refusing water; and the prevention of sleep for days on end. One account of a witch torture in 1629 read:

The woman was bound hand and foot and the executioner cut her hair and threw alcohol over her head, setting light to it; he placed strips of sulphur under her armpits and burned them. She was hauled by rope to hang from the ceiling for three hours while the hangman enjoyed his breakfast. Then he returned and threw alcohol over her body and burned it. He forced her body down on to a plank stuck with nails and squeezed her thumbs and toes in a vice. He whipped her repeatedly with rawhide and left her hanging for another three hours. Then her feet were crushed and her body stretched out to the greatest length; she screamed piteously and said all was true that they had demanded of her – that she had copulated with the devil, that she drank the blood of children whom she stole on her night-flights and she had murdered about sixty infants. She named twenty other women; and then she was hanged.

The terrors of Bamberg were at their height in the early 1600s; more than 500 witches were hanged between 1620 and 1632. A suffragan bishop led a committee of witch-hunters, made up of lawyers and local dignitaries. They employed a full-time bureaucracy of torturers and hangmen, using techniques which might have been a model for the Nazi Gestapo three centuries later. Informers were brought to a witch prison and made their accusations. The accused were then arrested and so effectively tortured that none who were brought there for interrogation escaped with their lives. Those who spoke out against the terror were themselves branded as witches.

In the British Isles, the Scots almost matched the Germans for their brutality and it was the practice of the local judiciary to join in a public feast after the witch-burning ceremonies; it became an event for the whole town to celebrate. There is one notorious record of such an occasion in Paisley in 1697 when seven people were collectively burned as witches. Earlier records of Scottish cases describe the kind of torture techniques used for many years. Alison Balfour, for example, refused to confess what the sheriff required of her, even after being locked in claspie-claws and pilniewinks, items of torture that were screwed down upon the limbs with such pressure that blood finally spurted from the extremities.

Overseen by the minister of the Kirk, the witch-hunters also took her seven-year-old daughter and locked the child's fingers into the pilnie-winks. Only then did Alison Balfour 'confess'.

Another of the more famous Scottish executions involved one of the present Royal family's ancestors, Janet Douglas, Lady Glamis, who was burned as a witch in 1537. At her trial, she was said to have conspired with other witches to assassinate King James V of Scotland by poison and magical powers. Some said she never practised witchcraft but was merely caught up in political intrigue, but those who support the witchcraft theory point to the fact that Glamis Castle is still haunted by the spirits supposedly conjured up by Janet Douglas.

There were other royal connections emanating from Scotland. In 1585, Reginald Scot wrote *The Discovery of Witchcraft*, in which he tried to bring some sense of proportion to the persecutions. He treated the whole business of witchcraft with scepticism, claiming that witches were merely a deluded bunch of old crones. He said manifestations were artful impostures, witches' claims were fraudulent and were supported only by the mentally disturbed – much the same argument that is offered today in many scholastic quarters.

James VI of Scotland, later James I of England, was something of a thinker. He had already written *Counterblaste to Tobacco* and described Scot's book as damnable and burned it. He chose to write his own, called *Daemonologie*, published in 1597 to dispute it. James was, it must be said, a man of certain peculiarities himself. He possessed a sadistic passion for interrogating witches personally and he showed a particular interest in extracting the fullest details about the accusations of demonic sexual activity that often featured in witch trials.

It was he who recommended the system of floating witches – binding them in cloth and throwing them into the village pond, on the basis that because witches had rejected the water of baptism, so the water would reject them. If they sank, it proved they were not witches – though many drowned, anyway. If they floated, it proved their guilt and they were brought to trial and hanged.

James supervised some of the tortures prior to another mass Scottish killing in North Berwick, where a young servant girl, who apparently possessed a natural ability for spiritual healing, was put to the rack by her master and confessed to being a disciple of the devil. When the thumbscrews were applied with greater force, she named several other prominent local people, including the local schoolmaster John Fian, and two women well up in local society, including one Agnes Sampson. Under torture, Mrs Sampson admitted she was a witch and was in league with other people who had once plotted to murder the king, in the hope of putting their own Grand Master, Francis, Earl of Bothwell, on the throne of Scotland. The circle spread, and more names were extracted until, in all, seventy people had been arrested. Most were burned.

The Scottish fervour for hammering the witches is further borne out by a relic that still survives – the Witches Stone at Forres, on the Moray Firth, which carries the inscription, 'From Clust Hill witches were rolled in stout barrels through which knives were driven. When the barrels stopped, they were burned with their mangled contents. This stone marks the site of one such burning.'

English witches, because of different laws, largely escaped the more barbarous practices of the Scottish and continental hunters. They could only be hanged, not burned, although some persecutors found ways around this rule. Unofficially, torture was widespread, especially during an infamous period in East Anglia following the Civil War which saw the rise of a lawyer named Matthew Hopkins whose declared intention was to rid the nation of witchcraft; he became the self-styled 'Witch-finder General'.

His first attack was on what he described as a 'horrible sect' of seven or eight witches in his home town of Manningtree in Essex. From there he began to tour the countryside, taking money from local squires and landowners and towns to rid their communities of the devil's whores and becoming very rich in the process. His favoured method of discovering if a woman was a witch was to see if she floated. He also used a team of walkers who would force his victims to run barefoot continuously for hours until they confessed.

One who suffered the 'walking' torture was a seventy-year-old parson from Bury St Edmunds. He was run backwards and forwards continuously for four days until he could stand it no longer and confessed to being a witch. It did not save him from the gallows. Eighteen were hanged for witchcraft in Bury in the year of 1645, and nineteen in Chelmsford. In the whole of the county of Suffolk in 1645, Hopkins administered sixty-eight executions. There is no exact record of his nationwide tally, but it ran into hundreds.

Hopkins was just one of many who enjoyed the profitable calling of witch-finder and trials continued well into the next century, both in England and throughout Europe. Not far from my home, to recall one rather sensational example, the two Witches of Oundle created something of a stir in these parts. Elinor Shaw and Mary Phillips were both from poor but honest families, but in later life fell into 'dissolute habits', becoming harlots and drawing the disgust of their community. As they were shunned by the women-folk, they swore revenge and so – according to the confession obtained under torture – called down the services of the devil. At midnight on 12 February 1704, according to their confessions, a tall black man appeared before them and said, 'Be not afraid. I too am one of the Creation, pawn to me your souls for one year and two months and I will assist you for all that time in whatever you desire.'

It was said that the two women agreed to the request of the devil's representative and made a covenant written in their own blood by pricking their fingers. One year later, they were arrested by the sheriff and accused of causing the deaths of fifteen children, eight men and six women, and numerous animals. They were also said to have killed four great hogs because their owner said the women looked like witches, and later sent two imps to destroy his four-year-old daughter. What evidence there was for such allegations cannot be imagined.

They were eventually found guilty of killing three people by roasting effigies in wax into which they had stuck pins. They were brought to Northampton for execution on 17 March 1705. As they stood at the gallows, they were asked if they wanted to say their prayers and to be forgiven for their sins. They laughed, according to the record, and called for the devil to help them in 'such a blasphemous manner that the sheriff, seeing their impenitence, caused them to be executed without delay, being hanged until almost dead and then they were burned.'

Pacts with the devil were a feature of a number of trials. At Taunton, where there were numerous witches' covens in the surrounding villages, two were said to have admitted signing in their own blood a written contract with 'a man in black' in return for 'money to live gallantly and have pleasure of the world for a period of twelve years.' They described in their confessions how they made effigies in clay and stuck them with pins, and cursed local people who had annoyed them. One of the witches, Elizabeth Styles, spoke of the anointment of the witches who were then able to fly very long distances in a short space of time. The man in black always appeared at their coven meetings when he was called, and supervised their activities. The stories were remarkable for their similarity.

There were several mass killings, the most notable in Europe, perhaps, was that recorded at Mohra, Sweden, which illustrated that there was no mercy for youngsters who were said to have become tainted by sorcery: 'Fifteen children which likewise confessed that they were engaged in witchery, died as the rest.' They were all burned at the stake.

In 1692, in Salem, Massachusetts, there occurred one of the most incredible outbreaks of witch fever, now familiar through Arthur Miller's play, *The Crucible*. Scenes of remarkable hysteria erupted after a group of pre-pubescent girls – overstimulated by voodoo stories related by a black servant – took to falling about on the floor flailing and shrieking. The local doctor pronounced them all bewitched, and fired by imagination and malice the girls accused various women in the village of forcing them to sign the devil's book. There seems little doubt that witchcraft was being practised in Salem – yet hardly in sufficient numbers to justify the arrest of 140 people of whom 23 were hanged, pressed to death or died in gaol.

Witchcraft had become an obsession that was hardly quelled even when the amendment of the Witchcraft Act in 1735 ended in England at least, punishment by death, although witchcraft remained a criminal offence punishable by imprisonment. The obsession had been on a scale so vast that no single cause can be pinpointed. The Black Death, the Hundred Years' War and the Civil War in England provided the social upheavals. The state of the Church and the opposing factions which permeated right down to community level were also a contributing factor.

That it existed and was widespread is beyond doubt. Observations that the British and European countryside was 'catacombed with covens of witches' is possible, but difficult to prove in the maze of untruths and enforced confessions. Many of the confessions were dictated and written down by the torturers, coloured and exaggerated until they are largely beyond either possibility or belief.

The witch-hunters also sent to their deaths hundreds of innocents and dozens of harmless old frauds whose greatest crime was their ability to charm away a wart, their adeptness at herbal healing or displaying an uncanny knack of seeing into the future.

Descriptions of the witches' rituals and festivals bore a striking similarity throughout Europe. The accounts of the rituals were filled with graphic descriptions of unspeakable events, such as 'kissing the arse of the devil' or being sprinkled with Holy Water, which was 'stinking urine', of eating loathsome sacraments of black bread, 'tasting like shit', all of which went totally against the holiest of Catholic ceremonies. All were to reappear in the 1980s, in rumour and in fact.

The Witches' Sabbath, for example, was widely held to be an orgy of perverted sex, human sacrifice and cannibalism, presided over by Lucifer himself, most commonly described as having appeared in the form of a black goat which then proceeded to have intercourse with all the women present – his penis was said by all to be rough and ice cold.

Witches, it was said in many of these confessions and descriptions, flew to the location of the ceremony on their broomsticks. According to legend, this was achieved by rubbing the stick with the witches' 'flying ointment' – a substance that Francis Bacon described as 'to be made of fat of children, of juices of smallage, wolfsbane and cinque-foil, mingled with meal of fine wheat; but I suppose the soporiferous medicines are likest to do it which are hen-bane, hemlock, mandrake, moonshade or rather night-shade, tobacco, opium, saffron, poplar-leaves etc.'

The stories of blasphemy and defilement became more and more frequent, and colourful accounts of exactly what witches did began to emerge as gospel truth. The accusations against them included killing children for sacrificial purposes; killing animals by magic; murdering their enemies by imagery, i.e. by forming an image in wax and stabbing it or roasting it; bringing harm to innocent people by just casting their 'evil eye' upon them. Behind these capital charges were other accusations which included human sacrifice, cannibalism, sodomy, incest and other forms of wild sexual practices, not to mention blasting crops and poisoning drinking wells – often the creative invention of ecclesiastical writers.

Other writers burst forth with superbly graphic and gory accounts, factual and fictitious, of the activities of witches, sorcerers and the devil's disciples, and the mysteries of the dark and dangerous worlds populated by evil. By the eighteenth century it had become an accepted fact, through *Malleus* and other writings, that witches were capable of some highly inexplicable activities – though the witch-hunters were no nearer verifying this theory or even explaining it. And what happened in these years – or at least the written version of what happened – ultimately became the research material for witches in the twentieth century.

As the witch craze began to die out, certainly in England, life for the village hags, wart charmers, healers and fortune-tellers became safer. There were still intermittent prosecutions, though by and large practitioners were loath to reveal themselves and what remained of the witch community in Europe quietly went about its business at the lowest of profiles for the next couple of hundred years.

What had become established in all communities, however, was the great fear of witchcraft and curses – still prevalent today. What housewife would refuse to buy a row of gypsy's pegs for fear of having a curse put on her house? And though the witch trials died down, stories of the unbelievable continued to appear in public record.

In 1896, a woman of Sourton, Devon, who was thought to be a witch, was brought to trial by magistrates at Oakhampton for stealing a sheep, a crime punishable by transportation. As the chairman of the bench passed sentence, she jumped from the dock and declared, 'You will be dead in a week and nobody connected with this case shall die in his bed.' Within a week the chairman of the magistrates collapsed in a field while talking to his farm bailiff and died instantly. Another magistrate committed suicide and the farmer who brought the prosecution died in a fire. A few weeks later, the clerk to the magistrates fell dead from his bicycle near Oakhampton. There were many such stories which abounded in the 'stranger than fiction' mode, and prompted a continual flow of literature, occasional prosecutions and an undying fear in society at large of anything concerned with witchcraft and the occult.

One of the more amusing aspects covered by the Witchcraft Act came to the fore in Victorian times – that of fortune-telling, clairvoyance and séances with mediums. As witches themselves had, by and large, returned to the shadows of society, the few prosecutions tended to be against charlatans accused of making money from what became a twentieth-century obsession – fortune-telling and contact with the dead.

One such case occurred at the beginning of this century when the palmist Cheiro was brought before Clerkenwell magistrates court accused of pretending to tell fortunes by reading his clients' palms, for which he was fined. Cheiro had the last laugh over authority, however. In 1925, he had the audacity to write a prediction for the then Prince of Wales, later to be Edward VIII and the Duke of Windsor, which read: '. . . his chart points to great changes affecting the Throne of England . . . [he] was born under peculiar astrological circumstances which make his character a difficult one to understand. He suffers intense restlessness, a lack of continuity of thought . . . has an absorbing love of travel . . . lacks any sense of danger . . . determined not to settle down until the grande passion. It is well within the range of possibility that he will fall victim to a devastating love affair. If he does, I predict he will give up everything, even the chance of being crowned.' Within ten years, the prediction had come true.

That obtaining money by fortune-telling or séances should be classed as witchcraft – and thus illegal – meant that it remained for many years one of the few continuing areas of prosecution under the Witchcraft Act until the repeal of the laws in 1951. By then, a revival in witchcraft was already under way . . .

CHAPTER THREE

REVIVAL

The history of witchcraft and black magic was researched, rewritten and regurgitated for the creation of modern cults, regardless of the dividing line between truth and mythology. And none was more adept at telling a good story than the man who has been credited with the rebirth of witchcraft worldwide, Gerald Brosseau Gardner, a controversial figure whose coven rituals became easily recognizable because of their content of sex and nudity. Others who do not follow what has become known as 'the Gardnerian Way' would argue that witchcraft would have resumed its active place in society without him, and perhaps they are right but it would have taken much, much longer.

The events leading up to the revival can be traced back several decades before Gardner came on the scene. It was a book that largely contributed to the crushing of witchcraft, and it was also a book which can be identified as a first turning point in its renewal at the end of the last century. The source was an unknown and almost illiterate young gypsy woman in Italy who was discovered to have written a manuscript entitled 'Aradia, or the Gospel of the Witches', which was turned into a book of the same title by American author Charles Godfrey Leland and published in 1899.

The story of how it came into international print, to become one of the standard works in the modern history of witchcraft, is enthralling, not least for the debate that has been continuing ever since as to whether witchcraft as practised today is a modern invention or truly predates Christianity.

Leland, by then already well known for books and essays on

many subjects, had long been a student of folklore and in pursuit of material for his books had travelled the world. He was as familiar in Europe as he was in his native America. He had an eventful life: while studying at the Sorbonne he saw the makings of the revolution in 1848. He was back in America for the Civil War and saw service at the Battle of Gettysburg. He ventured to the new frontiers of the Wild West, met General Custer and became a blood-brother in a tribe of Kaw Indians who befriended him. Based on these experiences, he wrote over fifty books and while researching a new work, which was a study on gypsy sorcery and fortune-telling, published in 1891, he and his wife went to live for a time in Florence.

There, he had a chance meeting with a wandering young woman he called Maddalena. He later wrote that she was 'a woman who would have been taken for a gypsy in England but whose face in Italy, I soon learned to know [as] the antique Etruscan with its strange mysteries to which was added the indefinable glance of the witch. She was from Romagna Toscana, born in the heart of its unsurpassingly wild and romantic scenery . . . and old legendary castles. I did not gather all the facts for a long time but gradually found she was a member of a witch family . . . whose members had from time immemorial told fortunes, repeated ancient legends, gathered incantations, prepared enchanted medicines, philtres and spells . . .'

Leland said that he had long ago learned of the existence of some papers which set out the doctrines of witchcraft that might well have been the remnants of pagan rituals, hidden away and secretly practised since the conversion of Rome to Christianity in the fourth century AD. When Leland heard of Maddalena's connections he implored her to help him in his search. He asked if she would question her sisters and her relatives about the hidden spells and the traditions of olden times. He knew that 'even yet, there are old people in Romagna of the North who know the incantations to Bacchus, Jupiter, Venus and Mercury and the Lares to ancestral spirits . . . and in the cities are women who . . . mutter spells known in old Roman times, who can astonish the learned by their legends of Latin gods . . .'

Nine years passed before Leland received, on 1 January 1897

the surprise parcel from Colle, Val d'Elsa, near Siena. It contained a manuscript from Maddalena entitled 'Aradia, or the Gospel of the Witches'. Leland, who never saw Maddalena again (he died in 1903), explained in his notes to the book:

> She succeeded, after many years, in obtaining the following 'gospel' which I have in her handwriting. I did not know definitely whether my informant derived a part of these traditions from written sources or oral narration but believe it was chiefly of the latter . . . For brief explanation I may say that witchcraft is known to its votaries as *le vecchia religione*, or the old religion, of which Diana is the goddess, her daughter Aradia, the female Messiah, and this little work sets forth how the latter was born and came down to earth, established witches and witchcraft and then returned to heaven. With it are given the ceremonies and invocations or incantations to be addressed to Diana . . . there are also very curious incantations or benedictions of the honey, meal, salt or cakes of the witch supper which is curiously classical and evidently a relic of Roman Mysteries.

Apart from the incantations and rituals, there were charms and spells, glue-making, legends and folklore which dated back through centuries. Ancient love spells were mentioned along with the most significant allusion to the worship of the goddess Diana ever discovered. The fact that it was written down in jumbled form, at times barely decipherable, by an uneducated travelling girl in Northern Italy made it more fascinating and romantic. Historical mentions of the goddess Diana had appeared briefly in the past, notably in the *Treatise on Witches* by Paulus Grillandus, published in 1547, and a Church Decree in the tenth century identified Diana as a Goddess of the Witches.

Leland's book, published by Scribner in New York, failed to make much impact at the time. Witchcraft was still outlawed, though it was visited as a subject occasionally by historians and anthropologists. Leland had also failed to discover any widespread organized cult of witchcraft or pagan religion, either in Europe or Britain.

Theosophy was all the rage among those interested in things

mystical in late Victorian London and New York, where the renowned occultists Madame H. P. Blavatsky and Colonel H. S. Olcott had formed the Theosophical Society with the intention of promoting their much publicized Universal Brotherhood of Humanity as a study of comparative religion and philosophy and to investigate the mystic powers of life and matter. It was a form of Kabbalism, another avenue of occult study which we shall examine in a later chapter.

There was talk of new secret societies, like the Great White Brotherhood, and other cults such as the Order of the Golden Dawn and various highly publicized occult personalities whose activities I will document later. Witchcraft, tainted by the lingering aura of satanic badness, remained firmly in the shadows of community life and stayed there for many years.

If there were surviving covens, whether they were in the British Isles, Europe or New England, they kept a very low profile, threatened still by the reality of prosecution. However, the publication of another book, by Dr Margaret A. Murray, an anthropologist and lecturer in Egyptology at University College, London, caused a flurry of new interest and created the next stepping-stone towards the legalization of the craft.

This time, it was an academic study and so carried rather more weight, coming as it did in the twenties during that great decade of historical exploration and archaeological discoveries such as Tutankhamun's tomb. Though she failed to make mention of it in her own book, Dr Murray admitted to Lewis Spence, a member of the Royal Anthropological Institute, that the work by Charles Leland was her inspiration, and taking up the Aradia gospel, she began an independent investigation into the origins and practice of witchcraft. The result was a book called *The Witch Cult in Western Europe*, first published in 1921. It came out at a time when women were still having to fight hard for any kind of recognition and where even academically confident females like Dr Murray were few and far between. Her conclusions went totally against the theories of the Church and the establishment for the previous nineteen hundred years. Even now, her conclusion that a witch cult attached to the Goddess Diana had survived, is attacked as romantic nonsense. Reporting on Dr Murray's findings, Lewis

Spence wrote at the time, 'She inclines to the hypothesis that witchcraft was in reality the modern and degraded descendant of an ancient nature-religion, the rites of which were actually carried out in deserted places and included child sacrifice and other barbarous customs. In brief, her hypothesis tends to prove the actual reality of the witch-religion as against that of hallucination which until recently was the explanation accepted by students of the subject.'

Spence added that his own recent researches had convinced him of the 'soundness of Dr Murray's views' and that he had personally encountered the 'existence of a witch cult precisely similar to that of Europe in pre-Columbian Mexico and I have seen the picture of a naked witch with peaked cap riding on her broomstick in the native Mexican painting known as the Codex Fejervary-Mayer'.

All of this represented a complete challenge to the established view of anthropology, that witchcraft was the creation of the Inquisition. Even so, writers continued to discuss the topic with a wonderful irrationality, seemingly taking as gospel the written down 'confessions' from the persecution era and using them as a basis for factual works or as a starting point for superbly colourful fictional writings.

Dr Murray's findings, though largely shunned by male anthropologists, dismissed the theory that witchcraft ought to be identified with satanism and devil-worship. She was personally convinced that it was basically a pre-Christian Dianic cult and said she had found the name Diana in writings about witchcraft all through history.

She believed that 'the man in black' described at meetings of witches' covens was a priest dressed variously in dark clothing, or in skins, and wearing horns or antlers. He might wear an artificial phallus from which he squirted goat's milk in order to perform the sex rite so graphic in all the confessionals. It was a ritual disguise, originally intended to represent the Incarnate God, that not merely existed in the practice of ancient ritual, and was copied by the witches of the Middle Ages, but still existed in contemporary witch covens she had experienced in Glastonbury, one of the most 'witch-possessed' areas of the British Isles.

Other covens, and many so-called hereditary witches, were thought to survive in the west country as a whole, in the Cotswolds, in Hampshire and especially around the New Forest, in Wales, the Channel Isles, the Isle of Man and certainly in Scotland. The survival rate seemed to depend on the strength and courage of the inheritors of the old traditions, and the predominance of witches in those areas in times past.

What began to emerge through the writings of authors like Dr Murray was a challenge to the belief propagated since the Inquisition that witches possessed diabolic powers given to them by the devil.

While giving credence to Dr Murray's theories, Lewis Spence, in his *Encyclopedia of the Occult*, also recorded that although witches undoubtedly possessed hypnotic and telepathic powers and extra-sensory perception, much of the vivid description which made up the confessions of witches during their persecution was either concocted by the prosecutors or was the result of hallucination from narcotic plants, drug-induced dreams and pure imagination. Leaders of the witches' Sabbatic meetings were able to convince the ignorant among the sisterhood that they were all able to draw down the diabolic powers and the assistance of the hordes of demons swirling through the air waiting to be summoned, by selling their souls to the devil.

As Spence pointed out, hypnotic trance and hysteria, drugs and salves, were used unsparingly. But the great source of witch-craft power was undoubtedly created by auto-suggestion, fostered and fomented by ecclesiastical and scholastic writings, and no less softened by popular myth and legend from the graphic accounts handed down through the ages.

What finally filtered through to demonologists was the acceptance that much of the descriptions were due to hallucination, yet they considered that the witches were no less guilty for *imagining* their diabolic acts. Even Dr Murray agreed that many of the executed witches undoubtedly did indeed believe themselves to be servants of the devil, and acted out their magical rituals for that purpose and there are ample descendants in the 1990s who are internationally recognized as being satanic witches.

There was still a large body of people who were ready to

requote the words of the Methodist founder John Wesley who declared, 'It is true that the English in general and indeed most of the men of learning in Europe have given up all accounts of witches and apparitions as mere old wives' tales. I am sorry for it. The giving up of witchcraft is in effect giving up the Bible. But I cannot give up to all the Deists in Great Britain the existence of witchcraft till I give up the credit of all history, sacred and profane.'

This theme was the one taken up by the colourful writer on demonology, Montague Summers, whose own books on the subject came soon after Dr Murray's with the publication in 1926 of his *History of Witchcraft and Demonology*, followed by three other works on the same subject. The difference between Margaret Murray, the anthropologist, and Montague Summers was that the latter was a total believer in the devil and in witches as his diabolical servants.

His writing, brimming with an intense knowledge of the occult, wholeheartedly supported the Roman Catholic Church for its persecution of witches and he made no secret of the fact that he believed an international conspiracy of satanists existed, and was growing. He believed in the incredible powers witches were said to possess, including the fatal powers of their evil eye and the ability to fly, and he wrote of werewolves and vampires as if they were each a true fact of life, and of the desperate evils of black magic – all of which he associated with witchcraft.

Summers was himself a colourful character. Often referred to as Reverend Summers or Father Montague, he generally wore the dark clothes of a cleric though no one was ever sure to which faith he belonged. One of the many stories about him was that he really was a Priest of Holy Orders on a Special Mission from Rome – to secrete himself into English society and take up the role of a roving attacker of all matters satanic, and specifically to counteract the damaging propaganda being put about by Dr Murray, which the Vatican authorities on the devil despised. True or not, Summers pursued his quarry with considerable vigour and never once showed any signs of disbelief, even of the most fantastic of occult stories.

His writings were also important to witches themselves, because he faithfully recorded some of the ritual practised in

England from the Middle Ages onward, which served as valuable information for researchers into what witches actually did in their covens, or more precisely, were *said* to have done.

The books of Margaret Murray inspired a further discussion that began to put the whole question of witchcraft into perspective, and awaken a new interest outside religious fervour. It revealed that a substantial amount of occult magic, superstition and cult practices still abounded in Britain.

It was almost a disappointment for many to discover a logical explanation, confirmed by scientists, to the popular theories encouraged by Montague Summers, that witches could fly through the air or were capable of transforming themselves into animals, both regular features of most confessions. Murray studied various ancient recipes for the preparation of witch ointments for these purposes, containing such ingredients as the fat of a deceased, unchristened baby, mixed with wolfsbane (leaves of aconite), poplar leaves and other potent herbs. By this means, said the old textbooks, the witch would be carried through the air in a moonlight night 'to feasting, singing, dancing, kissing, and other acts of venery with such youths as they love and desire mostly'.

The Brighton witch and author, Doreen Valiente, maintains that the ingredient of child's fat was merely a touch of the horrific; more likely it would have been hog's lard. But she does recount an interesting story of a German doctor who carried out a test, using one of these recipes. Dr Erick-Will Peuckert, of the University of Göttingen, and an assistant, followed the instructions to the letter, and then rubbed the ointment all over their bodies. They both fell into a deep sleep for twenty hours. When they awoke, they suffered a severe hangover and made immediate notes of their 'experiences'.

Both independently recorded wild dreams. Dr Peuckert said he dreamed of flying through the air, and of wild orgiastic rites, and of monsters and demons. The doctor concluded that his experiments proved the narcotic value of the salve which induced this kind of hallucinogenic response. And while strongly warning against amateur dabbling, Doreen Valiente herself gives other old recipes for salves which produce a narcotic-induced fantasy of images that could well have been the source of descriptions of the old-time witches' sabbats the witch-hunters obtained in their confessions.

It dovetailed with the claim that witches were able to fly off to these exotic coven meetings, leaving their bodies apparently asleep so that their husbands suspected nothing. There were many such stories, and these colourful accounts were certainly not unlike those recalled by the users of LSD and other psychedelic drugs which became fashionable in the 1960s.

In spite of this gradual debunking of the myths that had been the cause of so many executions, the popular image of witches remained surrounded by an aura of superstition and fear, especially to anyone who read the books of Montague Summers and his acquaintance Denis Wheatley, who sold the family business in 1931 to concentrate on his novels and quickly established himself as one of the most popular authors of this century.

His metier was an alloy of satanism and historical fiction, laden with research, which was immediately identifiable by the titles, such as *The Devil Rides Out*, published in 1935. There followed many like it and in one, *To the Devil – A Daughter*, he admitted that he used Montague Summers as a model for one of his characters, the strange and sinister Canon Copely-Syle. With this kind of attention, the devil was easy meat for the popular newspapers whose upsurge coincided with Summers, Wheatley and the rest.

The headlines soon began to appear whenever there was the discovery of the remnants of 'black magic' rites in some secluded wood, a set of chicken bones arranged in the sign of a cross, a desecrated gravestone or some other outbreak of witchcraft.

Any hint of witchcraft in a small village or town was sufficient to arouse immediate press attention and whip up a frenzy of interest, even as time progressed through this century. The reaction was generally the opposite in areas of the country where witchcraft had been prevalent; they preferred not to speak of it.

There was no better example of this than the murder of an old farmhand in the village of Lower Quinton, Warwickshire, in February 1945. It later became known as the 'witchcraft murder' when a writer discovered links with the occult. The victim, Charles Walton, a seventy-four-year-old farmhand and suspected witch, was found lying on his back under a willow tree, with a pitchfork driven through his throat and into the ground. A cross had been carved on his chest and the billhook which had been used was left lodged between his ribs, at the base of the cross.

Lower Quinton was in the heart of witch country, and surrounded by relics where spirits from the old gods were said to linger (those of pagan persuasion today find the place filled with atmosphere). Not far from where old Charlie was found, by the side of Meon Hill, stand the Rollright Stones that are thought to be as old as Stonehenge itself and where witches are known to hold their sabbats still.

The prehistoric stones, which form a correct circle, are located between Long Compton and Chipping Norton. The area is dotted with sinister names like Devil's Elbow and Lower Slaughter. And for those in the know it was considered no coincidence that Walton was murdered on 14 February, the day of Candlemas by the old calendar, one of the Great Sabbats in the witches' calendar.

Inspector Fabian of Scotland Yard took over the investigation. It was the sort of killing whose details he would relish. But Fabian came up against the proverbial wall of silence. Local villagers did not want to talk about the murder; they had convinced themselves that Charlie Walton was a witch. He was said to have bred toads and sometimes harnessed them to a miniature plough and allowed them to run in the fields. This was known to be one of the methods of an infamous and malicious witch of the eighteenth century and was said to make the fields sterile and the harvests fail. The previous year, during the height of the deprivation of the war years, the harvests had been poor around Lower Quinton. And, so the story goes, the finger was pointed at Charlie Walton.

Then another coincidence was discovered, which later investigators who followed Fabian saw as a precedent to Walton's murder – and which demonstrated the traditional methods of disposing of witches in these parts, that of blooding them so that as they bled their power vanished.

Seventy years earlier and just two miles from where Walton was found, an old woman named Anne Turner died in exactly the same manner – speared and pinned to the ground by a pitchfork and with a cross carved on her chest by a billhook. On that occasion, a local peasant named John Haywood confessed to the crime; he said the old woman had bewitched him.

Fabian of the Yard had no such confession to solve the Walton murder. His men took down four thousand statements in writing and acquired dozens of samples of clothing, hair and blood for forensic testing, but the investigation came to naught. In the annals of British criminal history, the Walton case was relatively unimportant, except to show how the fear of witchcraft continued in the countryside. Walton's death had all the hallmarks of being sacrificial, perhaps premeditated and planned. Even a black dog – identified as his familiar – was found hanged two days after the murder. Old fears die hard and Fabian packed up and went home, defeated. Old Charlie Walton had the dubious distinction of being the last known witch – if indeed he was one – to die a brutal death in England.

By then, the last major 'witch' trial had also reached its conclusion. Actually, Helen Duncan, whose case at the Old Bailey in 1944 lasted eight days, was not a witch in the true sense of the word, although she was charged under the Witchcraft Act of 1735. But her case, which became an interesting newspaper diversion to the final events of the war, highlighted the beginning of another significant step in the witchcraft revival. She was prosecuted after police raided a seance she was conducting as a spiritual medium. Her known clients included numerous well-to-do people, often anxious to make contact with the 'other side' after wartime tragedies.

Mrs Duncan was well known to the police, and the authorities. A senior police officer who led the raid said she had broken the nation's security laws by 'predicting the loss of one of His Majesty's ships before the fact was made public'. Mrs Duncan's daughter, Gena Brealey, explained that at one of her mother's seances, a young sailor who served aboard HMS *Barham* manifested himself and told how his ship had been sunk with considerable loss of life.

The sailor's mother refused to believe it, saying that if this had happened she would have been informed by the Royal Navy. 'You will be, mother, three weeks from now,' came the reply from the dead son through the medium. And according to Mrs Brealey, the confirmation came through exactly as predicted.

At her trial, Mrs Duncan offered to give a séance to prove her abilities. Witnesses also came forward in her defence, but their testimony went unheeded. The Old Bailey Recorder was adamant in his summing up of the case, 'If Mrs Duncan . . . by going into a trance or stimulating a trance pretended to hold communion with spirits that was the kind of conjuration which is referred to in the Witchcraft Act.' She was found guilty and sentenced to nine months' imprisonment; little more than two hundred years earlier she would have been hanged.

Unlike witches, who had no public support because they were deemed to exist no longer, the phenomenon of spiritualism and clairvoyance had grown immensely since the Victorian era and had many prominent people among its believers. There was also a strong lobby movement called the Spiritualists' National Union which immediately began a vociferous campaign over the injustice of the Duncan case, to which they enlisted the support of anthropologists, lawyers and even some policemen.

The laws that allowed such a prosecution were clearly obsolete and out of date; there was no place for them in the new free society of postwar Britain. Eventually, sympathetic MPs bowed to public opinion and agreed to repeal the ancient Act. Also repealed was Section Four of the Vagrancy Act of 1824 so far as it extended 'to persons purporting to act as spiritualistic mediums or to exercise any powers of telepathy, clairvoyance or other similar power . . .'

The two Acts were replaced by the Fraudulent Mediums Act, 1951 which, as the title explains, finally gave spiritualists and mediums the freedom to operate legally – unless they could be shown to be obtaining money or kind by fraud. Any payment for the demonstration of psychic powers for the purposes of entertainment was also freed from the dangers of the law.

The lawmakers had prised open the floodgates to allow easy passage for a new movement of witchcraft, paganisn, satanism, occultism, spiritualism, mediums, clairvoyance, fortune-tellers, tarot card readers and newspaper astrologers.

Authors on occult subjects were going to get a new lease of life too and, whether he knew it or not, Robert Graves, who had just completed a new novel, would figure strongly in the rebirth of witchcraft.

It was as if, he said later with a straight face, he had been forced to write the book by some supernatural force. For a man who professed to avoid the occult – 'I am no mystic; I studiously avoided witchcraft, spiritualism, yoga, fortune-telling, automatic writing ... I belong to no religious cult, no secret society, no philosophical sect,' he wrote on page 58 of *Five Pens In Hand* – Robert Graves could not surely have known how his book, entitled *The White Goddess*, published in 1946, would become so important a work for pagans the world over.

It was an oddly constructed and complicated book. He described it as the result of an obsession with the moon goddess and her sacred alder tree which gripped him while he was staying in the village of Glampton, Devon – another area of Britain where the energy and power of spirits of 'the old ones' is professed to abound. According to Graves's research, the deity he had discovered was the goddess of magic, the key to the subconscious and consequently the source of artistic and poetic inspiration.

His contention was that she was the moon goddess worshipped by ancient European civilization and was in turn linked to an African goddess; she was the young maiden of the new moon, the glorious lady of the full moon and the wise old crone of the waning moon.

Graves quoted from original evidence given in a Scottish witch trial of 1597 in which the goddess, or the queen, of the coven was described in detail; she, and all coven queens, were claimed to be the earthly representative of the goddess. More importantly for the pagan movement which was about to emerge from the shadows in twentieth-century Britain, and from there to spread into Europe and America, Graves discovered by a succession of coincidences that his goddess was a universal deity symbolized in pre-Christian mythology, appearing in all of the major old religions, whether they were Greek, Egyptian, Norse, Hindu, African or Celtic.

The strange and often incomprehensible book is filled with what Graves described as ancient secrets which had been 'thrust at him'. His obsession filled his days; he worked furiously at his project and now the coincidences began to arrive more openly, or as cynics might say, very conveniently.

On his desk was an old brass box he had acquired, with a

design on the lid which he had never been able to identify. On the top of the box he used to stand a bronze figure of a humpbacked man. While he was writing the book, a neighbour died and left him an antique carved figure with one eye, and soon afterwards he was given a carnelian ring by a friend, unaware of his moon goddess project, which bore three intertwined symbols. All these items were inextricably linked in their history – the box lid design he discovered ten years later represented the African Moon goddess; the humpbacked figure was the herald of an African Queen mother who claimed direct descendancy from the goddess; the antique figure turned out to be that of an Okrafo priest who was a sacrifice substitute for the White Goddess; the ring carried a seal depicting the three basic symbols of the moon goddess cult: a stag, a moon and a thicket.

'Please believe me,' said Graves, 'I was wholly unaware [of these connections] at the time . . . chains of more than coincidence happen in my life that if I am forbidden to call them supernatural then I must call them habit.'

Coincidence or not, Graves could never explain the speed at which he wrote the 70,000 word manuscript, writing furiously as if charged by some other force. His pen could barely keep up with the words that streamed from his thoughts.

When it was completed, Graves returned to his home in Majorca, drained and tired. Yet sinister coincidences continued. The first publisher to whom he sent his manuscript rejected it out of hand. That publisher died of a heart attack shortly afterwards. The second publisher to read *The White Goddess* returned it with a rejection slip which said he could not make sense of any of it, and doubted if anyone else would, either. He was later found dead, hanging from a tree in his back garden, dressed only in women's underwear and scandalously accused of sexual depravity.

The third person to receive the manuscript was the poet and author T. S. Eliot, who was a director of the publishing firm, Faber and Faber. Though Eliot was devoutly religious, having publicly announced his strict adherence to the Anglo-Catholic movement within the Church of England, he thought the work was of astounding depth and ability and recommended its publication.

The 'reward' was that the publishers made a profit and in the same year the book was published, Eliot was awarded the Order of Merit – an altogether better fate than that suffered by the two who turned it down. Only those with a deep belief in the possibilities of the paranormal would not immediately dismiss the two deaths as purely coincidence, as Graves himself said he would have done – up to that point. Afterwards, he remained altogether more receptive to the idea of some mystical intervention.

As in the work of Charles Godfrey Leland and Dr Murray, Robert Graves concluded that witchcraft was the descendant of primitive religions whose primary deity was a goddess who had been worshipped simultaneously in numerous countries.

What had emerged in each country, without reference to the other, were fixed and static concepts of numerology which were perhaps most simplistically demonstrated by Graves's notation on this point – that the witches' magical number is thirteen, there are thirteen full moons and thirteen witches' Esbat (the monthly meeting of witches' covens); there are thirteen lunar months in a solar year, and twenty-eight days to each lunar month, with one day over. The female cycle of menstruation is twenty-eight days, and menstruation is a word formed from the Greek *mene*, which translates as moon.

For those interested in witchcraft and whose earnest desire was to see it legalized and become respectable, all of this fell neatly into place. The detail from these three authors – allied to ritual described in the writings of Montague Summers and others – provided a broad outline for a new concept of witchcraft as it might be practised in the twentieth century, forging a link from the present day back to pre-Christian times through the re-creation of ritual passed down through the centuries.

There was no organized cult of witchcraft in existence through which this might occur. Knowledge was passed orally down through the ages; very little had been written. Those secret covens – and there were still a few – which operated in Britain and Europe were in no way formally linked by a network administration, secret or otherwise. There were a few national and even international groups which innocently harboured witches, such as the Folk Lore Society, but there was simply no overall body that could claim to represent paganism as an organized religion. And there was certainly no organization for witchcraft because of the law. With the exception of those considered to be hereditary witches, and thus initiated by a member of the family or someone close, witches and pagans might be said to have been in desperate need of some written, detailed analysis of the origins and form of their worship.

Apart from using the sources already mentioned – or embarking on long and meticulous archival research – there was no formal point of reference to confirm the theory and practice of the Old Religions. Nor was there readily available detail of the rituals which produce the power and energy a coven requires to perform its magic. However, for the latter mysteries, there were other authors and practitioners of the dark arts of the occult involved with more academic secret societies who could provide the missing links in the chain of knowledge.

There were two prime sources whose influence on witchcraft is now clear. First was the authoress and occultist Dion Fortune, pseudonym of Miss Violet Firth, who had, in 1927, founded the Fraternity of the Inner Light. This was itself inspired by the more acknowledged – and feared – secret society of the occult, the Order of the Golden Dawn. This society owes its recent fame to one of its former senior brethren, the most infamous of all modern occultists, Aleister Crowley – once dubbed by Lord Beaverbrook 'The Most Evil Man in Britain'.

The careers and influences of both these substantial and fascinating occult figures will be examined more fully in the second part of this book. Suffice, for the moment, to say that Dion Fortune's *The Mystical Qabalah* (published in 1935) and *The Sea Princess* (1938), along with Crowley's modern day 'bibles' of the occult *The Book of Law* and *Magick in Theory and Practice* are among the most consulted handbooks of modern occultists.

There were a number of parallel lines of thought which ran through witchcraft and the higher forms of occult study and it would not be a difficult task for an inventive researcher to merge the elements gleaned from all of these works with the rituals of the so-called old religions to produce an acceptable and potent new form of witchcraft.

*

The man who spotted both the gap in written knowledge and the lack of any kind of organizational source when witchcraft became legal in 1951, was a retired civil servant Gerald Brosseau Gardner, inventor of a witch-cult – and an old fraud.

Gerald Gardner was already a practising witch although he was almost sixty before he was initiated into a coven which operated secretly near the New Forest. It was an old-established coven by all accounts and among the more renowned – but secret – rituals the coven performed was their attempt to stop Hitler invading British shores in the early summer of 1940. They claimed responsibility for the historic mystery of why Hitler stalled the invasion of Great Britain. (The same coven, in the early nineteenth century, is said to have gone into ritual to stop Napoleon.)

The twentieth-century descendant of this New Forest coven was said to have been made up of a mixture of well-to-do middle-class people and poorer countryfolk. It performed its ritual on the full moons of June, July and August and the latter was the day Hitler scrapped the invasion plans. But then, he, too, was a moon person who relied on the prophecies of his astrologers and fortune-tellers.

The group were deadly serious about their secret rituals to keep Hitler at bay and decided beforehand that they could leave nothing to chance. But to be 100 per cent effective there would have to be a human sacrifice. It is said that the oldest and frailest member of the coven volunteered to die during the ritual, set for what proved to be the coldest May night in many years. According to Francis King, author of many books on the occult, all but the frail old man had covered their bodies with an ointment, which was in reality a heavy grease used among other things to keep the body warm.

The coven was also known to use an hallucinogen, the fly agaric mushroom, which could be eaten only in exceedingly small doses. Having formed their magic circle in the depths of the forest, the group, who were naked, made a line and held hands and then danced furiously around a small bonfire, chanting the incantation banishing Hitler from these shores. They performed the rite with such vigour that one or two of them fainted, a not uncommon experience when a serious amount of power and energy is aroused by the performance of ritual.

The old volunteer duly collapsed and died, and it is not known whether it was from an overdose of mushrooms, over-exhaustion or the cold. The great sacrifice had been made and the potency of their magic could only have been enhanced when two other members of the coven died from pneumonia in the following two weeks, and two others passed to the waiting room for reincarnation not long afterwards.

Hitler, meanwhile, decided he might be better employed on the Russian front.

Gardner had joined the coven in the early days of the war, having recently retired to the New Forest area with his wife, a former vicar's daughter, Donna Rosedale, whom he had married in 1927; she never joined him in his interest in witchcraft. He was a strange-looking man by the 1940s – frail and thin, white-haired and sporting a neat goatee beard. He had spent much of his adult life abroad, mostly in the Middle East where a latent interest in the occult had been strengthened by his experiences of eastern mysticism and folklore. Prior to his joining a government department, largely engaged in customs work, he had undergone the most curious of upbringings.

Born in Great Cosby, Lancashire, on 13 June 1884, he had been brought up almost entirely by a nanny who was provided with the funds to take him on travels to various parts of the world, to climates which aided treatment of his early chronic asthma. She was apparently given to beating her charge, which is said to have caused his own passion for flagellation in later life. He was also known for a peculiar habit – whenever it rained, he might take off all his clothes and sit upon them until the rain had passed. When the nanny married, he even went to live with her and her husband in Ceylon, thereafter remaining abroad, mostly in colonial service, until his retirement.

When he came back to England, he and his wife took a house close to the New Forest. Before long he heard of a group of people who were running what was then called The First Rosicrucian Theatre. The name intrigued him, because of the connections with the occult of that most secret of all secret societies, the Rosicrucian

Brotherhood. Unheard of before 1598, its very existence was so dark and mysterious that many even doubted it was real. Its aims and objects were various, ranging from the manufacture of gold through alchemy to the moral renewal and perfection of mankind.

It is said the Brotherhood eventually became incorporated into Freemasonry, though there are still rumours that it exists and it has inspired a cluster of fictional works including Lord Lytton's romance of *Zanoni* and Shelley's *St Irvyne the Rosicrucian*. The New Forest group ran under the title of the Fellowship of Crotona, administered by Brother Aurelius, but their relationship to the Rosicrucians was so diluted and distant as to be non-existent.

However, Gardner became interested in their amateur dramatics and it was while working with the group that he became suspicious of the existence of an inner movement unconnected with Brother Aurelius and his teachings.

Before long, Gardner discovered that the Fellowship of Crotona was being used as a front by a long-established coven of witches, made up quite well-to-do people from the Bournemouth area. He was initiated into the coven in September 1939 by the High Priestess whom he named only as Old Dorothy (later identified by Doreen Valiente as Dorothy Clutterbuck, the spinster daughter of a British army officer who spent her early life in India).

Excited by the ritual and the illegality of the coven, Gardner became an ardent student of witchcraft. Because his coven was made up entirely of elderly people who merely possessed partial knowledge of the old religion and the ritual, he began a comprehensive study of recent books (mostly those already mentioned). He believed there was an urgent task ahead of him, especially when five coven members died after conducting their rite against Hitler, and seemed to believe that it was up to him to save witchcraft from extinction – which many in the establishment of British society considered had already happened, otherwise the repeal of the Witchcraft Act might not have proceeded so smoothly.

Two years before the legalization of witchcraft, Gardner had written a book under the pen-name of Scire (so as not to be identified) entitled *High Magic's Aid* – an unreadable historical novel which barely disguised his intent to expound his beliefs about the origins of witchcraft and reveal some of the current practices of witch covens, including a thinly veiled description of the work of his own coven.

To his first-hand experiences in the New Forest, he added some of the ritual and historical research gleaned from books including those of Leland, Murray and Crowley – and added an overlay of nudity and flagellation largely contrived from his own sado-masochistic imagination.

Though nudity is a part of ancient rites, as is flagellation which was used to 'whip up' the dancers into a frenzy within their magic circle, Gardner's eventual conception of witchcraft rituals involved a good deal of sexual practice, actual and simulated. It was this area which was often challenged by the detractors of his guide to witchcraft when it became universally known; it might also be one of the causes of the constant and unconfirmed rumour that witches indulge in sexual orgies of a kind to make the Romans proud.

Gardner, like the acquisitive Romans, linked part of his ritual to his investigation of the cult of the Greek god Dionysus. This cult, which was adopted by the Romans in the name of Bacchus, was originally confined to women and degenerated badly when men were admitted to its mysteries, to such a degree that it was officially abolished by the Romans in 186 BC. The orgiastic rites which caused the controversy were continued in underground religious movements, especially in Italy where it surfaced again in Leland's *Aradia, Gospel of the Witches*.

It was Gardner's personal interest in flagellation and bondage that led him to study the mysteries of this cult which used it as part of the ritual for the raising of esoteric forces from within the body. Outside the occult, of course, flagellation had become more widely known as an aphrodisiac whose popularity rose amongst the gentlemen visiting eighteenth-century brothels.

Next, Gardner began to write out in longhand a compilation of ritual and ceremony, a sort of grimoire or magician's handbook of the type compiled by occultists and alchemists of old. He called it his *Book of Shadows* and claimed it contained the handed-down version of his own coven's centuries-old theory and practice of witchcraft. By tradition in witchcraft and the occult, practitioners of both were expected to write in their own hand a diary of their workings and rituals; printed versions were said to cause the loss of power.

It was this work that was to form the basis of the re-creation of modern witchcraft, and it is used in covens the world over as what amounts to the new witches' gospel. Other variations followed, and of course many covens and hereditary witches who do not practise the Gardnerian technique today were formed under other pagan regimes, notably Druidism, Odinism and eastern ritual. Lately, there has been an increase in the influence of the intellectual aspects of magical tradition.

None the less, in the Wiccan world, Gardner became recognized as having started the ball rolling immediately the opportunity presented itself. His *Book of Shadows* became hailed as a masterpiece of witchcraft and still is by the Gardner devotees today who revere his memory and regard him as a brilliant scholar, a wise and learned old man who restarted the craft single-handed.

In truth, it wasn't quite like that. Gardner claimed, or at least did not disclaim, that he was an MA and Ph.D, but had apparently won neither. He did not even have a formal education, having been taught by his governess and self-taught in the later years of his life when he embarked on various archaeological projects. Doreen Valiente, who was initiated into Gardner's coven in Bournemouth and later became one of his High Priestesses, discovered that his renowned *Book of Shadows* was not all that it was claimed to be – i.e. the handed-down ritual of perhaps a thousand years of witchcraft. She identified passages from Charles Godfrey Leland's book on Aradia; she found that the chant used in one of the rituals was adapted from a poem by Rudyard Kipling; and some of the magical rites were obtained from Aleister Crowley whom Gardner met a year or two before The Great Beast, as he was known, died.

Crowley initiated Gardner into his own international occult brotherhood, Ordo Templi Orientis, and passed him some of the order's rituals for a fee of £300. Ms Valiente recalls that when she challenged Gardner on this plagiarism, he explained that the rituals in his New Forest coven were fragmented and incomplete and it had been necessary for him to supplement the detail from the studies of other works.

Much later, Ms Valiente discovered that even the title of his grimoire, the *Book of Shadows*, which has become the internationally known name to describe a witches' book of working practice, was lifted from a magazine. She discovered it in an article next to a review of Gardner's book, *High Magic Aid*. The article referred to an ancient Indian system of predicting a person's destiny by the length of his shadow.

So it seemed hardly a coincidence that when Gardner had completed his handwritten book, amounting to a complete guide to witchcraft from initiation to the performance of ritual magic, he chose the title of 'Book of Shadows' to add the final mysterious touch. He must have thought this would give it a similar sort of authority as Crowley's notorious *Book of Law*, an often incomprehensible work which has become the essential handbook for all who follow the Crowley cult, and which is described in detail in later chapters.

So Gardner had pulled together all the essential elements of the last half century of research into the old religions, plagiarizing the novels and non-fiction, stripping in elements from Crowley's ritual magic, some from Dion Fortune and Denis Wheatley and even a line or two from the rites of Freemasonry; he incorporated the old rituals used in his own New Forest coven and added the exaggeration of his personal preference for nudity, flagellation and bondage. And modern witchcraft was born.

The whole was written in a kind of pseudo-medieval style which gave it the sound of ancient writings. He retained some of the warnings that belonged to witchcraft in the persecution era. The preface begins: 'Keep a book in your own hand of write. Let brothers and sisters copy what they will; but never let the book out of your hands and never keep the writings of another, for if found in their hand of write they may well be taken and tortured . . .' He advised any who had confessed to witchcraft to obtain relief from torture to deny their confession afterwards and warned that there would be no hope in this life or the next for any who betrayed the Brotherhood. But those who went steadfast to their death would experience the ecstasy of the Goddess.

*

One who knew Gardner and was initiated into one of his offshoot covens and has been associated with witchcraft ever since, recalled for me:

> It was a clever piece of work, well thought out and researched and had the appearance of being very authentic if you didn't look too closely. The original text is still widely used today and has an especially large following in America, Europe and Australia. But there were a lot of suspect passages which I think revealed the fact that he had copied bits and pieces from other books and writings; this was certainly not the truly ancient document he claimed it to be. There were no witch burnings, for example, in England, only in Scotland, and of course very few witches of that era would have been able to read, let alone set anything down in their own 'hand of write'.
>
> There were a number of things Gardner injected to add some excitement and sexuality and those groups around the world who follow his teachings can be recognized for them. His Great Rite of Third Degree initiation for witches, which is the last and highest level of the three grades of the craft, was based on the act of sexual intercourse between the priest and the priestess in front of the coven. This followed the five-fold kiss, when the priestess kissed her High Priest on the lips, the breasts and the genitals, the knees and the feet – all performed naked, of course. It was a powerful and striking ritual – although many successive groups felt that it was overdone, and curtailed it, so that the overtly sexual contact was between the parties in private. Equally, many did not object to it, and use it even today with great respect.
>
> Others did not like the bondage elements, like having their hands bound for one of the initiations, or having your blood flow controlled by the cords to lessen the senses when combined with flagellation in one of his rituals. Some especially did not like the line in his ritual to achieve power, where the witch tutor is recommended to beat the initiate with a flagellum 'with steady, slow and monotonous strokes . . . till blood came . . . but beware, it has been found that this practice doth often cause fondness between aspirant and tutor . . .'
>
> He was certainly controversial but in spite of it all, those

who eventually discovered the truth about his *Book of Shadows* realized, or convinced themselves, that it did not matter that he stole half of his material or copied rituals from other books and poets. They reckoned it was impossible for anyone to get a complete hand-me-down set of instructions for what witches do – and so, at the very least, Gardner can be credited with starting the whole thing up again.

He was heavily criticized by some for his self-promotional stunts and revealing the inner secrets of the craft by publicity. But he gave witchcraft a new lease of life and the old fool, sincere as he was in most things, seriously believed that it would become a leading religion of the future. At best, what he did was to whitewash witchcraft and create a beautiful image out of his imagination. It was a product of his research but in truth it had little to do with paganism and the old traditions. I was personally never quite convinced, however. I am an hereditary witch and though I worked with Gardner, I always had a feeling that at the end of the day, he just enjoyed seeing young women prancing about naked . . . and he especially enjoyed the bondage and flagellation.

But in 1951, it was suddenly all legal – and Gerald Gardner launched into a very public renaissance of witchcraft. He embarked upon a campaign aimed at trying to break the fear of witchcraft that still existed, at least in the minds of those who came into direct contact with it – and more especially in the minds of newspaper editors to whom the forthcoming emergence from the shadows of the naked, dancing, flagellating groups of witches was just what the doctor ordered to bolster the circulations of the Sunday papers.

CHAPTER FOUR

A NEW WITCH KING

In his ambition to banish the fear of witchcraft in society and make it more publicly acceptable, Gerald Gardner played right into the hands of Fleet Street and enemies in the Church who rose against him with a ferocity he might have anticipated but did not. One of his former coven members who described the years of post-legalization to me thought Gardner was 'naïve in the extreme' not to have expected the reaction. 'He dreamily and sincerely believed that by giving interviews and telling all, he could get everyone on his side, and especially the newspapers. He expected their reaction to be sweetness and light, to confirm that witchcraft existed for good and not evil. He was to be sorely disabused of that belief.'

During the three or four years after the old witchcraft laws were scrapped, Gardner had a new book published, entitled *Witchcraft Today*, and it gathered a fair degree of attention, confirming for the first time that witch covens still existed and revealing what he described as some of the ancient secrets of the cult – even though half of them were of his own creation. He followed up with lecture tours and broadcast on radio. He became associated with a witch museum on the Isle of Man that attracted a great deal of publicity, giving interviews to any reporter who came to call, in the hope that by spreading his message, many more people would become interested and join what he believed would be seen as an alternative religion – as indeed it was to those true devotees at its heart.

He saw himself as some kind of Messiah; his message was the religion of witchcraft. He stopped short of revealing some of the inner secrets of his cult, although ironically one of the vows of newly initiated witches was that they should not speak of the mysteries *at all*. By opening the doors of his covens and revealing some of the rudiments of ritual worship, he stirred up a new hornets' nest.

Although many people throughout the country responded and began enquiring about 'joining', the Sunday papers took up the gauntlet, and one after the other ran exposés of what witches do, under intriguingly lurid headlines proclaiming the dangers of black magic and the 'frenzied naked dance rituals' of the covens. A new witch fever developed; important churchmen spoke out against this infectious evil and there were immediate calls by some MPs for a re-imposition of the laws of prohibition. The *News of the World* claimed that Britain was 'plagued by the biggest upsurge of interest in black magic and the timeless secrets of witchcraft since the Middle Ages.' That was not an overstatement.

If they only knew it, these exhibitionist incidents which became public knowledge were just the tip of the iceberg. What had been emerging for some years was an astonishing revival in occult interest and ritual magic in particular. Witchcraft was just one relatively minor offshoot and, unfortunately for Gerald Gardner, the darker forces of the occult and the so-called black magic groups were springing up everywhere, especially in the Midlands and around the Birmingham area. They were in danger of out-publicizing the 'white and good' witches of the Gardnerian-style groups by the very nature of their activities.

For those newspaper investigators to whom the whole occult community could be wrapped up into one malevolent package, there was sufficient evidence from interviews with Gardner and others to show that the witch cult was very much alive and expected to expand. By the very existence of the mixture of 'white' and 'black' groups, it is only human nature that the worst should be expected, and that in assessing the impact and existence of witchcraft in local communities they were all pretty well tarred by the same brush.

In the eyes of the enquiring beholder, witchcraft, black magic, satanism and the rest, became one and the same. It was too much to expect that the differences between the cults, so obvious to the witch fraternity, would neither be seen nor understood by the general public. Magic is magic, black or white, and because the secrecy surrounding it, oddly still propounded by Gardner who maintained that all witches were bound by an oath of silence, the newspapers became intent on exposing what went on behind the closed doors of the witches' 'temple'. With rumours of sex orgies and blood-lust abounding, it made excellent copy, as did the outbreak of black magic, unconnected with Gardner and his group.

On top of it all, Donald McCormick published a book investigating the 'witch murder' of old Charlie Walton back in 1945 and the balloon went up again. Witchcraft became a national obsession. Gardner had contributed to it by going public in the hope of making witchcraft more widely acceptable, and then discovered to his horror that he could not control things when the press turned against him.

Nothing like it had been seen for many, many years and suddenly the media were filled with witch stories. Although the decade was fast approaching the onset of the 'swinging sixties', in austere, post-war Britain most children still went to Sunday school, skirts were long and pretty well everything revolved around family life in which Christian values were generally the norm. Nothing had changed in the public's perception of the occult and the paranormal.

This was perhaps understandable, especially when such things as nudity and flagellation were involved. Sex was still a dirty word and the only nudes to be found were motionless in Soho sleaze clubs, the National Gallery or in photographic magazines. To have naked witches prancing about the countryside was regarded as nothing less than shocking. To have them flailing each other with scourges was considered nothing less than perverted.

Gardner disregarded, or ignored, the possibility that he might be taken to the village stocks and pelted with rotten fruit. Not content with trying to organize the complete revival of witchcraft as a religion, he also became involved with a nudist colony which operated at Ricketts Wood, near St Albans. He bought the land where the naturists met so that he could rebuild a small white, timber-framed cottage that apparently had once been owned by a witch and had a 'special atmosphere', for his meetings. His London coven used to congregate there for a number of years and the naturists who used the adjoining land provided a very good cover in the early days from prying neighbours who were already aware of the eccentrics who used the woods.

One Hallowe'en, several carloads of Fleet Street reporters descended on Ricketts Wood, with a huge searchlight mounted on a lorry, expecting to discover the Gardnerian coven engaged in ritual activity. All they found were a couple of people taking wine in the cottage and they retired without story or pictures. But Gardner's cover was blown, and the witch cottage was demolished.

There were several landmarks during this new witch craze and not the least of them was a front-page story of a particularly gruesome desecration of a grave in the village of Clophill, Bedfordshire, which is still spoken of today. A local resident, Robert Watson, who lived nearby recalled for me:

> In village life, especially then, anything untoward was a major event. Our villages were still largely unaffected by commuterization and the population didn't really change a great deal from one year to the next. So the discovery of black magic rites being performed on their own doorstep put the fear of God into the community. There was always a suspicion of a witches' coven locally. People used to talk vaguely about them; witches, black magicians, no one could differentiate because they had no knowledge on which to judge. One morning in March 1963 it was discovered that a huge granite slab covering one of the graves in the village churchyard had been moved, and the remains of the body of a girl called Jenny Humberstone who died in 1720 had been removed . . .

The story gradually unfolded when one of those taking part in what transpired to be a black mass staged inside the old Clophill church confessed to a newspaper. The skull and bones of Jenny Humberstone had been taken from the grave and arranged inside the church over a makeshift altar. A Celtic cross in a circle was painted in blood-red paint on the wall and a white chicken was sacrificed in an hour-long ritual.

Almost thirty years later, locals still talk of the witches of Clophill because at the time, it caused an uproar of protest culminating in a powerful article published by the *News of the World*, which dismissed talk of white witches who heal and do good and thundered 'in our considered opinion witchcraft and black magic are a state of mind . . . youngsters out for kicks will find only depravity, disillusion and destruction in this thing called witchcraft.'

This was the way witchcraft and black magic touched local communities; in fact it was generally the only form of occult practice – discounting mediums and fortune-tellers – which would come into general contact with everyday life. That there existed on a higher level an abundance of high magic ritual, performed in privacy by some leading academics and local pillars of society in their various secret societies, ranging from the Temples of the Kabbalah to, at the other extreme, the satanists in whom interest was already beginning to emerge, was never mentioned – largely because in those areas secrecy was maintained.

It was at a local level that witches were exposed and the Clophill mystery demonstrated the apprehension that still existed.

Another example occurred later that year, when a witch called Sybil Leek, who lived in the village of Burley, Hampshire, where she ran an antique shop, suddenly sprang into the headlines. She was well known in the area because she was seldom seen without a noisy pet jackdaw, named Jackson Hotfoot, that perched on her shoulder. She was married with two sons, and occasionally appeared on local television talking about folklore and the antiquities of the New Forest area, about which she was knowledgeable. It was only when she revealed that she was a practising witch, and had witches among her ancestors, that things began to go wrong. And yes, the jackdaw was her familiar, she admitted.

In September 1963 the *Daily Herald* headlined her confession that she was a witch, had been initiated by her grandmother in France in her youth and was a member of one of four covens operating around the New Forest. The commotion which followed stirred up unrest in the village and soon there was a concerted campaign to get her to leave. A Canadian television company arrived to do a special programme on her, visitors began looking for the Witch of Burley and the local church people were up in arms.

It hardly seemed coincidence later that the landlord of Sybil's antique shop refused to renew the lease, and evicted her, or that the owner of her rented cottage decided he wanted it back for his own use. The two sons began to get abuse at school. Sybil, a substantial woman of fifteen stones or more and renowned for her eccentric mode of dress, her green eye make-up, golden snake bracelets and golden sandals, was not one to be scared off easily.

'It wasn't as if I was a black witch,' she recalled later. 'Everything I did was for the benefit of others. I spoke out against all satanic practices and my coven was wholly concerned with good work. But people around me, my neighbours, could never grasp that; a witch is a witch and that's that. One to one, you might get a sympathetic ear but collectively people you thought were your friends took on the form of a lynch mob.' Before long Sybil and her husband went off to America where she had been offered a lecture tour – and the response was such that they decided to stay.

She became quite successful, appearing on television and writing for magazines. 'I was lucky in that respect – but I was left in no doubt whatsoever that I had been driven out of my home and business because of my involvement in the craft.' She and her husband eventually set up home in southern California and she found she could talk openly in America about her spells and potions without an immediate outbreak of witch hysteria. In fact, she claimed to act as occultist and astrologer for several well-known personalities and public figures.

And so the hounding of Sybil Leek in Hampshire had a happy ending for her. But at the time the story merely added to the crescendo of witch-craze publicity that year and before long, questions were being raised in high places.

On 21 November 1963, Commander John Kerans, Tory MP for Hartlepool, asked Home Secretary Henry Brooke if, in the light of newspaper reports on witchcraft, he had considered introducing laws to make it illegal. He said it was clear to everyone that so often it was merely a cover for sexual orgies and other misdemeanours. Brooke replied that he did not intend to reintroduce laws prohibiting witchcraft and pointed out that there were sufficient laws to cover any such malpractice, including the Sexual Offences Act.

Gerald Gardner, seen by many to have brought this massive press interest down upon his own head, had gone to ground; five or six years of relentless publicity had made him an internationally known figure. Though he had revelled in his fame, it had turned sour. His coven was split by disillusionment. Some of his early followers had left because of the publicity, others never quite forgave him for misleading them over his claims that the *Book of Shadows* was anything other than the genuine article, the record of handed-down tradition which it was not.

In spite of those misgivings, however, his writings on witchcraft were taken up by students of the craft, as well as anthropologists, the world over. In ten years, he had accumulated what can only be described as a substantial band of followers, some taking his work as gospel, others using it as a guide and adjusting his theory and practice to their own requirements.

From there its influence continued to expand and flourish into the 1990s. Past doubts were forgotten and the Gospel of Gerald Gardner had become witches' law, together with the belief that he had handed on the tablets of knowledge from time immemorial, even if he had been forced to improvise.

That winter of 1963 Gardner left the witchcraft furore behind, and headed off for a holiday in the sunshine of Beirut, then one of the jewels of Middle Eastern tourism. Later, he went aboard a steamer, the SS *Scottish Prince*, to sail the coast of North Africa. On the morning of 12 February 1964, he collapsed and died of a heart attack while having breakfast. He was buried at Tunis, the next port of call. The death of 'The King of Witches' was recorded in newspapers around the world.

Did he possess important ancient knowledge or was he just an old crank? No one cares, least of all the many Gardnerians who still pursue his original Book of Shadows and they would say that it matters not if he invented half the ritual, so long as it works.

The Wicca movement was left leaderless but there were two contenders waiting in the wings, both controversial characters for different reasons. The first was Robert Cochrane, an angry young man who claimed to be an hereditary witch and could not be doing with Gerald Gardner's niceties. He was initiated into the craft at the age of five and said he was able to trace his witch ancestry to the eighteenth century when two of his predecessors were hanged. He ran a coven from his home in Sussex and initiated many of today's leading occultists, some of whom went on from witchcraft into higher forms of ritual magic.

Cochrane has been described by some as a genius who berated Gerald Gardner's brand of Wicca as Sunday school material. As his activities grew in the early sixties, he veered towards the grey, if not black, magic. He spoke angrily about the publicity given to witchcraft and the various writings that had made it popular. He believed they not only gave the wrong impression of the truth, but also undermined what true witchcraft was about; and that, according to him, was power: the power of will over others.

His beliefs were aligned to serious occultism and he wrapped everything he did in mystification, claiming that nothing should ever be written down that could either solve the mysteries of witchcraft or even confirm its existence. His initiates all had to wear jet-black robes and he was the organizer of some of the archetypal outdoor coven meetings, especially on the Sussex downs, that would go on all night. Descriptions of them sounded reminiscent of old-time witches' sabbats: dancing around a fire until his coven members were ready to drop with exhaustion, calling up what he believed was enormous energy that he could use to his own authoritarian ends.

Cochrane's work became the talk of witchcraft, but gradually his expertise in ritual magic began to take on more sinister tones. He had become obsessed by his authority over all others, claiming to be a Magister of Witches – the person of highest office – and threatening anyone who went against him with dire consequences. His wife Jean rebelled against his sexual activity with new members of his coven, and left him. Worse, Cochrane was experimenting with the use of various ancient potions made from poisonous or narcotic herbs and mushrooms that would heighten the spiritual experiences and assist in the passage of his members to a higher plane of working.

He even forced a young couple who went through the ritual witches' marriage ceremony, known as handfasting, to drink a potentially lethal mixture of herbs and berries of deadly nightshade; if they survived it would show that the gods approved of the wedding. The couple were so violently sick that the poison was fortunately ejected from their bodies almost immediately, otherwise they would probably have died.

Not long afterwards, in 1966, Cochrane became the victim of his own stupidity. He drank a fatal cocktail of deadly nightshade berries and psychedelic mushrooms laced with crushed sleeping pills. Needless to say, he did not wake up and left his followers trying to work out the inexplicable mystery – had he committed the ultimate ritual self-sacrifice on their behalf or had he just accidentally overdosed himself on his magical concoction? No one will ever know, and the coroner assumed a more Christian stance, that he committed suicide while the balance of his mind was disturbed. But his death gave new impetus to his somewhat renowned form of witchcraft which is still widely practised today, and has an especially devout following in America.

Coincidentally, the departure to the other side of these two founding fathers of modern witchcraft marked the arrival in the public eye of the man who was to become self-proclaimed King of the Witches, although he appears to have engineered the proclamation of his succession himself. There was no heir apparent to Gardner or Cochrane; the movement was leaderless again and the new man, named Alex Sanders, made his bid and launched what eventually became known as the Alexandrian movement, which rivalled the Gardnerian way for international acclaim among the world's witches.

He also carried the witch cult forward into another bout of highly publicized activities that, in the beginning, had all the hallmarks of being perpetrated by a conman and a fraud.

Like Gardner, Sanders carried the flame of controversy wherever he went, and it rages today, largely over discussions of his authenticity. Born in 1926, he was a curious man, small and thin, with a receding hairline and bandy legs. He made up for his diminutive, Nero-like appearance by a flair for flamboyance and self-promotion that made Gerald Gardner look self-effacing. His most favoured mode of dress was a dark cape with a touch of glistening braid, and he wore jet-black-lensed spectacles long before wearing sun-glasses when the sun wasn't shining became fashionable.

He, too,had a curious background in the north of England (he was born in Manchester) and his early days in the practice of witch magic certainly had a charlatanesque air. He claimed his introduction to witchcraft came from his maternal grandmother, Mary Bibby, who told him that he was a descendant of a medieval King of Witches, the Welsh chieftain Owain Glyn Dwr. His first initiation into witchcraft came at the age of seven and I quote from a recorded interview with Sanders for his description of it:

I was sent round to my grandmother's house for tea one day in 1933 and as usual I just barged straight in through the front door; it was never locked in those days. I found her in the kitchen. She was naked and her grey hair, which she usually had tied up in a bun, was hanging down around her waist. She was standing in a circle drawn on the floor in white chalk, and there were a number of odd things lying around, such as a knife and a sword and there were other items on the Welsh dresser including a small statuette of a goat-like figure, all neatly laid out.

I don't think she was expecting me at that moment, because she seemed a bit angry. But she told me to take off my clothes and step into the circle. This I did, half scared to death. She told me not to be frightened, and to bend over. She spoke some strange words and then took her knife and nicked my scrotum, drawing blood, and said something about me being one of the clan, now. She explained that she was a witch and said that not all witches were bad. I was told we must keep it secret; I should not even tell her daughter who was my mother, and over the months and years, she gradually taught me things like studying the craft, casting spells and how to enduce powers of clairvoyance.

Some time later, on my tenth birthday (in 1936) my grandmother took me on a journey to London and we went to a boarding-house – I have no idea where, now – and I was left with a man she called Mr Alexander. In fact it turned out to be the magician Aleister Crowley who was a friend of hers. She left me with him for the rest of the day, and while I was there he performed The Rites of Horus. He also gave my grandmother a ring, which was to be handed over to me when I was eighteen. It was an engraved silver seal ring which was apparently once owned by Eliphas Levi, the great French magician of the nineteenth century. I never saw Crowley again before he died in 1947, but I eventually obtained the ring and of course I will remember the ritual he performed until my dying day.

After this, I used to continue with the spells and rituals at my grandmother's house, until finally one day she told me I was going to achieve the highest form of priesthood, which was the Third Degree rite where I had to lie on the floor, and she lay on top in a token sexual position – and thus I became a fully fledged witch.

Sander's grandmother died during the war and as a young man, he moved to Manchester, where he continued secretly to practise witchcraft. Gradually, he turned towards black magic, with the sole purpose of attempting to influence his own life and bring himself wealth and success.

He claimed that his spell-casting worked, because one day in the late forties, he was walking in Manchester when he was stopped by a couple who said he was the absolute double of their son who had died some years earlier. They stood chatting for a while and the couple asked him if he would like to go home with them for dinner. He went, and stayed on, living as their adopted son for the next four years when they bought him his own house and gave him a bank account with his own money. 'I can't put that down to anything but the magic I was working,' Sanders claimed. 'I had everything I wanted but I always felt that I was going to have to pay for it in some way.'

There were other rumours that Sanders had gained a hold over the couple by involving them in seances to contact their dead son. Sanders never talked about that, though his former wife Maxine did tell me he was a 'natural medium' and claimed he could call up a Red Indian spirit guide named Red Feather.

Maxine, whom I interviewed in Notting Hill, London, where she and Alex once shared a home, took up the story:

> Before Alex became known publicly, he practised in the Manchester area as a medium and in black magic. He accumulated a sizeable personal fortune. How? People just gave it to him, for helping them or involving them in his seances or magic. In those days, he operated under the name of Paul Dallas and was quite famous locally. He actually used to work in churches as a healer on occasions, though they did not know of his black magic activities. He became a very well-known healer. People who joined his group kept it very much a secret. Any involvement with witches had become a great scandal again, and especially in black magic. One of the newspapers discovered there was a black magic coven operating and had identified two men in his group who would have been ruined if they had been publicly exposed. So Alex took responsibility and told the newspapers he would do a ritual for them. He performed it on Alderley Edge, a romantic beauty spot near Manchester which has ties with the wizard Merlin and King Arthur.

Maxine said that they had a 'body' of a man under a white sheet inside a white circle and surrounded by four lighted candles; the ritual was supposed to show the death of the man's former lifestyle and the rebirth of his new, clean self. Next day, 15 September 1962, the *Manchester Evening News* carried the headline 'Amazing Black Magic Rites on Cheshire Hillside'.

'It was all a fake for the specific purpose of pleasing the newspapers and throwing them off the scent of the other two coven members,' said Maxine. 'The ritual was something like a Swiss roll recipe read backwards and meant nothing. But the headlines went all over the place and that's where the publicity broke for Alex Sanders.'

The death and rebirth of a lifestyle might well have applied to Sanders himself because life had gone sour. According to Maxine, he had discovered that going down the path of black magic – generally known as the left-hand path – was highly dangerous; to get personal wealth and good fortune there would also have to be personal sacrifice. She said that he eventually found out there would be a debt to pay.

In his case, it was his beloved younger sister Joan who contracted cancer while quite young. He became deeply affected by this and very morose, convinced that his activities in black magic had brought about this tragedy, which was heightened by the extent of her long and terrible suffering. He spent eighteen months nursing her, hardly away from her bedside. Maxine added, 'The difference in the working of witchcraft and black magic is that one is for the benefit of others. Black workings are usually for personal gain, either in money or power and influence. But there is always a price to pay. And that is what Alex discovered.'

The death of his sister was followed by other family tragedies and the suicide of a girlfriend. Sanders' money had also disappeared as quickly as it came.

According to Maxine, Sanders denounced black magic and began to devote himself, like Gardner, to furthering witchcraft. For a man who would attract a large following over the next few years, his methods in the early days were strange and often irresponsible. Some would say that this was a kind description.

In fact, many to this day challenge his credentials in witchcraft, pointing out that although he claimed to have been initiated by his grandmother, he wrote to a well-known Sheffield witch, Patricia Crowther, in 1961 to ask if she would initiate him in one of her covens. Mrs Crowther invited Sanders to attend an interview for assessment and he also attended a coven meeting. Mrs Crowther says today that she did not care for him much because he boasted that he 'could make the front page of the *Manchester Evening News* any time I want' and she declined to accept him into her coven.

This became the source of the rumours that Sanders was not an authentic witch. Thirty years later, it still causes controversy within the rivalry that exists between some witch groups since the position of Sanders' Alexandrian movement within international witchcraft depends on the credibility of his lectures and teachings – and therefore on his being an initiated witch.

In 1991, Mrs Crowther was still denying she ever initiated Sanders, stating vehemently, 'I totally refute this allegation and would like to make it clear that I did not at any time initiate Alex Sanders into the craft . . .' She explained that he had written to her after seeing her on a television programme and quoted a line from his letter: 'to be a witch is something I have always wanted and yet I have never been able to contact anyone who could help me . . .'

Sanders was undeterred by this rebuttal and apparently went to see Gerald Gardner on the Isle of Man eighteen months before he died, and persuaded the old man to allow him to copy some of the rituals from his *Book of Shadows*. According to Maxine, Sanders was initiated into the modern craft not by Patricia Crowther but by one of her coven maidens and they set up their own coven together.

The Alexandrian movement was on its way, in spite of an accusation made against him at a meeting of witches by another of Mrs Crowther's initiates, Alan Wharton, an academic and now a High Priest of Wicca. Wharton accused Sanders of being 'a menace to society . . . you have no true knowledge of witchcraft and created more damage to the newly emerging craft than any person I have ever known.'

Maxine, then a stunningly attractive teenager, was to play an important role in his rise to fame. She had first met Sanders when he came to visit her mother Mary Morris who, though a strict Roman Catholic, was interested in the occult, seances and tarot readings, especially after her husband died.

Maxine had already been initiated into the occult world herself, in a ceremony that today could well be classed as satanic ritual abuse. She became fascinated by a young woman who used to visit her mother. The woman, it turned out, was a member of what Maxine described as 'a hightly secret occult lodge of masters and adepts – not witches but more like priests – who followed Egyptian traditions.' One day, the woman took her on a journey to Cheshire for initiation into the lodge, involving a long ceremony deep in underground caverns. She recalled:

> I was driven by car and helped by two initiates who removed the greenery to reveal an entrance to the caverns. They took me into a vast cave, already lit by five flares. Here all my clothes were

taken off and I was washed and purified and dressed in pure white linen robes. I noticed the shadows began to dance in the flickering of flames of the flares . . . I was led down a tunnel and through more caves and across ledges for what seemed like ages . . . until I came to another vast underground cavern which was filled with light. When my eyes got used to the flares, I looked around and the cave was filled with forty or so people each in colourful robes and wearing masks. These were the assessors of the occult lodge and this was their Hall of Judgement . . . I was led into another cave where there were other initiates waiting. My body was anointed with oils and perfumes and I was dressed in fresh robes. I was laid out on a cold rock slab, like a corpse, and was instructed in meditation.

Maxine said she went off into a deep trance – probably caused by the narcotic effect of the substances rubbed on her body – which she compared with an experience she had later while experimenting with LSD. She believed she had travelled on an astral journey and also thought she was in the underground chamber for several days. It is unlikely that she was, because when she awoke and was told the initiation was complete, her mother's friend dressed her and took her back home, where she remembered nothing untoward in her reception.

Maxine's future as a witch was sealed in her early teens when Alex Sanders first began to call at their home. At first, she did not like the little man over whom she towered by several inches, but over the weeks his visits became regular and the group invited by her mother to listen to his talks grew larger. Eventually, Maxine said, she became intrigued by the secrecy of witchcraft and decided that she wanted to be part of it, though her mother refused permission and there was a rift between them resulting in Maxine leaving home and moving into a flat on her own.

At the age of sixteen, she was initiated into Sanders' witch coven, along with a young man named Paul whom she had met quite recently. Sanders had plans for them both. Maxine was to be his Witch Queen, and Paul her High Priest. The first degree initiation as witches was simple compared with what followed in later weeks.

She was told to be afraid of nothing, because fear caused an interruption of the magical powers of witchcraft. Everyone was naked for the ceremony. Maxine was apprehensive about being blindfolded and having her hands tied behind her back and her ankles bound with cord. She and Paul stood on the outside of the magic circle while existing members of the coven performed their ritual, with the High Priestess saying, 'O thou who standest on the threshold between the pleasant world of men and the dread domain of the Lords of the Outer Space, has thou the courage to make the assay?'

The point of the sword was placed against her heart and the ritual continued: 'For I say verily, it were better to rush on my blade and perish than to make the attempt with fear in thy heart . . .'

Maxine, the postulant, was moved to the centre of the circle while the coven members danced around her chanting pre-learned verse. At this point the initiate was given the five-fold kiss by the initiator: a kiss on each foot, to each knee, to the genital area, to each breast and finally to the lips. The initiate was then given forty strokes of the scourge in increasing strength and asked to swear a solemn oath of allegiance that 'I will ever keep secret and never reveal the secrets of the arts . . . mindful that my weapons may turn against me if I break this solemn oath.'

A few weeks later, the last stage of Sanders' plans for Paul and Maxine's promotion to the stars of his magical circus went ahead. This is Maxine's description of the night of her initiation into second and third degree witchcraft:

I stood blindfold again and I was conscious of being led into a room where the incense was so all-pervading that I had to adjust my breathing to it. I had not seen the circle cast but it obviously had been by the other witches present before my arrival in the room. Four candles would have been lit at four points and upon an altar there were assembled a censer that has burdened the room with the incense, an athame [the witch's black-handled knife containing a magical inscription], a pentacle, a wand, water and salt. The water and the salt are consecrated by the touch of the athame. Salt is mixed with the water before the witch walks

the right-hand path around the circle and prepares to enter it at
the north-east point of the pentagram within the circle. Still
blindfold, I heard Alex's voice . . . it is less gentle now. I could
also hear the swishing of the scourge. Everyone present has to be
purified for the initiation and the scourging is part of the
purification.

Then I heard Alex say: 'Hail you mighty one. Maxine, a
duly consecrated priestess is now properly prepared to be made
High Priestess, and Lady and Witch Queen. Hail Mighty One.
Paul, a duly consecrated priest is now properly prepared to be
made High Priest . . .'

Paul was close by me, but blindfolded, I could not see him.
Breathing the heavily pungent air, I was conscious of nothing
but the single voice that was moment by moment taking on new
undertones and becoming barely recognizable. The voice says,
'None may enter this circle, other than naked.' I feel my robe
being opened and hands reach over me to take it off. I am led
into the circle, and I kneel as I hear a bell ringing. Then I felt
the scourge lashing my buttocks, forty strokes in all. It didn't
hurt too badly but I flinched at every stroke. Now I hear Alex's
voice: 'I give thee a new name which I will say is Veda.' I feel
his lips on mine as he pronounces it and I must say . . . 'I Veda,
swear upon my mother's womb . . . I will never reveal to any at
all of the secrets of the Art . . . this I swear in my hope of
salvation . . .'

The ritual continued . . . the cords that bind me are loosened
and the blindfold comes off. Alex is in the circle and he gave us
the cords and said 'Use them!' We must now bind him and he
tells us to take the scourge and return triple the strokes that he
had given me; he looked so frail, I was frightened of hurting him
with the leather thong . . . Paul took over the scourge and there
were one hundred and twenty lashes in all. We untied Alex and
he began to read from his Book of Shadows until the rites of the
second degree initiation are complete.

The third degree rites began immediately. Maxine was laid down
on her back within the circle with arms and legs outstretched so
that her body coincided with the five points of a star. This begins

what is known in witchcraft as The Great Rite and is the culmination of the highest form of the craft.

The preliminaries were much the same as in earlier initiations, with the opening of a magic circle, the chants and the ritual recitation and flagellation. As Maxine took her position spread-eagled within the circle, her High Priest, Paul, was positioned kneeling between her legs and was brought forward to lie on top of her. The coven chants became more intense, and finally a thin veil separating their bodies was drawn away so that they were touching, his to hers. It was designed as a fertility rite, demonstrating the joining of the gods and goddesses but now is a symbol of the 'fertility of the mind'. Maxine explained, 'Although it is totally sexual in nature, the Great Rite is to us intensely sacred. In my initiation with Paul, it was a token act – sexual activity did not occur – and usually in the Alexandrian movement if consummation does take place it is between husband and wife, regular partners or consenting adults; the other witches would normally turn away or leave the room. That is the procedure in white witchcraft. In black workings, it is a vastly different matter which requires merely a fertile imagination to complete the picture.'

The ceremony continued, lasting in all about three hours, and finally Maxine was dressed in robes of white linen, heavy with rows of seed pearls and a black velvet cloak. On her head Sanders placed a silver crown with a stone in the shape of the moon. At the age of sixteen, she was Witch Queen, the representative of the goddess they worship. The other witches surrounded her and kissed her and congratulated her.

As such, she came to be the star attraction at Alex Sanders' coven meetings and outdoor ceremonies, which he arranged mostly at Alderley Edge, and at the private lectures he gave in an increasingly busy calendar of engagements.

His fame was spreading among the witch community, and the number of covens which sprang up from his own mushroomed. By the end of 1965 he reckoned he had between eighty and a hundred associated covens in the north of England. Sanders continued to seek publicity for his movement and, like Gerald Gardner, considered it the only way to spread the word of his craft.

'He maintained,' said Maxine, 'that the more publicity he

received, the less likelihood there was of persecution. To me, the ritual and ceremony is important to everything we did and I am only sorry that it has been cheapened and devalued by sensational publicity. But Alex always said that for the craft to go forward, there had to be publicity. He was accused by some in the craft of undermining the basic principles of a closed community, with its secrecy and silence which had remained since the worst days of the persecution of witches. Alex saw it differently; he wanted it opened up, and was prepared to take the consequences and deal with them as they arose.'

Maxine was very much the central figure of the ceremonial as his Witch Queen. Sanders next announced that he had been made King of the Witches, elected by a council of elders in the craft in recognition of the 'expansive work' he was doing. This statement has often been challenged, detractors pointing out that those who elected him were members of the covens he had formed. At best, he might be described as the King of the Alexandrian Covens. The Witch Queen is a generally recognized title for a youthful member of the craft who may be adopted as Queen provided she is High Priestess of at least three covens.

Maxine reckoned that by 1966, there were 107 associated covens in the Sanders movement and thus she amply qualified for the title. The Witch Queen, it is said, should be young and beautiful, therefore by the very nature of that definition the Queen has a limited timespan. Her function was to be the representative of the goddess, in meetings, rituals, festivals and so on.

When Sanders began to arrange public meetings to give lectures on witchcraft, Maxine would sit on the platform in a silver robe, white gown and headband and say nothing. Sanders told her, 'All I want you to do is sit there and look beautiful and represent the goddess.' In those days, Maxine admits now, it was shocking to the public at large that a witch should actually stand before an audience and identify himself as such, even more shocking that one should actually speak in favour of it.

There came a time when Sanders went too far, however. He had arranged for his coven to meet on Alderley Edge in pitch darkness. Maxine and the other witches were naked, as usual, and while performing one of their ritual dances they noticed occasional flashes appearing somewhere from the undergrowth. Sanders had tipped off a local photographer and that weekend the front page of the *Manchester Comet* was filled with a story and photographs of witches dancing pagan rites at the local beauty spot. Much trouble followed. Maxine's landlady evicted her, and her mother summoned her back home. A Roman Catholic priest was waiting when she arrived and he threw holy water over her, accused her of communing with the devil, declared that she must confess and repent and tried to perform a banishment of her ties to witchcraft.

Amid shouts and screams from the priest and mother, Maxine – barely seventeen years old – fled. The following day she was informed that her family had disowned her. She remained estranged from her mother for some months until, just before Christmas that year, she was called to hospital where her mother lay seriously ill. She died soon afterwards, having succeeded in extracting from Maxine a deathbed promise that she would recite a novena occasionally.

Maxine was then alone and after the funeral returned to her mother's house in a wealthy neighbourhood of Manchester, intending to move back in. 'Normally it was a quiet residential area,' she said, 'but some crazy fear seemed to catch hold. Someone called out "Witch!" and threw a stone. Then there were people running after me throwing stones. When I finally got to my mother's house, they broke every window and set fire to the shed outside. I collapsed in the doorway, covered with bruises.' Thirteen days later, she married Alex Sanders in a witch wedding ceremony, known as handfasting. He was forty-two, bisexual and twice divorced; she was eighteen. A wealthy witch lent them her house in Didsbury, near Manchester, for the wedding, involving a ritual binding of the arms of the bride and groom, slicing their veins so that their blood mingles and then jumping over a broomstick – a phallic symbol of fertility. Since a witch wedding lasts only a year and a day, they took the vows in a civil ceremony, in time for the birth of Maxine's first child, Maya.

In the meantime, another ordeal presented itself to the King and Queen of Witches. Not long after Myra Hindley and Ian Brady were arrested for the horrific Moors murders towards the end of 1965, police discovered that there were hints of witchcraft in the case. It transpired that Maxine and Sanders had been holding outdoor coven meetings on Saddleworth Moor, half a mile from where one of the murdered children had been buried.

Sanders was asked to go to the inquiry headquarters at Manchester Central police station along with his High Priest, Paul. They were shown photographs of a stone circle which had been identified as witches' working. Sanders agreed that it was his coven who met on Saddleworth Moor but denied any knowledge of Hindley and Brady who apparently had books on witchcraft in their home.

Then, according to Maxine, the police played to Sanders extracts from the horrific tape recordings of the death agonies of the children and wanted to know if they could identify anything that might be construed as ritual. They could not. Later, Maxine herself was asked to go to the police station for questioning, and she remained there for eight hours – though she refused to listen to the tapes of the children.

Eventually, police were satisfied that the Sanders coven had nothing to do with the Moors murders. Though the questioning was never publicly revealed, Sanders was appearing in the newspapers in his role as King of the Witches more frequently than ever. Even Hollywood came looking for him in March 1966 when MGM was making a film on witchcraft and asked him to act as a consultant. The era of the Swinging Sixties was in full flight and the centre of attraction was London. Sanders and his Witch Queen saw the opportunity to expand.

With the interest generated by publicity about Sanders' activities, along with the natural expansion of the craft through more traditional witches like Patricia Crowther, the north of England was well endowed with new covens, far more so than the south – as demonstrated by the fact that a number of northern groups had members from London who travelled by rail for the Friday night meetings.

By moving to London, Maxine and Alex Sanders began to spread the message south. Even Doreen Valiente, no admirer of Sanders' methods, acknowledged that the years Sanders and

Maxine spent together in London running their coven from their home in Clanricarde Gardens, Notting Hill, were 'the most productive and successful of Alex Sanders' life . . . another facet of this extraordinary and complicated man shone forth; so many people have testified to the genuineness of his healing powers and clairvoyance that one is compelled to accept it. Moreover many people who now run a coven of their own were first initiated by Alex Sanders . . . their sincerity and dedication to the Old Religion is known to me . . . and they acknowledge they learned this from Alex and Maxine Sanders.'

They moved to Clanricarde Gardens in 1967 and the emerging psychedelic scene around them began to take on the hue of a giant witches' festival. The Beatles had gone mystic and Indian gurus were much in evidence. Interest in witchcraft and the occult rose, along with all the other extravagances of the age, and it was quite remarkable that in the space of ten years, much of what witches did – according to the Gerald Gardner Book of Shadows – had suddenly become publicly fashionable.

Nudity was no sin; the *Sun* newspaper introduced Page Three girls in 1969; the young were said to be seeking new mystical experiences – along with those induced by cannabis, LSD and magic mushrooms as prescribed by Dr Timothy Leary in America in his famous speech, 'Tune In, Turn On, Drop Out.' Oddly enough, the elders of witchcraft were far more prudish than that and would not recommend such an attitude. But the prevailing wind certainly caught the imagination of some of the younger covens who began experimenting in other, more sinister, directions.

Alex Sanders became the first 'pop' witch in history, quickly establishing himself among both the avant-garde of London life and those seeking alternatives to orthodox religions and following the likes of the Beatles down mystical paths.

Sanders even made an LP record of witchcraft ritual, and tried to promote a stage act with himself and Maxine as the stars of a magical and sinister drama 'drawn from secret powers known only to the inner circle of witchcraft'. The King of the Witches became something of a knave. His stage act ended in fiasco and those of the traditional witchcraft looked on with horror at some of his antics. His television appearances and press interviews continued and his statements were sometimes outrageous even in those liberated times.

His belief, for example, that bisexuality was the norm was splashed across the pages of *Men Only*. Even Maxine, who had produced two children by the Witch King, a daughter Maya and a son Victor, became disillusioned and upset by the sensationalism he had brought down upon them by his quest for fame. A further disappointment in their marriage must have been his growing search for young men to join him in sexual activity.

In 1973, Alex and Maxine parted and were eventually divorced. He moved to Bexhill and his life as the world's most famous witch began to take a downturn. He was in dire straits financially after his divorce, and in the enlightened seventies the kind of witch buffoonery that Sanders displayed in his later years could no longer be taken seriously by the media, or anyone else for that matter. He went into decline and Maxine became what she described as the spiritual head of the Alexandrian movement – which itself continued to grow, unaffected by Sanders' shenanigans.

His lectures and writings on the subject of witchcraft were published and republished around the world. Maxine, meanwhile, disillusioned by it all, sought solace in the Liberal Catholic Church, a semi-occult organization which had its beginnings in the Theosophical Society of the earlier part of the century. She turned away from witchcraft temporarily, though returned to it and began holding initiation soirées at her flat in Notting Hill. She runs an active coven, and from it many others have been formed – stretching throughout the country.

As for Sanders, his power and influence were burnt out. He drifted in and out of the headlines, largely over his romantic liaisons. He married again in 1982, but his wife left him amid a blaze of degrading publicity, accusing him of spending her £50,000 divorce settlement from her first marriage, and of a lacklustre bedroom performance brought about by his insatiable 'desire to have sex with young men'.

In 1987, it was confirmed that Sanders had contracted lung cancer. He died the following year, on 30 April – the eve of May which is one of the great sabbats of the witch calendar. A service at Hastings Crematorium was arranged by two old friends, the

London witches Nigel Bourne and his wife Seldiy Bates who publish the witchcraft magazine *Ace of Rods*. One hundred friends turned up for the service which was pagan based, with the burning of strong incense, guitar music and Old Testament readings.

The king was dead. And this time there would be no replacement.

CHAPTER FIVE

CONVERSATIONS

How could it possibly be called a religion? The imagination is stretched to breaking point. A religion, surely, involved all the people, men, women and children in their communities. Could children, even teenagers, really be included in ritualistic worship that involves naked men and women who are not their parents? It seems that witches are asking for trouble, and this has in fact become a talking point among themselves. In a loosely scattered organization so well populated with oddball characters, extroverts and not a few charlatans, the public relations exercise of those who prefer to call themselves pagans becomes a constant battle of defining the good from bad, white from black. The issues are clouded by secrecy, myth and legend to such a degree that discovering a case for the defence becomes almost an impossibility. At each turn of the page there is some new example of malevolence, some new headline of perverted sorcery.

The witches themselves realized, after all the publicity surrounding Alex Sanders in the 1970s, that in order to survive in a legalized form they would have to project an aura of goodness. This was obviously going to be difficult, given that the activities of black witches and magicians who continued to carve up graves and cut heads off cats showed no sign of abating. All they could do was try to achieve it by having an organization to speak for them, one to project the better side of their nature.

The term 'white witch' became the symbol of witches working for what they call the 'benefit of mankind'. Such a perception was not going to be easy to purvey, especially since even the so-called white witches managed to get themselves pictured in the *News of the World* wearing precious little but a lucky charm and a funny hat. Today, they say the rule for the majority is goodness – though even some of the more famous of their number admit to a blurring of definitions on the darker edges of their craft, that their rituals might stray from concept of 'an harm none' into what might be termed as grey or black magic. Those who are decidedly 'black' – and there are many – look upon the 'white' movement with considerable derision.

The arch-satanist Anton Szandor LaVey, founder of the Church of Satan and popularly known as the Black Pope, attracts as much hate mail from pagans as he does from Christians. He has poured scorn on Gerald Gardner's brand of witchcraft and said he could have no truck with people who tried to justify what they were doing by calling themselves pagans and who had a 'simple belief in religions of the old wise ones, using herbs, charms and healing spells for beneficial purposes.'

LaVey proclaims in his book, *The Satanic Witch*, that in order to be successful, a witch *does* have to make a pact with the devil, at least symbolically . . . 'She must worship the Luciferian elements of pride within her' and anyone who professed to be a white witch was 'either kidding themselves or has much to learn'.

There is a wide gulf between the two camps, and to try to discover a perspective and a justification for the continued existence of witchcraft as a legalized religion under the umbrella of paganism, I interviewed more than thirty practising witches on both sides of the divide. I taped my interviews and, listening to them afterwards, I found that all shared a basic philosophy that was expressed in remarkably similar words. The glaring difference came in the extent that they pushed their quest for so-called magical power and how it should be used. For the remainder of this chapter, I will recount some of the views of white witches.

Even after all that had happened to Maxine Sanders in her reign as a Witch Queen, she is as committed to witchcraft as she ever was, probably more so. She is the spiritual head of the worldwide Alexandrian movement and there are those who would say that she was always more of a witch than her husband ever was. Her life, after the turmoil and publicity of her latter years with Alex Sanders, is more peaceful and after a period of disillusionment, she returned to witchcraft with a more balanced view of it and life in general. She still has many enemies, and in a cult that is also known as bitchcraft, she reckoned that she was being cursed by opponents 'every Friday night'.

The past is past, she says philosophically, and where once she had 'the most photographed bum in Britain' she has settled to a more routinely quietish life of almost total devotion to witchcraft and coven magic. And where once her late husband was the man the witch establishment loved to hate for his flamboyance and stunts, she now finds herself critical and outspoken about those who bring witchcraft into disrepute and points the finger immediately at impostors who pretend to be witches and psychics just for the money – a growth industry of the 1980s.

She hates inexperienced dabblers who she says do not realize, or seem to care, what damage they can cause to themselves and those around them by summoning and releasing uncontrollable forces into their homes. 'Things can easily go disastrously wrong,' she admits. 'I was in a house quite recently where bad spirits had been brought down and were not properly banished. The room was wrecked, the television was smashed, curtains pulled down, ornaments flung around the room. There was blood everywhere . . .'

She chastises those who corrupt and degrade the ritual and the ceremony for their personal ends, whether for sexual pleasure, financial gains or to satisfy a distorted lust for black magical powers.

Maxine, in her early forties when I visited her in October 1991, still lives in the same street off the Bayswater Road that she moved to with Sanders in the sixties, though with her children grown up she moved into the basement apartment. Her son Victor, it was once reported, was earmarked to become his father's successor, King of the Witches. Victor was having none of it. He is not interested, though naturally both children have seen plenty of strange events in their home during their lifetime.

There is a warm and friendly welcome for anyone not put off

by the trappings of the occult and the distinct aroma of incense and hermetic oils and herbs that is common to many witch homes. The living-room walls were lined with what must be one of the largest private collections of books on the occult outside the Vatican; her small dogs, a whippet and a chihuahua, lay peacefully on the settee and might be her familiars.

On the sideboard, a blue flame burned from a wax holder, a permanent light to the goddess because her house is a temple and she is a priestess, and undoubtedly one of the most experienced in the world. The house is overtly occultish in every way; books and tools of her craft cover almost every surface. In the back room there is the permanent temple, with its red altar on which her pentacle, knives, scourge, god images and wands are on display. They are used so frequently that the temple is never dismantled. Most of the neighbours know she is a witch, and quite a few seek her advice. She says her door is always open and having faith in the craft is not a prerequisite to seeking her help.

She smiles, lights a cigarette and talks confidently with still the trace of her northern brogue:

I am a witch. Not a pagan – a witch. The craft is a religion to me and not pagan history; it is addictive, at least it is as far as I am concerned and for many like me. For more than twenty-five years, I have explored its myriad opportunities and as I grow older I have merely become more intense about it; more sincere and love it more deeply than ever. I have also become more tolerant. I look at people now and I am able to say that's your point of learning whereas once I would consider these people as shallow, and disapproved of their practices. Nowadays I think that's a point of their evolution, and hopefully they will grow out of it. However, it worries me that on the way, the inexperienced might get hurt. There are a lot of bum groups around and many people are merely naïve and know-nothing dabblers. I get angry about the commercialism in witchcraft and rip-off merchants who prey on those seeking help or guidance.

Maxine explained that she did not disapprove of witches being paid for what they do; she charged for certain services. But there were witches and witches! If she was going to work magic for a businessman then she would charge, as she would for working her powers on emotional issues, helping to quell marital problems, bringing back an errant husband and the like. She said that if she gave advice without charging for it, people would immediately turn round and say the advice was worthless. She knew that there were extraordinary numbers of people who do pay large amounts of money – £1,500 or £2,000 – to people who have no real business charging in the first place, people whose advice was indeed worthless because they were not true witches; and, of course, many fortune-tellers and tarot readers talked absolute rubbish.

The charlatans, she said, found an easy route to money because many more people were being drawn to the periphery of the occult, for various reasons. In some cases it was a genuine quest for knowledge, but also because there were more neurotic people around, more people who are seeking help because they felt inadequate through the hardships of being jobless, or from the pressures of life. There were many who also genuinely sought some spiritual guidance and involvement that they could not find elsewhere, and especially not in the organized Christian religions.

She felt that increasingly people were being pushed by circumstance and pressure towards an alternative to religion – a fact which the Church of England might well be forced to concede. There was nothing especially new in that, at least, not in the second half of this century. Apart from businessmen wanting their problems solving by her magical influence or spells or seeking the benefit of her foresight, there is a lot of the problem-page element who contact her and she had to do a lot of sifting before deciding whom she was going to help.

A typical recent 'case history', she recalled, was that of a young woman who had a relationship which had broken up about a year earlier. Her male partner had become possessive and obsessional, refused to accept the break-up and became violent. She pleaded with Maxine to try to make him stop. And so, within her magic circle, they had to bind this man – not literally but using an effigy – and put something else into his mind to try to make him become interested in something else and forget the girl.

She agreed that some people would say that they were attempting to influence the mind and free will, even taking his will away from him. Maxine countered that it was clearly for his own good. He would probably have ended up in gaol. They were saving him from himself. She said it worked. The man stopped his violence and the woman had not been troubled since. This was one of the more common ways that witchcraft helped those who sought her assistance. There were many others, such as healing techniques.

Naturally, I asked for proof, because as yet I had seen none. How does it work? What is the power that witches have that others do not?

To understand, she said, I would have to see a coven at work, and there were not many witch groups who would allow outsiders casually to observe their rituals, which are long and complicated, and learned through experience. (I eventually found one that would, and I report on my findings in the following chapter.) The basic training of a witch lasts two years – and that was just the basics – and it would be very unwise, said Maxine, for anyone to contemplate such workings before this training had been completed. Beyond that, it was a continuing process of becoming more proficient in the craft over the years.

I can describe a way that you can visualize it; we'll take an image – be it in Plasticine, dough, wax or whatever – and we'll bind it. We'll have a photograph of that person and we may put a face on that image; we will name it and get into sympathy with it, and then incline its mind. And yes, we do try to incline people's minds. Does it work? I would say that whatever results from witchcraft is ninety-five per cent psychological, four and a half per cent coincidental and a half per cent magic. But when that half per cent of magic works, you really know it's happened.

There is no physical contact with the subject; we do not go out and throw things over his garden wall. What we do, our influence, comes from the energy generated by the group, which is transferred to the man's mind; a form of telepathy if you like – but it reaches him. Of that I am convinced, because I have seen the results of workings so often over the years.

What we produce, as a group within our magic circle, is a consciousness, a different energy. There is, for example, a positive change of temperature in the room which has been empty; you fill it with say twelve or thirteen people who are working within that circle, you would imagine the temperature would go up; it doesn't. It drops. That provides scientific proof of a change but as far as the magical proof goes, I cannot prove the power is there. I *believe* the power is there; I know there is power from my experience. We do influence people's minds, but with good intent; someone needs the magic that we perform. It has to be that way. We are not allowed to harm anyone; that is the fundamental rule of the craft and all those who are in it are governed by this rule, and abide by it. If they do not, they are not true witches, or even pagans.

Magic is only a small part of our work. People tend to imagine, when they hear the word witchcraft, that we are out every night working magic and casting spells. I am very careful these days about working spells. It's not that often we do them, anyway; I'm involved with witchcraft because it is my religion and because I am a priestess. I spend many hours studying. Out of the worship comes the magic; it doesn't have to go anywhere. It can merely be my experience, my magical experience, my mystical experience which is totally, totally personal. There is not necessarily always an end product to what we do, though we never waste power generated by a group meeting. If there is a lot of energy there, because witches are generally concerned about the things around them, the ecology and so on, we would direct that energy into the well-being of mother earth.

Maxine said she had become more earthly in everything. Astral journeys and out-of-body experience, for example, was a practice she had studied and performed frequently, but no longer. They were still important, and she was able to teach astral projection to newcomers. It is one other part of her work and not one on which she especially spent a lot of time but she was surprised how many people tell her they have had some sort of experience. She reckoned people draw on psychic phenomena when their emotional life is upset; they become psychologically disturbed to the extent that they talk rubbish.

Operating from her home, as a working temple, she attracts

activity without any kind of publicity at all, and she keeps a very low profile. Businessmen are among her biggest external clients. Healing rituals also form a large part of coven activity, although she has had to curtail it; she said she received so many requests for help on health that she used to hold healing sessions once a week. Those with romantic problems or sexual inadequacies believe that by weaving some magic spell, she might solve their problems; there had, over the years, also been a preponderance of bald men seeking instant new hair. She turned most of them away because either she could not help or felt uncomfortable about trying. Others, she says, were not so honest. This activity is merely a by-product of the traditions of witchcraft. To her, the religion of the craft itself is fundamentally more important.

> The craft is a fertility religion, though we do not have the sacred orgies any more because we do not need children. If anything, we are overpopulated. But the craft is still a fertility religion, hopefully aiming for the fertility of the mind and spirit now.
>
> The sacred orgy remains as a ceremony. There is a good deal of misconception about sex and witchcraft. After all, what is the definition of an orgy? [*Collins* says: secret religious rites of Dionysus, Bacchus, etc. marked by drinking, dancing and songs.] I do not know many witches who practise sexual magic, although there are the dabblers who seem to think that sex is all witchcraft was invented for; there are abuses of the Great Rite – we know that goes on and that is why I and others to whom the craft is everything continue our fight to keep it pure. Our sexual ritual tends to be part of the high ceremonial. The sex act is part of that ritual, and it is done either in actuality or in token. It is a very intense ritual, lasting over three hours. And it is very pure, because you can imagine or visualize the subject and the circle being purified and purified, and the ritual going higher and higher all the time. You could not be smutty about it in any way. It is very devout and very holy. If the sex act is performed in actuality for the ritual, then it is usual for this to be between husband and wife or between established lovers – and only ever between consenting adults – with other members of the circle facing outwards. If not, then it's a token act – as was my own.

I live a much calmer existence now but the house is still a hive of activity. I have my own covens and join in national, even international festivals. I hold soirées here for those who have expressed interest in joining the craft. These are people who have contacted me or a member of the group; I cannot ask them – they must ask me. And they come around, a dozen or more at a time, and we have wine and then I sit down to allow them a question and answer session. Some decide that the craft is not for them; others may ask to join. Even then, membership is not guaranteed. I might decide that they are emotionally or psychologically unsuitable, or their reasons not quite right. It is a common and well-known fact in witchcraft that one single misfit in a coven can cause total chaos and disruption, sometimes leading to the break-up of the group. The people we accept for initiation have to be mentally stable, they have to be whole in body and limb. If it was a mass religion, it could not work.

I could practically guarantee that a third of the people who dabble in witchcraft, opening their circles and playing around with spells and ritual, would develop psychological disorders and emotional disturbances because they are opening their subconscious without the training and knowledge of how to handle it and the discipline to control the force they are opening up.

Sometimes we guide people towards other religions, perhaps to Buddhism or to transcendental meditation. We look for certain qualities and won't budge. I am frankly disappointed by the dilution of the craft into the broader base of paganism. Now, we are being lumped together with pagans whose interests may not lie with witchcraft, but with the green revolution or animal rights. These are not witches – and I am not a pagan. The craft is not a congregational religion; it is based upon small groups around a priesthood, in private temples. Witchcraft is a minority religion – and that's the way it should stay.

One thing I discovered very quickly was that the philosophy of modern witchcraft is as variable as the weather. The outward concept depended on the level of activity and the intent of those who are involved, ranging from the benign and harmless rituals of the white witches through to the extremes of the black ceremonies involving animal sacrifice and desecration of graves.

The discussion I had with Steve Jones, a High Priest running his own mixed coven near Leeds and a professional man in his early thirties who is at the heart of modern witchcraft, provided an informative and occasionally amusing insight into what attracted him and others of his age group and middle-class social background into such a controversial and much-criticized activity. Jones is perhaps a classic example of a white witch. He is an area organizer for PaganLink, one of the three main national groups that act as an information exchange and help-line for witches in trouble. I will let Jones tell his story in his own words:

> The trouble is that when you try to define the word pagan these days, it is so diverse that it is difficult to generalize. In many ways it has replaced the word 'witch' but then again, many pagans are not witches and may not be members of covens. Pagan activities range from the traditional witch covens, through to feminist covens, 'green' groups, animal rights groups, even travelling pagans. A lot of the older people in the movement would claim to be solely Wiccan and would like to remain as such but nowadays the majority prefer to be called pagans.
>
> Like the Christians, we have Wiccan fundamentalists who say that if you are not organizing yourself and working exactly in the way it is written down in the *Book of Shadows* then you are wrong – that is like Evangelists telling Christians they must follow exactly the teachings of the Bible.
>
> People who call themselves pagan today have a more relaxed attitude than that. They would say, as we do in our coven, look, if we want to do a ritual we will sit down on the night and discuss it – decide whether we want to have a few drums and chant; or if we want simply to light a candle and meditate, then we'll do that. We do not follow the written down rituals with such precision as the Wiccan fundamentalists would want.
>
> This is why the activities of a lot of modern groups differ quite widely. They discover what works for them as a group of people and follow their own forms of ritual and celebration,

though using their *Book of Shadows* for the basic format. A lot of groups are into guided meditation.

The general object of the rituals we perform is to be in touch with the energy that surrounds us, call it a god or a goddess, or whatever. Most groups I know of use this force to send out energy for purposes of healing and other reasons of good intent.

Most of the rituals are connected with the seasons of the year, revolving around the eight major sabbats of the year. Thus the groups try to tune themselves into these eight celebrations, basically going back to the old agricultural cycle to which the whole of life in the countryside was once attuned, old Mother Earth – and, incidentally, which a lot of pagans now seek to get back to, opting out of the rat race.

We have an altar and I act as High Priest. If we are performing a healing ritual after the initial ceremonies, we all gather round in our circle holding hands, focus on the person to be healed, who will have been described by the person requesting the ritual. We then concentrate on getting the energy out of our own bodies. It does work; you can feel it. Some people who are clairvoyant say they see blue light. I don't. I tend to get a tingling feeling all over, and you can feel the energy powering up and being passed out of your body, around the circle, going faster and faster, always focusing on the task at hand, until it leaves you.

Does it work? We don't make any outrageous claims about that – at least true pagans do not. Most of us are able to quote examples and I have observed the results of our healing rituals for people who did not know we were doing it. I was working with a coven in Doncaster and there was a case of a guy with multiple sclerosis; he was in a private nursing home and feeling very depressed. One of the women members of the group asked that we meet to send her friend some energy, to try to help him. The way we performed the healing ritual was for her to form a mental picture of her sick friend, and then we joined hands and we sent energy via her.

Now I would not claim to know whether we helped the man or not; all I know is that afterwards, those taking part felt very drained and when the woman member of the group visited her friend in hospital, he seemed much brighter and actually spoke of having renewed energy, starting on the night we performed the healing ritual. Now all of this could be coincidence, and self-delusion. But I don't think so, and certainly none of it can do any harm.

We always work naked when we are inside. I'm not one of these naturalist pagans who goes dancing around starkers in the dead of winter, I am afraid, because it's bloody cold. The other reason why we are careful about stripping off and running through the woods is that no matter where you go in Great Britain, there is always someone who has a valid reason for wandering around the countryside in the middle of the night when the covens usually go out. On one occasion, I remember, when a coven was performing a ritual celebration deep in some woods, they were confronted by a group of people studying owls, who were quite amazed to discover a group of adults dancing naked in a circle around a small bonfire in the pitch black night far inside the woods.

The reasons for working naked often baffle the uninitiated. Simply, it is because the energy does come out of your body; it radiates from your whole body – you tingle all over. By consciously taking off your everyday clothing you are putting yourself in a state of mind for doing something special, within a magic circle. Oddly enough, there is another reason – the safety factor. When you are in a circle and there are lighted candles or bonfires around, and when people are waving their sacred knives around – which should be blunt but often aren't – you can have a nasty accident, so people tend to take a lot more care and concentrate on what they are doing when naked. Again, it brings the mind to a state of alertness.

A lot of groups these days work robed, which is naked but covered by a robe. But there again, I have seen people forget. Once a woman in a group I was with wore a long robe which trailed behind her, and it caught fire and we had to rip the robe off and stamp on it. I have also seen one member in a dark robe back into someone who was brandishing a knife in a ritual, which might not have happened if she was naked. I have never seen it happen in a circle where people are naked, because they are more safety conscious.

Finally, there is also the fact that if you are naked, then everyone is equal; no one is trying to impress anyone else. The richest person there might have the worst-looking body.

Everyone comes down to the same level. We do not like to work on a hierarchical system. We don't work on the basis of someone saying, 'well, I'm highest grade witch here'. That's a load of bullshit. There are covens which strictly adhere to recognizing that a member might be a second-degree witch or a third-degree witch, which is the top one, and they do it all by the book. These tend to be the more formal groups who follow the principles set down by the likes of Gerald Gardner and Alex Sanders to the letter. As I have already said, my group and many like us, tend to be more relaxed about it.

Most people do keep their own Book of Shadows, recording their own experiences and rituals which were carried out in the coven meetings.

My own initiation was quite hilarious really. I started off back in 1984 when I actually decided to do something positive about my interest in witchcraft. The problem was finding a group; covens do not normally go out looking for members because each group works its own thing out, and the members of that group get to know one another well, like a family in many cases. Sometimes, a new member of a group can be a disruptive influence. They've only got to fall out with one person and the whole group can split up. It's all built on trust and the period of acceptance into a group is traditionally a year and a day.

So consequently many of the established groups do not look for members. I went through the route of trying to find a group and thought they would welcome me with open arms – which they didn't. Eventually I managed to get in contact with an initiated witch and we formed our own coven in Blackburn.

I wanted my initiation to be done properly and we arranged it for the night of a full moon in May 1985. We all travelled in a transit van with our gear and wine and food for a ritual and feast on the shores of Lake Windermere, to arrive there to perform the initiation at midnight in a grove of oak trees. It sounds very romantic but the basic truth was that it was a complete balls up from start to finish.

We went up to find this place which had been recommended to us; markers had been left on the spot. It was supposed to be a nice site, well away from the road and private. By the time we got up there, it was pitch black and we were driving around for about half an hour looking for this track which would take us to the site.

The site itself had been marked with stones for future use – by the likes of ourselves – but unfortunately the track that led to it had not been marked out and we had forgotten the torch. So we were all wandering around in the darkness, looking for the track. I went off on my own, and unfortunately fell into a stream and shouted Help! They looked at the map and said that if I could find a trail near the stream we were on the right track, which I did. So we found the site and the circle of stones and we had to strip off and jump into Lake Windermere.

The high priestess dived straight in and let out a tremendous echoing scream because she hadn't considered how cold the water would be; I couldn't swim so, apart from paddling, I sat on the bank watching until they all came out. They lit a bonfire inside the circle and began to perform the initiation ritual while I, the newcomer, had to stand on the outside blindfolded. It was very cold, especially for me on the outside because I couldn't feel the warmth of the fire.

I was pretty blue before I got into it; another difficulty was that the man who was acting as high priest for the initiating ceremony could not remember the words and had to read it from a book by torchlight so it took longer than normal. That is one ritual that must be adhered to, to demonstrate the seriousness of commitment to the craft. If people are not properly initiated, then it affects their own attitude towards the group.

It also proves their own seriousness towards entering the craft – to show that they are not coming into it for a bit of fun, or for nudity or hopes of joining in an orgy for sex. If that's the case, I always advise them to go to Soho or somewhere like that.

Personally, I haven't come across one of these so-called sexual orgies.

So, anyway, that was my initiation. Eventually I formed my own coven and followed the practice of most pagan groups which is to meet regularly for discussions, meditation, perhaps, and ritual.

Yes, there is always a lot of confusion about 'white' and 'black' witches; all the groups I know can be classed as white. The rituals and the magic are produced for specifics like healing and helping people. Black magic is really used by people who frankly don't give a toss for anyone else, when they want to influence someone's thinking. Pagans never use black magic.

True pagans would class themselves as good witches – especially because there is the belief among us that whatever you do, you get back tripled. So whatever you send out is returned in kind and similarly if you call upon your energy for self-interest or bad purpose, that will also come back to you, only worse.

Curses and spells aimed at influencing people and done for selfish motives are not part of pagan ritual, though I know it does happen among some unscrupulous groups who may argue that, ultimately, they are doing it for the benefit of others – I don't believe that; you are doing it for your own ends. This is black magic. Black magic is where you are influencing someone else's life to give you some sort of benefit.

True ritual magic is more the preserve of occultists whose activities go much deeper and are far more involved than our way. A pagan would not call himself an occultist and conversely occultists tend to look down on us. They go in for serious ritualistic magic. It is the same culture, only somewhat advanced. A lot of it comes from the Golden Dawn tradition, which Aleister Crowley revised in his order the Argentum Astruma or Order of the Silver Star; it is a sort of elevated masonic ritual magic and there are quite a lot of lodges – some dubious ones – that practise this kind of thing. It is a lot more precise, and things can go seriously wrong if you don't do it at exactly the right time and under the right conditions, with the right robes, and the right surroundings, so they say.

You tend to get the more scholarly types going in for ritual magic which attracts them because it comes from old traditions, including the old grimoires and the Kabbalah. The people who practise it are, like the masons, generally middle-class people, often university educated. The occult – as opposed to paganism – has also attracted some groups of people whom we would warn against; in fact not just warn against, but positively and actively discourage anyone from joining. There are groups who are out for power only and there are people who do call down the forces of evil for their own purposes and are actively opposed by all the people I know.

I am not saying that the pagan movement is entirely populated by the uncorrupted or the incorruptible; we have our extremists at both ends of the spectrum. But at least, the movement itself is supervised, for want of a better word, by a responsible body of people who are ready and willing to give advice when called upon to do so.

There are three international movements in witchcraft based in Britain, formed to protect, project and publicize the religion of paganism: the Pagan Federation, PaganLink and Green Circle. The largest group is the Pagan Federation whose president is Elen Williams. Elen was a member of the coven that Gerald Gardner originally started in St Albans and has been a practising pagan for many years. She is an intelligent, well-read and articulate woman in her fifties, who lives in north London. She spoke first about the formation of the federation in 1971 in the wake of some of Alex Sanders' extravagances and an attempt the previous year by Mr Gwilym Roberts, MP for South Bedfordshire, to get the Home Secretary to consider introducing new laws to prosecute those who admitted indulging in the practice of witchcraft:

The Pagan Federation began life as the Pagan Front in 1971, with a newsletter, 'The Wiccan'. Its main function at that point was to counteract what witches believed was an extensive pagan defamation appearing in the papers and the media. It pedalled along for quite some time and then some other people became interested, notably the author Vivianne Crowley who is the secretary of the PF. Their view was that there were so many pagans, it was time we started making ourselves known, or at least putting forward our views, and so its aims began to broaden at that point – not merely to carry on the anti-defamation work, but to provide a forum for all pagans and a networking set-up to put fellow pagans in touch with each other.

From there, the Pagan Federation further extended to cover the three main esoteric groups of paganism and Wicca, Odinism and Druidry.

In spite of organizations like the PF, it is still impossible to tell the overall number of pagans and witches. Elen Williams said they get hundreds of letters, an increasing number from people who say that they now realize that they are pagans.

The federation asks its members to accept an oath to abide by three main principles which fall under the general edict to 'An harm none – do what thou wilt'. Members are encouraged firstly to become part of nature with the high ethical stance of not harming any living thing. The second principle urges them to discover their worth and pursue their true will and destiny but not by riding roughshod over other people. Thirdly, they accept the polarity of deity, which is something of a hallmark of paganism distinguishing it from Buddhism. They believe that running through nature is a male and female principle that they think of in terms of a goddess and a god – or several goddesses and gods. It is a Pantheistic religion – the Divine is in everything and everything needs to be nurtured and cared about.

There are many paths in witchcraft for communion with the Divine and any particular group or coven is free to select any mythology which is most familiar to them or that attracts them. Some are very attracted to Egyptian, some to Greek or Roman gods, some to Celtic or Norse gods, some even develop their own and their own names for gods and goddesses. Very often they talk about the Great Goddess, the triple goddess who is Maiden, Mother and Crone – reflecting the stages of the moon from waxing to waning – rather than actually using names. Sophisticated pagans recognize that they are dealing with archetypal images; there is a conscious awareness that the image they want to work with, whether it is called Aphrodite, or Demeter, is used merely as a way of parcelling up the Divine image, the point of worship. They consider the whole formulation of a Christian God and a Devil as irrelevant.

This seemed a good opportunity to raise with Elen Williams the question of black rites and the satanic view, as propounded by LaVey, that true witchcraft involved a pact with the devil. She replied that she did not think it a useful dichotomy to talk in terms of black and white witches.

We don't think of the division of good and evil or of there being an all good God; our belief is that the divine includes all that there is. Something is evaluated as evil from a particular perspective – even Hitler thought he was doing good from his perspective. We regard it as an imbalance which needs to be corrected. Unlike the satanists, pagans do not recognize the existence of the devil because it is part of Christian mythology with roots in the pre-Christian religions. It is possible to see that some of the pagan gods were demonized. The horned god that figured in so many accounts of witch meetings in the Middle Ages, was classed as the devil, yet the image was around long before the devil appeared in mythology and legend. Pagans now tend to associate themselves with the Stag God, rather than the Goat God, though Pan is quite important to those who follow Goat mythology. The demonization of witch gods and the stigma of the witch-hunts remain a continual source of battle among pagan revivalists who try to live down the bad history. Yes, the term witch-hunt remains part of the language.

Gardner tried to get people to believe paganism was a religion of the future and would tend to publicize it and let newspapers come in. Sanders did much the same. Gradually, it has become more accepted and known. Compared with thirty years ago, paganism and witchcraft are remarkably widely accepted and widely known about, even though there is still a long way to go.

Gardner should have called it paganism from the outset and not witchcraft; he was courting trouble. But then it was perhaps an act of defiance. People like Alex Sanders seemed to enjoy the publicity, and liked to be demonized and seen as a Black figure.

Black magic is quite often difficult to define. Some people define black magic as the use of curses and spells, but much of that goes against the pagan stricture of 'harm none'. But equally, perhaps it could be said that using magic for healing purposes could be seen as self-interest. Gaining power, influence or money is seen as being black but then working to achieve abundance, having enough, seems to be OK.

Those who participate in today's witchcraft come from a diverse cross-section of the community. In Elen Williams' own groups, there are several quite well-to-do, well-heeled people which shows that paganism now embraces the full spectrum of opportunity. For instance, there seem to be a high proportion of computer program-mers joining pagan groups!

This diversity of members brought with it a diversity of opinions within the group, best illustrated recently when the Gulf War was looming. Some pagans were so anti-war that they went all out for peace with their workings – much as Gerald Gardner's covens had done to repel Hitler's invasion. What they did in their ritual and incantations was to try to achieve 'the optimum outcome for all peoples'.

Increasingly, Elen said, the Pagan Federation was discovering that many people, young adults especially, were seeking new values, to do with their personal disposition and the ecology in general, which were not led by materialism. There were extremists who felt that all pagans should go back to nature and live in mud huts but what the best pagans and the best New Agers were looking for was a synthesis, a new development where the values were not all materialistic and self-centred and which had a non-dogmatic spiritual dimension.

The thing I think many people find appealing is that there is no orthodoxy in paganism. There is no hierarchy, or central govern-ing movement. People come together because they want to come together not because they have been told that they must; small groups form and it all very much fits the third-wave (as Alvin

Toffler defines cultural waves) type of development of society. There is some merit in the great New Age slogan which says this is the Age of Aquarius, and that the attributes of that age are greater individual responsibility, less mass thinking, less coherence in mass domination; there should be much more reliance on individual points of view and much more individual responsibility for your own ethics, rather than these being imposed by the stone tablets from on high.

If one tries, it is possible to see some kind of reasoning behind pagan beliefs; at least their right under international law to worship whom, what and where they wish without interference from others must be accepted. And when one surveys the various alternative religions scattered around the world, there is in paganism, at least, no apparent brainwashing of the participants, as there is known to be in some Christian sects.

There remains a problem, the problem that I outlined at the beginning of this chapter. I put to Elen Williams, as spokeswoman for the Pagan Federation, that the activities of some witches do the movement a considerable disservice with their variable forms of alleged magic that veered towards the black end of the spectrum and often involve sexual rites which attract sensational publicity. Williams replied:

> As far as the sex magic is concerned, it is always going to be the sort of thing that draws the sensational news coverage. But again I think attitudes are changing here, especially as people begin to understand what is actually meant by sex magic, what a responsible and sacred thing it is, and what the pagan attitude to sex is, and how it is handled. It is almost always between regular partners and certainly always only between consenting adults. People are discovering that there is more responsibility in the pagan attitude than there is in your average suburban wife-swapping group. Pagans regard sex as the highest expression of love and respect and a celebration of mutual beingness. The Goddess says 'All acts of love and pleasure are my rituals'; relations between men and women are not hedged about by property laws but each is responsible for the ethics of their own

behaviour. Affairs and temporary liaisons, or even occasional sex between friends (perhaps in some groups) are not frowned upon provided it 'harm none'.

Sex magic is intercourse within a ritual setting in which the god and the goddess are invoked through the participants. It is a sacred act designed to awaken and empower the very highest elements within the participants. It has no connection at all with, say, people who indulge in magic with love dolls and the like. To me, that is the lowest form of magic, followed by the oppressed and the powerless. I do think that is bad, and it doesn't do anything for our movement. Using spells with such things as bats' eyes and hearts, and such things, simply does not figure in pagan rituals, not at all; that's all based on old stuff which absolutely does not apply any more. Rubbish that I am not at all interested in. We had someone who was absolutely in love with someone in our coven and wanted us to work to help capture that person, and we said no, that's not responsible. We said you must not override their will because it would only lead to trouble and would not be to your benefit. All we would work for would be to help you to be yourself, and be as attractive and interesting as possible. Which in a way sums up what we do.

We are constantly trying to correct a lot of the misconception about what we do. A recent exposé in the *News of the World* caused quite a lot of dissension in the pagan community. One allegation was about a couple who were seen to share a joint. In the original article it was described as just that, in the second it became 'drugs were used'; that sort of thing caused deep concern. I spoke to the couple concerned and they said it was just a purely personal thing; not widespread, not handing it around. He said he never used it in rituals.

Lois Bourne, on the other hand, is a witch alone. She claims to be an hereditary witch who recognized her powers of vision during childhood. The powers and feelings merely strengthened in adulthood so that her clairvoyance and mediumship, both of which she believes were an essential element of medieval witchcraft, became more developed as the years went by.

As a practising occultist for thirty years, she is now regularly approached by people seeking help from an alternative source to that offered through community channels; she is the nearest there is to an old-fashioned local witch, working alone with her potions and herbal remedies, her spells and charms.

Though once a member of Gerald Gardner's St Albans coven, she is now seldom involved with other witches and is amused at the description of her as the Claire Rayner of the Wiccan world – though perhaps Claire Rayner would not be. Lois is the author of two books on witchcraft, she lectures and gives free advice to all who write. She is exactly the kind of community witch who would have been sent to the gallows a couple of centuries ago.

In the privacy of her own home she performs the kind of magic that she claims has been handed down through the centuries and she talks wearily, if not cynically, about some of the so-called witches in the British Isles:

> The study of the occult and the metaphysical is a lifetime's endeavour and there are so many diversities around today . . . I am in constant touch with most aspects; I get about one hundred letters a week. I cannot just ignore them but they take up a lot of time and energy. I must tell you that I am not part of the Wiccan world or the New Age philosophy.
>
> I tend to agree with Colin Wilson that witches are born, not made, but you will discover that this is not the general opinion and you will fall over 'witches' everywhere. I think that a lot of people are looking for new answers to old questions and are disillusioned with Christianity and organized religion. They read a book, fancy paganism, find someone who has also read a book and start a coven. They become initiated and there is another instant 'witch'. It is true that our ancestors worshipped the Old Gods but they were not all witches, for Pete's sake! Real genuine witches are few and far between. They are often solitary and work alone. I know a few. Most of the real witches start by resenting their gifts and their abilities. I have been through that too and then one comes to terms with it all and realize that it is the path one is intended to follow and you just get on with it. I work with a select few people and we do not associate with other

so-called witches, most of whom could not summon up enough power to boil a cauldron of water between them.

I must warn you that you are likely to find among the great unwashed a lot of disturbed people; some are dishonest and a large proportion downright phoney – the sort who demand £1,000 for a fertility spell that could never ever work. Real witches never accept money for the magic they perform. I am currently helping a woman who paid over £1,500 [to someone else] for a spell to solve her recalcitrant daughter's problems. How? Don't ask. It is a trade secret. But a lot of people have written to me and to my publishers to thank me for work I have done which they say has saved their lives. A lot of them become friends. I have received literally thousands of letters from people seeking help to solve domestic crises, make someone love them, help sell their house quickly or even cast a spell to ensure that they should win on the football pools. I have had success with selling houses, but I don't enjoy doing it; it is very boring magic ... my instinct is generally to avoid interfering in marital relationships – although I do occasionally when someone is desperate – but in financial situations I have to tell them that I am very reluctant to work magic for financial gain because of the risks involved. Witches utilize primitive energy which attempts to fulfil itself on a basic level ... a simple request that Mrs Jones should receive £5,000 is full of potential danger and could result in an accident, such as losing a leg and receiving that exact amount in compensation.

True witches possess a fairly high moral code in their dealings with people and we are forbidden to interfere too much with a person's free will. Binding and enchantment spells can be worked to heal a disintegrating love affair ... but I consider it slightly immoral to use magic to influence a man to stay with a woman he no longer loves.

I am no one special and nothing special. I just happen to have been born with a few abilities which I use every now and again for the benefit of others. I am not Queen of the Witches (you will come across a lot of these; there are more chiefs than Indians). I am very ordinary.

And so, as in any fairy story, there are good witches and bad witches. And to summarize from this cross section of working views, it will be seen that by and large they *are* ordinary people, as Lois Bourne says, who are either born with a modicum of natural psychic power which they learn over the years to extend or who join a coven and learn how to become a witch. The lone witches like Lois generally stay apart, the rest are a fairly mercurial movement of people who follow basic ground rules in their faith and who are kept in touch with each other by a mass of underground contact magazines.

One such magazine, called *Ace of Rods*, is run by Nigel Bourne and his wife Seldiy who are well known in the Wiccan world; they were among those who arranged the send-off for Alex Sanders. Their magazine is a forum and post drop for like-minded pagans and white witches seeking contact with others, i.e. 'Pagan couple, 30s, into witchcraft, nature, tarot, sacred sites, Earth energies, dreams, ritual magic, astral projection, Celtic art, conservation, healing, would welcome contact with like-minded folk . . .'

They are open about their association with witchcraft, and their small daughter Madelaine is allowed to watch her mother preparing the altar that they construct to celebrate witch festivals in the front room of their London home. Both have been associated with a south London witch coven for many years; Nigel, who runs a major recording studio, and Seldiy, a former actress, are high priest and priestess.

Although most of the people he works with know he is a witch, this has never caused difficulties in Nigel's day to day business. 'I've never thought I should stop being what I am because of someone else's inability to cope with it. Secrecy only leads to people making the wrong assumption,' he says. Even at the height of the child-abuse scare when all occultists were going through an uncomfortable period, the Bournes said they did not experience any unpleasantness and their daughter felt able to discuss her parents' beliefs at school. However, Seldiy admits to caution. 'We are very particular about whom we are lumped together with,' she told me. 'We are sensible harmless people and try to avoid being juxtaposed with senseless harmful fanatics . . . the wallies can make prats of themselves while we get quietly on with our work.'

However, the association of children with witchcraft has been a matter of discussion and concern among its practitioners, not least inspired by the fear that after the satanic ritual abuse hysteria a neighbour might complain to the NSPCC and before long the witch parents could find themselves facing an official from the social services department bearing a child care order. The Pagan Federation became so concerned at this possibility that in 1991 Elen Williams appealed to members to contact her immediately with details of any case of pagan parents having difficulty over child custody because of their beliefs.

The problem also strikes at the roots of the federation's attempt to place witchcraft under the heading of paganism. In the federation's magazine, *The Wiccan*, a discussion on the subject highlighted the dilemma of committed witches. James Pengelly pointed out that paganism as a system of religious belief and *without* the [witch]craft tag seemed to be becoming more socially acceptable, even fashionable. He said that the rites of paganism could often be staged without occult overtones and as such it was easier to involve children. He cited the case of one couple who included their children by staging the rituals as if they were parties, playing games and telling stories. He admitted that pagans needed to be much more circumspect when involving children in witchcraft. He quoted a line from the rites of the First Degree initiation. 'The Craft is not for the weak . . .' Everyone participating needed to be advanced in tuition and alert. Children were weak physically and spiritually, he said, and thus to open a child's mind to the demands of witchcraft 'could be termed irresponsible and is potentially dangerous.' Children versed in the ways of paganism could in time make contact between it and the craft and would then be in a position to make up their own minds.

Another well-known occultist and author who is known simply as Robert, issued a sterner warning. He agreed that active paganism involved things that could be shared with children such as daily meditation, alone or as a family, looking after plants, talking to animals, blessing the food before meals. These provided no more danger to children (or, he added, from bigoted social workers) than the celebrations of any religious faith on earth. But he warned that initiated witchcraft circles were a different matter altogether, pointing out that their purpose was to raise power for healing and other uses and one of the main ways of raising power used the polarity between sexes. Prepubescent children who were naturally physically very open could easily find the energy raised in such circles very disturbing and might be damaged by it. They might also talk about it at school and this would 'quickly bring the social workers down in force. Adolescents would probably take to raising power like ducks to water but lacking discretion would teach all their schoolfriends how to give a disliked teacher indigestion – if not levitate him out of the classroom.' It would be better, Robert concluded, to maintain a lower age limit of eighteen for all participants in witchcraft. He also felt it unwise to pursue the practice – followed by some Wiccan covens – of allowing children into the cakes and wine after an evening's main business had ended. He warned that this was especially dangerous if the adults were still skyclad (naked), as a lot of the raised power lingered on.

Lingering power? It is, for an outside mind, difficult to dispel the sinister or to contemplate the presence of children anywhere near the rituals. Indeed, it is not difficult to see how witches can become targets of social workers.

CHAPTER SIX

IN A WITCH'S TEMPLE

In spite of the public excesses of some of its number, witchcraft in Britain flourished in the eighties. Covens were springing up everywhere. Today there are few major towns where there is not a coven, and where one is established it invariably spawns another, and the chain reaction begins. Some die out, but the pattern has clearly been one of expansion. Some follow the Gardnerian tradition, others are in the Alexandrian camp, and both have spread abroad. The two schools of witchcraft became the basis for the formation of large witch followings in America, Canada and Australia as well as elsewhere in Europe. America and Canada especially have seen witchcraft expand into legalized churches and it has crossed social boundaries virtually everywhere.

For a clearer view of what witches do in the privacy of their own covens, I travelled to Leicester to gain some practical experience.

It was a clear and crisp evening and at around 8.30 there was already a full moon suitably rising, to shine down on a row of large Victorian houses where nine members of the coven were beginning to arrive for their regular gathering. Behind the net curtains of this ordinary suburban house in an English city I sought to answer the question: does witchcraft have any meaning or purpose? Or are witches merely, to put it bluntly, a bunch of weirdos performing their rituals for obscure, even obscene, pleasures? Do they really see themselves as being part of a religion? And if so, how do they equate their actions with modern society? Above all, is there real justification in believing, as they all seem to, that they are continuing ancient traditions and not just performing some cobbled-together junk rituals which have no historical consequence?

This particular coven included two married couples. The rest came on their own but the sexes matched in number, except for the High Priestess; two of the others were married and the spouse of one of them did not know he was a witch; he used the cover that it was a bridge club – though how he would explain the pervading aroma of sandalwood incense that wafted from the cellar and was absorbed into our clothes and hair was beyond me. There was an architect, a council employee who did not wish to specify his job, a pa/secretary and the manageress of a boutique; the remainder did not wish to divulge their occupations or their names, and some were apprehensive about being observed, fearing that their identity would be revealed.

Society's fear of witches is matched by the witches' fear of society. As in most covens, this one was made up of like-minded people generally drawn from the same sort of social background – in this case middle class and comfortable.

Like seems to go with like, socially and sexually. The coven originates from an Alex Sanders' initiation but they have long since discarded his Book of Shadows as being definitive; they have studied further and added more ritual from standard textbooks on magic. 'You tend to make up your own rituals as you go along,' said High Priest Barry Roberts, in whose house they were gathering. 'When you are new to it, you tend to think that Gardner or Sanders or some of the other Wiccan stars must be followed to the letter – then you realize that it is all very flexible, as long as the fundamentals are in place and you follow very rigidly the formula for magic.'

As Steve Jones of PaganLink explained earlier, there are fundamentalist witch groups who stick to tradition, there are those who follow a more loosely associated pattern of activity, there are groups who go for a particular path or cult, such as the Shamanistic or Dianic, Gardnerian or Alexandrian, there are feminist groups, lesbian groups and a smaller number of homosexual groups. They do not tend to mix and match.

There are also family groups who bring their children to some of the more general festivals. The Leicester group had five children between them; one of the couples brought their first child to a group meeting to be laid before their coven altar to celebrate the birth but generally the children are not involved in anything they do.

Apart from their coven meetings, they do not see each other during the course of a normal week for any purpose, social or otherwise. They meet as and when they feel like it and attendance is entirely voluntary – 'no pressure whatsoever, in fact quite the reverse,' said the High Priestess, a tall, blonde woman still in her thirties. She has two children aged eleven and thirteen who do not yet know she is a witch but she will tell them when they are old enough to appreciate 'the practicalities of paganism'.

There are several set dates that coven members must try to attend, such as the thirteen (lunar) monthly esbats to coincide with the full moon when the power source of the Triple Goddess is at its height. Then there are the witch sabbats, eight in all. There are four greater sabbats which are Candlemas (2 February), May Eve (30 April), Lammas (1 August) and Hallowe'en (31 October). These sabbats coincide with the four great festivals of the ancient Celts and were traditionally held during night-time hours from midnight to cock-crow. The four lesser sabbats are the two solstices at midsummer and midwinter and the two equinoxes of spring and autumn, whose dates vary each year.

The belief that the esbats and sabbats are celebrated now as they were in pre-Christian times is also central to paganism as a religion today. This may well be the case but as far as I could see it was not possible to prove that pre-Christian pagans were witches. They were almost certainly not. It seemed to me that witches now wanted to be called pagans because it had not been as easy as was once thought to shake off their bad name, or the fear they caused. Otherwise, why had the elders of witchcraft in Britain thought it necessary in 1971 to form a Pagan Federation whose aim was basically to defend witchcraft from attack? The fear of attacks and exposure to neighbours and friends was well founded. 'Good' witches they might be, but there was an unfortunate underlying badness attributed to the movement through the deeds of the extrovert black magicians and devil worshippers that would not go away simply by calling themselves pagans.

It also seemed a very loose form of worship – whereby any coven or even any witch could choose the deity, worship whom, what, how and when they pleased; yet they were not really worshipping that deity at all because they did not believe in an overall creator, merely a central core of the Divine. The focal point of their worship was the earth and the universe, as a total entity through which mankind passes again and again.

The Leicester coven members disagreed. Everything they did related back to pagan times; that was their heritage. True the gods and goddesses were invoked in name as a convenient receptacle of coven prayers but they were as sincere as any Christian worshipper might be in the God they worshipped. There had always been the badness and indeed those who propagated it today were doing so at the behest of primitive tradition which demanded sacrifice for the continuance of power and life.

And that, said the host Barry Roberts, was where the difficulties lay. There were satanic groups who practised such dark arts and whether occult elders liked it or not, the pagan witches made a point of dissociating themselves from this black and satanic activity. The pagan ritual attempts to work for the good things of life, symbolizing the fertility of the land, animals and the family – all at one with Mother Earth.

Witches still prefer to meet outdoors for their festivals, in some secluded spot selected for its historical associations and generally related to the pagan worship of the Earth, the sun, the moon and the stars. The ancient sites of early civilizations, stone circles, standing stones, natural sources of water, such as wells and springs, or just a grove of trees, are sought because they are considered to be centres of natural energy that in modern terms is described by witches as magical. Just as a water-diviner – who would have been called a 'witch' in an earlier age – sought power vibrations from deep in the earth, so witches drew on this energy as they performed their naked rituals.

This search for 'power centres' in many ways explains the proliferation of traditional witch covens in areas where these sites are most common, such as the West Country. Thus if it is to be accepted that modern witchcraft is indeed a proper descendant of the old religions and not some puerile bastardization invented less than fifty years ago by the likes of Gerald Gardner and popularized by dubiously charismatic figures like Alex Sanders, then the celebration of the sabbats must be seen to be performed with a precise correlation to past rituals.

I posed the question again. How can it be a religion? The collective answer came back that most religions include a good deal of plagiarism and invention. Paganism provides its followers with a traceable history of gods whom they could worship and a tradition of primtive ritual they could copy. This was their interpretation of primitive sacrificial magic which they, and sorcerers of the first millennium, could copy and develop as their own.

What exists now, out of this study, for the more sophisticated witches like those in the Leicester coven, is a link to these past traditions and ancient gods which they see as their source for tapping into the earth's energy – the sun's power, the moon's cycles – that provides the underlying theme of their worship and ritual. They take it all very seriously.

It was, they said, a sign of a coven moving towards black magic when these points of worship, in other words their selected deity, faded into the background of their working and the search for the manifestation of demonic forces within their circle became obsessive. That was when a coven was heading towards a dangerous liaison with a force they might not be able to control.

The Leicester group maintained it had no such ambitions, though Barry Roberts admitted that everyone I spoke to in witchcraft would probably say exactly the same:

It is always someone else who strays into the greyness and then the black; but not us – we are simple witches. We do not eat babies, sacrifice animals or do nasty things to naked virgins on black altars. It just does not happen in any witch coven I know. But of course we have all heard stories about people who do these things ... To understand it, you have to remember that magic is as old as man – in fact, it is believed by some to be a precursor to religion and there are many historical examples of how magic and religion actually went hand in glove, until the Christian movement decided that all magicians were heretics.

Magic is the power within oneself that is the key to what we do, and sometimes we can whip up a great deal of power. The magic we are capable of is almost indefinable. Our magic, according to Aleister Crowley, is the art of causing change to occur in conformity with will. In other words, we attempt to raise enough etheric energy between us, by our ritual, to use our paranormal powers to force a desired result by our will-power. The odd thing is that the ritual and methods of magic are basically the same whether it is for good or evil, white or black, witchcraft or occult lodge.

The difference lies in the symbolism; we, the white witches, see it as our form of worship from which we can develop our inner selves and grow in all kinds of ways, whereas the black magicians and satanic witches pursue magic for its own sake and end up consumed by it. And in any event, I frankly do not believe there are a great many pagan witch covens who have either the ability or the desire to experiment in the serious stuff. What we do is child's play compared to some groups in the higher levels of the occult arts. Even at our level of operation, unless absolute care is taken, a coven can still get into difficulties, and this is especially so for witches working alone.

The discussion broadened, because discussion and study are the fruit of many coven meetings. It was agreed that what witches did in private was usually a form of lesser magic. It was one thing using the supernatural powers of the human mind to try to compel something to happen, but it was quite another matter summoning up the assistance of spirits and demons, whether benevolent, malevolent or neutral. Mistakes in the ritual or failure to observe the minutiae could lead to disaster.

None present had ever witnessed any kind of apparition although one member, a witch for twenty years or more, recalled being invited to assist a magician who practised the darker arts. The magic went wrong and the room they were working in was virtually wrecked by lingering, unseen spirits. The leader himself was mysteriously injured with a stab wound in his shoulder, though no one saw the knife go in or where it came from. Many guides to higher ritual magic issue a health warning with their instructions: the practitioner must be confident he is totally in control of all the techniques and disciplines otherwise he faces physical, psychological and spiritual dangers of a most serious kind if any attempt to invoke spirits goes wrong.

By and large, witchcraft – and certainly paganism – seemed not to be about chasing demons, though they do claim to make spiritual contact with the gods invoked during their worship. Witchcraft, as practised in this Leicester coven – a fairly typical example of what was known as a working coven – was about 'tuning in to Mother Earth, improving your own karma and helping others, all tied into the traditional mystic elements and powers that witches are renowned for . . . believe it or believe it not.'

The coven members did not wish to force their belief upon anyone, but asked who could honestly say that they had not experienced some kind of paranormal event in their lives which they could not explain? The group offered an abundance of 'evidence': the feeling you had been in a certain place before when, in this life at least, it was your first visit; the uncanny foresight of witch fortune-tellers; the 'proven' success of powers of auto-suggestion; the out-of-body experiences that witches claim to be able to learn; the sixth sense of animals, a dog barking at the spot in an old house where the occupant died years ago and the seemingly psychic abilities of witches' familiars, usually cats. The list goes on and on. But where is the evidence? Could they prove to me that what they are going to do now, their coven 'working', will have the slightest or even the remotest chance of success?

The architect, polishing the gleaming blade of his witches' knife, the athame, interjected: 'This kind of discussion has been going on for centuries, but it was not until quite recently that we could actually talk about it without fear of being prosecuted or hanged. In our most basic and simplistic forms of magic, there is little difference between us and more orthodox faith healers, like the Spiritualists, only we don't have a hierarchical system and our ritual is more ceremonial and dramatic.'

There have been endless experiments with auto-suggestion, relating to the powers of a witch healer that triggers in the body of the patient a healing process, usually on more simple medical matters such as wart charming or even some forms of pain. There are easily definable and scientific explanations for many; less easy to explain is the healing process which the witches claim they can prove had occurred when the patient is totally unaware that they had been working in their coven on his behalf. Furthermore, how do you begin to explain some of the more sinister forms of witch magic – the black sort – with the use of pins stuck in effigies where there are numerous examples to be quoted? Where did they get this 'power' and more pointedly why should I, as an outsider, believe it even exists?

The strength of their power, they said, was linked to their calendar of meetings – special nights of lunar importance – but they might also get together for special reasons, perhaps to perform healing magic or some other specific purpose for which a member of the group might wish to enlist the aid of the others, such as providing him with a karma of confidence for a new job interview.

Sometimes they would meet for study, or meditation, or deeper trances, or to practise tarot reading, clairvoyance or scrying (crystal gazing) or the art of enhancing their psychic powers. Only three of them had seriously studied the art of astral planing, and claimed numerous out-of-body experiences. Otherwise, their meetings were for the pleasure of it just as Christians met, it was pointed out, for a variety of church-linked events, only in covens they came for the enjoyment of the ritual and the ceremony.

The Leicester house was no different in outward or internal appearance from any of the others in the row. With all the accoutrements of modern society, it bore no signs of the mysterious when the witches began to arrive in their similarly normal attire. The neighbours might indeed believe that the visitors were arriving for a bridge night, though they must surely have had their suspicions, especially if they could hear the strange music later in the night.

The witches took off all their clothes and put on their coven robes in the front room; the women first and the men afterwards. It seemed odd that they should perform this disrobement of street garb separately since all would normally be conducting their rituals naked and they have been together as a coven for several years, the newest member joining eighteen months earlier. This was the norm, and not for my benefit I was assured. Getting undressed remained a separate function and no one could quite explain why this was; embarrassment seemed to be the most common thought. Tonight, because of my presence, they were going to perform the part of their normal coven meeting that I was allowed to observe in their robes, which were variously brown, red and dark colours.

I noticed that, as they came out of the room, each female witch wore or carried a beaded necklace. This apparently symbolized the lives through which they pass to achieve perfection, the circle of rebirth. To many exponents of Wicca, the beads represent two things, a rebirth of their own self through initiation into Wicca, and reincarnation. The rebirth during life is supposed to follow the three stages of initiation into Wicca. The initiated witch is given a new secret name, and the idea is that the mysteries now to be learned will change his or her personality and inclinations, resulting in the individual becoming a better person – hence the rebirth.

The suppositions of rebirth during life and reincarnation after death are central to the craft as practised by this coven. What struck me, in the continual discussions which arose, is that all of them seem to be extremely well informed on their subjects, well read and studious. The Greeks, they told me, called reincarnation 'metempsychosis', or the transmigration of souls. The doctrine of reincarnation was widespread. Ancient Egyptians, Hindus, Buddhists, American Indians and other pagans believed in various forms of reincarnation, though the Wiccan view was much in line with the Kabbalistic theory that each life is offered to achieve progressive perfection before final acceptance into a glorious hereafter which is available to all; thus past mistakes can die with past lives and recurring opportunities to improve are offered.

It is totally at odds with the Christian teaching that man's single life on earth will be followed with eternal damnation in Hell or eternal ecstasy in the Kingdom of God, depending on his level of goodness. 'What kind of threat is that?' asked Barry Roberts. 'It does not seem a very encouraging proposition made on behalf of their apparently all-loving God.'

Discussion followed; reincarnation remains, even to Christians, another of the great mysteries on which we can only speculate, and occasionally offer up new purported evidence of a past life, related by someone under deep hypnosis or recovered from dream memories. Pagans study such reports avidly, ever questing for more knowledge. It is a general belief in the Wiccan world that after death, the physical body is shed and the spiritual body moves on to the astral plane to await rebirth in another earthly body.

History is littered with examples, especially in recent years when the preponderance of practising hypnotherapists has increased, their techniques heightened and recording equipment becoming ever more sophisticated. I, the sceptic, offered the Leicester coven my preparedness to be convinced. One told the story of a naval rating who served under Earl Mountbatten and continually recounted stories about his previous life as a naval gunner at the time of the battle of Waterloo. Mountbatten was not in the least sceptical about the man's claims; he was himself a believer in the paranormal, the supernatural and the ability of the human mind to hold secrets that were inaccessible to normal recall and too incredible to imagine – that's exactly what he told his astrological and psychic friend Dolores North who wrote in the magazine *Prediction* under the name of Madeline Montalban. Dolores, who hailed from the area of Broadlands, the estate which Edwina Mountbatten inherited from her father, later moved to London and became Mountbatten's personal witch.

He consulted her on many matters, and was especially keen on the astrological influences that affected the enemy. He was equally interested when he heard the authentic details of the rating's recollections of serving in the British navy at the time of Waterloo. Mountbatten, who was a great one for the electronic devices of the new film age, went to the trouble of having the man's recollections recorded on tape and played it to his colleagues in the naval hierarchy.

'But that,' said the Leicester high priest, 'is one of a hundred stories that can be drawn on to offer some evidence of reincarnation. Many could be explained away, and have been dismissed. There are those that remain intriguing.' They are the stories that those who would consider themselves to be 'real' witches love; they absorb them to give evidence and a sense of history to their beliefs.

*

Meanwhile, the Leicester coven was preparing for the evening's ritual to begin. They all moved towards the cellar steps and down into a large but gloomy underground chamber, lit only by a single lamp in the small ante-room leading to the temple, which itself was lit only by candles. It was a normal cellar room, with a low, boarded ceiling and the only source of light, a grating once used for emptying the coal sacks, was boarded up. As we entered the air was thick with the incense being burned on the altar, a combination of sandalwood shavings and dried berries and herbs which exuded a sweet and oppressive odour that, close-to, makes you catch your breath.

The walls were decorated with drapes of a kind of net curtaining, green in colour, covering old prints depicting witch and folklore. There was no furniture at all in the room, although there was a hi-fi system with speakers pointing inwards, alongside which was a large selection of tapes of ritual dance music, to be used in the process of raising magical powers. The floor was covered with grey fibre carpeting and at the centre was a white painted circle made up of two concentric circles, with symbols between the inner and outer lines.

Apart from the necklace symbolizing rebirth, the priests and priestesses wore other jewellery, including rings and bracelets, which they claim retain some of the ritual energy they generate and can help boost the strength of their own magical powers considerably. They did not explain how, but it seems that these items absorb the energy which is raised during a ritual and retain it; there is only one stipulation to the wearing of jewellery – that the necklace should be made by the priestess herself, even if this entailed merely taking the stones off two necklaces and rethreading them in alternate colours. No watches or timepieces are permitted within the circle because time is of no consequence on the higher level of consciousness that they seek to achieve.

The High Priest explained that normally they work naked and robes are only worn by new initiates. This is because they believe that the human body holds within it a latent power which can be released by certain ritual exercises that witches perform. This power is widely known as etheric or spiritual energy, similar to that aroused by exponents of yoga. Some spiritualist healers and clairvoyant witches can actually see it, like a rainbow. Many British witches believe that ordinary clothes absorb the power and inhibit its full value; even robes can act as a block. There is, I am assured, historical confirmation of nakedness among Europen witches, though this practice is almost unheard of in American and Canadian covens. Some covens perform all of their main rituals in robes – the colour of which may be chosen by the individual; the initiate must have done some work on the robe. Neither shoes nor underclothes are worn, unless they are working outdoors when sandals are allowed. Colours are chosen from astrological symbols – yellow for the sun, green for Venus, silver or white for the moon, but most seemed to select darker colours representing the other planets.

A belt or girdle is worn around the waist to keep the robe in place; it also forms a circle about the body signifying that the witch is in tune with the elements by living and working with nature. It is usually red, the colour of life and the life blood, and symbolizes the life of the martyrs who died in the persecution.

The inner of the two circles painted on the carpet was, by tradition, nine feet across and it butted on to the farthest wall of the cellar. A smaller circle is set up if a witch alone desires to contact spirits or elemental beings, weave a spell or meditate; a larger one may be used outside – but in fact the size of the circle turns out to be immaterial. The whole room may be consecrated as an operating circle if it is desired. The circle, it was explained to me, is the centre of all occult activity and was drawn to concentrate the occultists' power and to protect them from hostile spirits. Within the circle, the spiritual journey begins and their efforts are directed to produce what they call their Cone of Power.

The High Priest explained that it is only within the circle that the gods and the spirits of the astral world can be safely contacted. It was, he said, like a clearing in a dense forest where the physical bodies can meet the spiritual.

Before entry into it, the circle was swept clean of every speck by the priestess, using a witch's broom – just like the one of popular image. The process is twofold, again physical and psychological – to sweep away any lingering unwanted influences which may be absorbed in the dust and to inspire the coven members to begin the process of opening their minds for their journey to a higher plane, clearing their minds of earthly problems and worries so that they may open their 'whole being' to the singular concentration of the work before them, tapping now into the energy centres of the body. The priest confided, 'It is at this point, as the broom passes to and fro across the floor, that we really have to put our earthly existence in abeyance; with experience one moves quickly into the state of readiness and any cares and woes simply fade out.'

Lighted candles were placed at strategic points on the circle, defining like a compass the north, south, east and westerly points. These are the Watchtowers, through which contact will be made with the Lords of the Elements – air, fire, water and earth. They are regarded as the guardians of the circle. In the centre of the circle, the altar had been arranged; it was small and unobtrusive, allowing the witches ample room for their activities around it.

The arrangement of items on the altar is apparently important: in the centre was a pentacle – a copper badge, normally nine inches in diameter, which is the symbol of Mother Earth, bearing inscriptions on one side and the triple circles (representing the Triple Goddess) on the reverse. The rest of the altar was arranged around it. To the left stood the statuette image of the goddess whom they are to invoke and to the right a god image, the Horned God of Pan. Across the centre of the altar lay the sacred sword with the tip pointing westward.

There was a small silver plate containing salt and a bowl containing water which are used for the consecration of the witches' tools. A censer contains the incense smouldering on glowing charcoal and is said to provide a 'conducive atmosphere', not merely for the witches but for the gods and spirits they invoke during their rituals.

There is a chalice of wine which will be offered to each member to drink a toast to the gods, a white-handled knife for work within the circle, a wand to summon up spirits and genii and the scourge to use in the rites of initiation and creating 'vision'. Each witch carries his or her own black-handled knife, the athame, which is consecrated at the time of the witch's initiation and is reckoned to be the 'most powerful' tool they possess. At the beginning of each working session, the High Priestess uses her knife to open the magic circle; the holder of the athame is the 'ruler of the magic circle, and has power over rebellious spirits and demons.'

Inside the magic circle, no force of darkness can stand against the athame; with this knife in hand the witch is said to hold complete domination over the spirits. It should be used by no one other than the witch who owns it, and for no other purpose than the ceremony. The witch's secret name, given at the time of initiation, is inscribed upon the blade, along with a pentacle.

With all the witches inside the circle, the High Priestess begins the proceedings which I have shortened in description here to give just the flavour of a fairly lengthy night of magic. She blessed the water and salt with her athame and the coven, I was told, visualizes the bodily power of the priestess moving in the form of a blue light through her hand into the athame and out through its blade as she says, 'Blessings upon this creature Salt. Let all malignity and hindrance be cast forth hencefrom, let all good herein enter.' The salt is the sterilizer of the circle and she added it to the water before consecrating each member of the coven with the mixture.

Then she consecrated the circle itself, starting at the north, the sacred place and home of the gods, with arms outstretched and brandishing her knife amid more incantation and recital. The Wiccan tradition of honouring the north is in principle the same as Christianity's eastern direction or Islam's prayer direction towards Mecca, the birthplace of Muhammad.

Next, using the incense, the circle was purified in a similar manner to complete the conception of the coven working within a space of purity and protection from all external impurities and influences.

Finally, the whole coven took part in invoking the attendance of the Lords of the Watchtowers, following the words of the priestess, as the ritual opening of the circle reached its conclusion.

The coven was now ready for its work, raising power for the magic. A reminder of the definition of witches' magic is perhaps called for; they say it is the creation and use of energy to cause a change in consciousness, usually achieved by a ritual, a factor common to the rites of ancient tribes the world over.

The Leicester High Priest had a large selection of specially recorded music from which a choice was made at this point. It was of bongo-like drumming and ghostly flutes and oboes playing a totally unidentifiable tune. They join hands, march and commence their dance which is one selected for a night of the full moon. (In Wicca they follow the latest scientific discoveries on research into how the full moon can affect the human mind, and thus attune their ritual towards it.) They performed what is called a spiral dance, where the witches are together in a ring, going around faster and faster, creating an energy which moves first from the priestess, then into the priest who adds to it and passes on around the circle until it returns to the priestess.

When the base circle of energy is complete, it is added to by the dance, each member of the coven drawing up all the power they can muster from within their bodies and exhaling it into the centre of the circle so that it builds up into what is known as the Cone of Power.

By that time, although they were going faster and faster, there was an aura of icy coolness and no one was perspiring; the eyes of some were closed, and the eyes of one had gone upwards so that only the whites were visible. The dance had had a trance-like effect and, according to the High Priest, those with powers of second sight would now see the energy spiralling from each coven member like blue lightning into the central reservoir of energy which the group was creating. I am afraid I saw nothing.

The energy is created and stored in the circle and can be drawn upon when the dance stops to perform magic. The intent is now held in the minds of each member of the coven, who had been told beforehand the purpose of the magic, and they focus on it with intensity and 'send' the energy on its way to perform their magic ... and during all of this three-act drama, there was a chant intermittently made.

The last of the four verses went:

> Queen of Heaven, Queen of Hell,
> Hornéd Hunter of the Night
> Lend your power unto our spell
> And work our will by magic rite.

The descriptions above are necessarily truncated, and I have not attempted to detail in full the very wide range of activities in which these covens indulge, other than to give the flavour of the formalities.

The invocation of gods and goddesses or their attempts to attract angels and genii into their circle involve long and complicated rituals which I believe can only have any meaning, or understanding, to those who are actually intent on performing these rites, and thus I will not venture into the complexities.

The last act which takes place before the circle is dissolved is worth mentioning. It is the dedication of cakes and wine and it is seen as a major part of the ritual of any coven gathering. It can be compared with the Christian communion – the symbolic partaking of bread and wine, representing the body and the blood of sacrificed Christ, in memory of the Last Supper.

In Wicca, the ceremony has its origins in the most primitive form of ritual and was based on cannibalism, whereby the actual flesh of the sacrificed Divine King was eaten and his blood drunk so that his powers would be passed on and multiplied among those consuming him. In the same way that the bread and wine are consecrated in the Christian Eucharist, so the cakes and wine are blessed in the coven circle to symbolize the actual blood and body of a divine sacrificial victim. They are seen by witches as the magical food from which their spiritual energy is drawn.

The blessing of the cakes and wine represents the final ultimate invocation of the gods and goddesses so that their power flows into the circle and energizes the food they then consume, as the High Priest passes the cakes among them and kisses each female member of the coven. Many covens also use this as the starting point of a celebration or feast, with music, dancing and singing. Others tend to use the solemnity of the ritual quietly to end their evening's work. The circle is finally and formally dissolved and any lingering spirits sent peacefully on their way.

At least, that is what I was told . . .

CHAPTER SEVEN

THE SORCERER'S APPRENTICE

The title of this chapter is also the registered business name and trademark of a man who stands at the epicentre of international occultism today and who is in many ways a linchpin in the exchange of information and views between witchcraft and other forms of occult pursuit.

His name is Christopher Bray, a vociferous and prolific defender of the rights and beliefs of occultists and equally vociferous in his attacks upon all who dare to question them – or him. He is a businessman and magazine editor who carries on his worldwide mail-order supply empire from a suitably sinister-looking corner building in a run-down area of Leeds; two minutes away by car he has another shop, called Astonishing Books.

The Sorcerer's Apprentice shop has windows which are covered entirely with black-painted boards; the shop is accessible through a heavy timber door where all who pass are monitored. There is, perhaps, justified reason for Mr Bray's obvious security consciousness. The Astonishing Books shop was fire-bombed not long ago and much of his collection of occult paraphernalia and huge library of books were burnt to a cinder. In times past, he too would undoubtedly have been put in the stocks, at the stake or on the gallows.

He worked to rebuild his business, reopened the bookshop and kept the mail-order side running without a break. He has boasted of a customer list kept on a highly efficient computer file and consisting of 40,000 names and addresses (including my own, since I bought a number of books from him) from sixty-six countries. He has made the point that he is not a satanist himself, though he does have about 300 clients who are known satanists, and says there was nothing in his catalogue that was illegal.

Mr Bray, a practising witch, is one of many proprietors running occult shops now operating throughout the country but few can match his stock, his contacts, his power or his influence in the occult world. He adopts a tough, uncompromising stance on the whole issue of the occult and clearly dislikes the polite approach of some of the neo-pagans and says that 'unlike many so-called occult shops, the SA never had any truck with the hypocrisy of self-interest or pseudo-bigotry'.

This is, in effect, justification for doing business with a wide spectrum of occult practitioners and it follows attacks upon him for stocking a selection of books and magazines on satanism. He has accused Christian fundamentalists of inspiring these attacks, and described their attitude as 'twisted ignorance'.

I wrote to Chris Bray as I began my research on this book to request an interview. An aide replied that Mr Bray had become extremely cynical about the manipulation of the subject by the media and believed that a high-level conspiracy had been formed in Britain against the occult so that it was 'virtually impossible to get the truth out.'

Later, I discovered that Mr Bray had warned at least one of those I interviewed not to talk to me, a warning which was disregarded by my contact, and when I wrote back to tell him I had received excellent co-operation from the witch community and that I would be quite happy for him to see my copy on him so that he could make a response, I received a second letter informing me that anyone giving me information was not to be trusted.

He did, however, say he would review my manuscript for any inaccuracies and enclosed with this letter a review he had just published on another book, the one by Tim Tate, entitled *Children for the Devil*, published by Methuen in 1991. The review, unsigned but with a familiar ring to it, and printed in a twenty-three-page pamphlet issued by the Sorcerer's Apprentice, was apparently circulated to hundreds of Mr Bray's clients and the occult media. It was highly critical of the author and the controversial issues he raised.

Tate and Bray had crossed swords before. Tate was a former

researcher for Roger Cook, the television investigator who had once had one of his typical television confrontations with Chris Bray when the latter refused to take part in a programme on satanism. His book, portrayed on the jacket flap as 'a deeply disturbing account of the systematic torture, abuse and murder of youngsters and a searing indictment of official and public complacency' pulled no punches.

Upsetting though some of his claims may well have been to the 'respectable' satanists, it did not, in a free society for which Mr Bray campaigns, merit the attack heaped upon the book in his pamphlet. Mr Bray himself spoke three years earlier, long before the outbreak of publicity over satanic ritual abuse, in an interview with Kim Fletcher for the *Sunday Telegraph*, on the issue of blood rites among satanists, claiming that real or arch-satanists were very gentlemanly, very polite and very gentle to ladies. He added that injury was not necessary as part of the ritual for satanists and that life-force blood can be released from a finger or by breaking a fertilized egg. Gallons of blood were not needed to consecrate a talisman, only a microscopic amount. The trouble came, said Bray, from pseudo-satanists who had no intellectual appreciation of the tasks performed by those they sought to emulate but who derived satisfaction from violent and often perverted sexual acts.

I will return to the issue of satanic ritual abuse in later chapters. Meanwhile, let us take a closer look at the self-styled 'world-famous Sorcerer's Apprentice' who happily boasts that his shop is a microcosm of the occult in Britain and that its evolution is of national importance.

I will start by asking why Mr Bray is so suspicious and touchy while others around him in the occult world go more calmly about their business?

Since he declined an interview, I will answer for him, as best I can. There are numerous reasons, which will unfold as I relate his story. First and foremost, it must be remembered that apart from being his passion, the occult is also his livelihood. He is obviously proud of his business, which he markets with considerable vigour and expertise. If he wasn't running an occult shop he could have made it big in advertising copy writing.

There is little in the way of equipment any member of any

occult group could want that he doesn't sell. A glance through the catalogue for autumn 1991 is fascinating reading for those who, like myself, do not normally come across this kind of merchandise. There is, for example, a complete home study course in the occult with thirteen books and lecture cassettes for £182, or a 'genuine 2000-year-old altar incense boat' for £40.81 or an 1800-year-old altar lamp, fully functional and with a supply of oil for £42.07.

There are idols and Baphomet statues [usually for satanic worship], a giant-sized one at £173.97 or a crossed-legged Goat of Mendes for a mere £22.22. The Goddess comes giant size at £164.77. There is a card kit for developing your ESP for only £5.67 or a dowsing kit compleat (five items) to enable you to find water immediately for £15.60; there's a crystal ball for £66.36 for your visions of the future – for a de luxe future, consult a five-inch model with covering cloth for £99.30; alternatively you can buy a quartz crystal ball for £204 or a larger one for group focus for £332.

There is a '3000-year-old knife handle block' authenticated by carbon dating and ready for carving and shaping into knife handles' for only £8.97. It seems a pity to carve into such old wood! A life-sized skull, at £38.48, that 'looks' hundreds of years old and 'will fool anyone first time round'.

Among the 'special items' the Sorcerer's Apprentice can supply is a magic carpet – 'genuine eighteenth-century' – for £273.15 or there is a complete temple kit with thirty-six items for only £171.88. I rather liked the sound of the mobiles – super eighteen-inch vampire bat and castle silhouettes with Tower of Horror centre-piece, but were they really 'ideal for kids' at £3.66? Definitely not for children is the Satanic Pendant Goat's Head, exclusively manufactured by the Sorcerer's Apprentice; a solid brass disc etched with a sinister seal that 'captures and reflects the Satian current, similar to the seal used by the LaVey Church (of Satan), recognized universally'; £10.01 (which reversed is £10.01).

I turned the page to sheet number six in the 'world famous Sorcerer's Apprentice equipment price-list' and discovered a list of products that benign witches might despair at: there is a spellkit for a job or promotion at work – 'the acclaimed spellkit the media tried to discredit' – a snip at £57.23; or a spellkit for success in business, cheaper at only £50.61 – the same price as a spellkit for drawing wealth, or one for passing your driving test which ensures you reach perfection on the day. There's one for your love desires – 'many testimonials' – for £52.80; another to get revenge, £51.93, but should I fear such acts, then I may merely purchase a spellkit for psychic protection for a similarly modest outlay.

If that doesn't work, I might choose to chase away my cares by smoking the 'painstakingly hand-blended to a secret recipe' Herbal High, the only herbal pot that actually smells good, tastes good and produces no rough side effects; comes with free Rizla papers for £16.97 for a four-ounce pouch – 'so powerful our staff wear breathing masks when bagging it otherwise it's pandemonium for the rest of the day.'

I found the list for ritual incense oils, baths and powders particularly interesting and I suppose that from the massive selection on offer by the Sorcerer's Apprentice, the customer's selection is governed by the level of seriousness of the task at hand. The code B30 in the A to Z spellguide, for example, brings a potion to bathe with your lover, or to rub on prior to an assignation for increased ardour. Apply oil to groin, breasts and sprinkle powder in underclothes; £6.09 an ounce. The list is long and mysterious.

You can buy anointing oils to aid astral travel or powder to rub on your hands for good luck at the roulette table – one of a long list of gambling aids, including Powdered Bat's Blood to burn as incense in your home before opposing card players arrive, or to sprinkle on your chair in the casino. The catalogue does not explain what Bat's Eyes, at £6.09 per ounce, might be used for; but I liked the sound of Bon Voyage, an ointment to break up an undesirable relationship or to drive away enemies. Finally, I was intrigued by a substance named Graveyard which, it seems, will solve all my financial problems. I should merely write on a strip of parchment the amount of money I require, place it in a small red bag with the graveyard powder and put in my left shoe.

Flicking through the pages of his catalogue, it struck me that they seem to go against all the things that the white witches were saying about the superficiality of such spells and curses that, for the true pagan, had no place in witchcraft in Britain today.

But that, it would seem, is exactly the point – if Mr Bray had to rely on the neo-pagans and white witches for his trade, he would not find a very good living. He complained in his editorial that occultism today was becoming 'more and more a social club rather than a Path of Being'.

He bemoaned the fact that neo-paganism had become far removed from the true concept of witchcraft, being based today on anthropology and mythology – echoing a complaint by the satanist Anton LaVey in his book *Satanic Witch*, in which he said British witchcraft was revived by the writings of Dr Margaret Murray and the myths of the persecution era as written by Montague Summers, and was as exciting as a Christian sermon.

Chris Bray, writing in his own magazine *Lamp of Thoth*, was horrified that the magical side of paganism was being diluted and that other aspects of occultism were 'being similarly castrated' – ideas such as those which say that homosexuals have no place in a male–female coven; or that occultists should just concern themselves with nice things; and that animals are so sacrosanct that any human found harming them should themselves be harmed. He argued that the real work of the occult path lies in plumbing the depths of one's psyche and releasing the shackles of self.

It is this uncompromising, but entirely legal, stance on the occult that has made Bray a target for Christian fundamentalists and other critics. They see Bray as being at the heart of the occult movement's attack on the Christians' decade of evangelism.

More topically, he was to become the focus of an attack when fundamentalists were alerted to the prospect of huge publicity in the offing resulting from a case in Nottingham where, on 20 January 1988, Carl, a four-year-old boy in care, whispered things to his foster-mother that indicated he had been sexually abused by his aunts and uncles.

Although there were alleged to be elements of ritual abuse present, the case was prosecuted as one of the offences against children, largely because the police felt the children's claims were so fantastic they might not be believed. I shall deal more fully with these cases in my discussion on satanism. The point at issue now is that the Nottingham case coincided with the beginning of a campaign against the occult that was to be taken up with considerable vigour the following year by the newly formed Evangelical

Alliance and promoted as a warning of what was secretly happening in Britain on a large scale. Bray was a natural target.

In April 1988, Geoffrey Dickens MP first alerted the nation to what he described as despicable acts and drew attention to the operations of Chris Bray with a speech in the House of Commons deploring the activities of the Sorcerer's Apprentice and its sister business Astonishing Books, both founded to serve the needs of practitioners of witchcraft and other occult practices.

True enough; but then Mr Dickens turned the accusation to a more pointed direction: 'It is common knowledge that witchcraft rituals involve the abuse of children.' Mr Dickens offered no concessions to Westminster sceptics and said that he had been assisted in his efforts by benign witches from 'every corner of the United Kingdom', some of whom had named Bray's shop as being a prime source of witchcraft regalia.

Very soon, when anti-satanic literature and videos were being pumped into Britain from America, and passed on courtesy of the Evangelical Alliance to social workers and child care agencies such as the NSPCC, Bray became the focus for what has become a long and bitter battle between himself and the Christian fundamentalists. He called them the Gang of Five: Geoffrey Dickens; the Reverend Kevin Logan, a Blackburn vicar and ardent anti-occultist; Dianne Core, founder of the Hull-based Childwatch; Maureen Davies, then the director of the Reachout Trust, a religious rescue mission for survivors of occult experience; and Audrey Harper, a former witch and reformed heroin addict.

In the welter of publicity that followed, Dianne Core and Maureen Davies were repeatedly interviewed. As I mentioned in the introduction, incredible figures began to be quoted – such as the allegation by Dianne Core that there were 4000 children sacrificed each year in Britain for these rituals. These figures were repeated and taken up by the media, and received widespread coverage.

Bray, meanwhile, was already in the process of forming his answer to this first wave of allegations. He had for some time been working on a theory that Britain's occult community extended well into the upper-middle-class reaches of society and in 1989 began an Occult Census, sending out a questionnaire to several thousand witches and occultists. He received over 1000 responses, which was disappointing compared with the number he posted, but an adequate return on which to base fairly accurate findings.

The census produced some revealing facts, even down to the newspaper-buying habits of occultists – 20 per cent were *Guardian* readers, the second most popular newspaper was the *Independent*, while *The Times* and the *Mirror* shared third place.

Two-thirds became interested in occultism in their teens or early twenties; few became involved once they were over twenty-five. Sixty-nine per cent of practising occultists were between twenty and thirty-nine years old; 12 per cent were over fifty. Ten per cent were without jobs, the remainder were in a variety of occupations and a sample band of 200 occultists included 4 scientists, 4 homeopaths, 2 social workers, 1 vet, 4 musicians, 1 hotelier, 3 booksellers, 1 bank clerk, 1 soldier, 2 doctors, 2 farmers, 5 salesmen, 4 teachers, 1 psychologist, 5 typists, 4 electricians, 2 postmen, 1 policeman, 1 journalist and so on.

Three-quarters of those who answered the sample said they had no interest in satanism but listed sixteen different occult paths, with astrology, tarot cards, paganism, witchcraft and the Kabbalah being the most popular. Again, about three-quarters of those sampled thought involvement in the occult enhanced their social lives; 82 per cent believed alternative religions such as paganism should be taught in schools. And three-quarters believed that even if they did not learn about the occult this time, then they could probably do it next time around – in other words they steadfastly believed in reincarnation. As many as 43 per cent thought that the occult could be harmful to society, especially when abused.

And clearly there was abuse. One satanist who responded said he had worked evil magic more than a hundred times; otherwise, 14 per cent admitted they had worked evil magic an average of 3.3 times and 22 per cent 'knew others who did'.

More than 90 per cent had experienced a psychic occurrence or magical phenomenon yet surprisingly fewer than 25 per cent had a committed belief in astrology – far less than a sample of the non-occultist population. And politically, the colour of occultism is virtually a reverse of the national image. In order of preference came the Greens, the Liberal Democrats, Labour, SDP, Marxism

– the Tories were eighth, just ahead of the Trotskyites and Anarchists. From this research it was estimated that as many as 250,000 people indulged in witchcraft and paganism.

Armed with their own version of these facts, and the colourful evidence of Dianne Core, Maureen Davies and others, Tim Tate and Roger Cooke began putting together a programme on satanism. In the meantime, at a conference in Rome organized by the Martin Luther King Tribunal, Mrs Lyndon La Rouche, wife of the right-wing, anti-communist who runs a quasi-religious organization based in America that once promoted the view that all AIDS victims should be isolated in prison-like compounds, spoke of the work of Dianne Core and projected a ten-foot-high portrait of Bray to the assembly as being the occult's Mr Big.

By then, Roger Cook had interviewed numerous people, and also brought to England Michael Aquino, the head of the US satanic organization Temple of Set, who was originally associated with satanist Anton LaVey. Bray refused to co-operate with an interview because the programme, entitled *The Devil's Work*, was based almost entirely on the facts provided by his sworn enemies, so naturally he fell neatly into the mould of the Cook doorstep villain, refusing to be interviewed. 'Why won't you talk to us Mr Bray . . . ? What have you got to hide Mr Bray . . . ?'

Bray began to feel the pinch and the old fear of witches began to show once again. Graffiti artists attacked the front of his shop with aerosols, trade delivery suppliers refused delivery to his business, neighbours became unneighbourly and his daughter was suddenly friendless.

One month after the programme was shown, the wiremesh grill over the front of Astonishing Books was severed with bolt cutters and the intruders smashed down all the bookshelves, especially those on witchcraft and satanism, and made a bonfire in the middle of the shop. The bookstore was burned out, though the mail-order offices upstairs remained operative. When donations came in to help him re-establish, Bray formed what is now known as the Sorcerer's Apprentice Fighting Fund and he decided to try to build up a cash reserve to fight those who libelled himself and other occultists.

He warned witchcraft parents to be on their guard from prying neighbours, otherwise they may find themselves in court facing a child custody case. And he turned the screw with a drawing of three witches hanging from gallows . . . 'look into the eyes and imagine the horror and suffering, twisting and spinning in the death throes.'

So the fighting fund was in place, and continues today, giving Bray the wherewithal to fight back on behalf of witches and pagans who themselves may feel somewhat reticent now about coming out from behind their box-number addresses and publicly revealing their names.

If there is a common factor emerging from all of this research so far, it is that witches are all coy about identification. Few will allow their real names to be used, fewer still want their addresses known. Very few are as forthcoming as Chris Bray who continues to dish out attacks on the attackers, and in many ways this move towards the defensive was a natural reaction to the new interest in witchcraft and the occult which began emerging with the new offensive by the Christian fundamentalist campaigners and their allies.

In fact, from its 1989 beginnings when Geoffrey Dickens launched his attacks in the Commons, a new media interest in witchcraft and the occult mushroomed so that the year 1990 became one packed with claim and counter-claim. Tracking back through the files and the case histories, it is now quite simple to pinpoint the explosion of these stories as being inspired by the Evangelical Alliance, one feeding on the next, and indeed the most bloodcurdling accounts of those who had flirted with the devil were brought to public attention by leading personalities in the Alliance.

Bray, in his role as the great defender of the occult, would claim that though they had accused him, by implication, of being at the centre of a massive web of evil, no evidence had been produced to support these allegations, especially none against himself. In his now familiar and colourful invective, Bray trumpeted, 'Through being targeted by the fundamentalists, I have suffered a concerted and intricate attack on many different levels all designed to put me out of business and deal the occult a death blow.' He added that newspapers had printed the most appalling lies linking him with child abuse, abortion and the skinning and eating of foetuses. Yet not one of them, he pointed out, printed anything about the fire-bomb which gutted his shop.

It was not sufficient, he said, to fight off the Christian fundamentalists whom Bray cast in the modern-day role of the sixteenth-century witch-hunters. It was necessary to pursue them and the media into the courts and make them realize that they had to stop persecuting those who had alternative beliefs. To this end he appealed for money to be sent to him for a fighting fund to be run on a basis of trust, to be administered by him and used to conduct a defence against newspapers and television companies who show themselves to be 'actively anti-occultist'. This plea has been supported from all quarters of the occult and when readers of the official magazine of The Society of the Dark Lily, which bills itself as the voice of satanism, were somewhat tardy in sending donations, its editor chided: 'This is war. No one has been killed yet (for which you can thank Lucifer) but there have been injuries, mental and physical and property has been damaged.' He reminded his readers that they did not have to stand in the front line or put themselves or their livelihood in danger. Chris Bray was doing that for all of them, to ensure that they continued to have the right to practise their beliefs.

And so, Chris Bray became not only the self-appointed freedom fighter and voice of occultism but also, by his own account, the prime target of its opponents. This is only a slight exaggeration of his importance in the occult world but it remains a fact that he was one of the few publicly defending his friends and customers.

He has submitted many valid points in his summary for the defence, written in many thousands of words, mostly published by himself as he tried to stir the occult movement into some concerted effort of response to the wide-ranging allegations concerning every known practice which falls within the sphere of occultism.

CHAPTER EIGHT

A DARKER CALLING

The cries of 'Innocent!' from the white witches are drowned by the furore surrounding their counterparts who stray down what is known as the left-hand path into darker regions. Even some of the most benign souls we have so far encountered agree that it is not at all difficult to step over the imaginary line into the area of black magic and immediately distort the undertaking to harm none, as laid down in the witches' creed. There is no difference in the magic, purely in the intent and the setting.

There are distinct areas where it occurs. Sometimes a perfectly normal witches' coven will begin to move towards black magic through boredom or inexperience and suddenly become excited by the danger of treading in forbidden territory. There are also covens which are formed specifically for black workings, though often they do not last long, either being arrested for damaging gravestones or scaring themselves half to death. There is also the calling of Satanic Witchcraft, spawned by the Church of Satan in San Francisco, which spread fast; it is totally allied to the Satanic Bible of Anton LaVey and is a selfish creed which is both anti-Christian and anti-pagan. Finally, there are black hereditary witches, working alone, and perhaps the epitome of the old-time hag: bad-tempered, casting spells and uttering curses to all and sundry – and known for a remarkable success rate.

Every witch has a story about such a woman (or man) who might cast spells regardless of the consequences, using a variety of herbs and potions. There is the familiar story of the man who consulted a witch because he wanted promotion at work, but his immediate superior was younger than himself and unlikely to move on. Soon afterwards, the younger man fell dead from a heart attack and his assistant gained promotion. It's that sort of confused assistance that may be expected from a black witch.

A black witch describing these matters to me said I ought to believe it, and if I did not I very soon would. I do not know what she meant by that remark and at the time of writing I still have no idea. 'It's common knowledge . . . you should never make an enemy of a witch,' she said menacingly. I could not see her face, because she was on the other end of a telephone, I having made contact through a box number address in a witch magazine. She called herself Anna and this is a précis of her monologue on black witchcraft:

I knew I had powers when I was a child; I could will things to happen and often they did. I suppose it was natural that I should be drawn to it eventually. By chance, a neighbour had formed a coven; she didn't know what she was doing and I didn't and it all went wrong. There were eight of us; there used to be twelve but the three men and one of the women left. We had been deliberately corrupting our original workings, which we had largely copied from Stewart Farrar's book, *What Witches Do*. It all became a bit boring and we tried to spice it up and one of our group spent a lot of time researching some old grimoires for the rituals said to have been performed by witches who were hanged or burned. Plenty of these writings exist, and we found a museum which still has scraps of parchment bearing the witch's original scribble; we got very excited about that when we heard but when we got there, it was totally illegible. So I think in the end we began taking notes from Denis Wheatley novels and combining these with the spells and curses we had found from books about the sixteenth century. It was only then that I realized I must be an hereditary witch, because I was capable of a lot of the things that were written down, quite naturally. Everyone said so. I didn't even have to think about it.

Our coven historian did come up with some interesting classifications that were apparently used for rituals three hundred years ago; you know the sort of thing – magic to ensure opulence;

to incite hatred or vengeance; and, for men, to secure the love of a virgin; to open every kind of lock without a key; to cause a dead body to rise – all that kind of stuff. It's a bit better than sending healing energy that might get lost in the post, I can tell you. Whether it worked or not, we had a lot of fun with it. We were throwing curses and casting spells all over the place. We studied the old rituals for bewitchment, the type that got a lot of old hags hanged, and wrote out as many as we could. There were these spells rather like voodoo where we made wax effigies, or you could even use a dead animal like a toad or a mouse, and you would run a nail or hat pins through the body of the image of the person for whom we wished to cause trouble. You had to know all the incantations and the maledictions but learning them made it all the more interesting. That was just the start of it.

We went through a whole list of old rites, and that's where you begin to find occultism truly interesting. We began to study necromancy, for instance. That's raising the dead by sacrilegious rites – talk about bringing the dead back to life; it scared us to death. We performed this really old ritual to raise the soul of a man who had just died; his wife wanted us to do it though we warned of the dangers. I mean, this is not to be confused with Spiritualism, where contact is made through a medium and it's all sweetness and light. Necromancy is a far more dangerous undertaking, the ultimate black art. You know, it's surprising what those old biddies used to get up to, far more exciting than this modern rubbish. Necromancy was used to consult with the dead and discover, for example, where an old miser might have buried his treasure, that sort of thing. It wasn't always pleasant. The method we used was one where we drew our magic circle in the house of a recently dead person, in front of the armchair where he used to sit, and we put a photograph and his favourite belongings beside it. This is supposed to attract the spirit back. Then we performed the rites which lasted about thirty minutes. Nothing happened the first time or the second time, but the third time the room went cold and you could feel a presence. Suddenly ornaments crashed off the sideboard and pictures fell from the walls . . . we had made contact but whoever it was was obviously unhappy about it so we had to give up. We did not give up experimenting though . . .

The black witch went on to explain some of her other talents which were enough to make any self-respecting white witch cringe with embarrassment. However, her telephone call prompted me to examine more closely the art of necromancy and I discovered that in its worst form, it is often the cause of occasional outbreaks of attacks on graveyards where misguided occult dabblers believe they can make contact with the dead no matter how long they have been departed, though in truth a graveyard is probably the last place the spirit might wish to join his callers for an evening's discourse.

I then discovered that in March 1988, the cemetery where Denis Wheatley is buried in Woking, Surrey, was the scene of some bizarre rituals that puzzled even experienced occultists. More than twenty graves were ransacked; old-fashioned lead-lined coffins had been 'ripped open like a tin of beans' and the bodies or remains were carried away.

Whole skeletons are used in various forms of old black magic ritual and there are those who believe that to perform a ritual for necromancy over complete remains has a better chance of success in achieving the desired result. Undoubtedly, for many who pursue this darkest of experiments, necromancy is the touchstone of occultism, especially for black witches. If, after careful preparation, they are able to carry through what they regard as a successful contact they have reached a certain pinnacle in black magic conjuration. It is fruitless discussing whether or not this feat is possible; belief by the practitioner is all that is needed for the ritual to proceed and some psychological or drug-induced trance may well convince the adepts that they have indeed succeeded.

Necromancy has a particular appeal to black witches seeking confirmation, for example, of the mysteries of the afterlife but more often necromancy is pursued by the skilled masters of ritual magic who we will meet in greater abundance in the next section.

In its blackest form the art of necromancy has produced fairly evil recipes for success. Graveyards are indeed a common place where contact might be attempted with the dead for the expressed purpose of evil; other places conducive to apparitions are darkened, suffocating rooms or beneath a mock swinging gibbet (hangman's noose).

The old grimoires are full of colourful descriptions, and since they were often written by clerical scholars when they took down the confessions of witches prior to their burning, it is difficult to know what was true and what was invention. To the black witch and black magicians who might care to consult these old rites, it does not seem to matter. What is apparent, now in the 1990s, is that the material can be easily identified in the accusations laid at the door of witches and occultists of the current age. The procedure for the black art of necromancy, for example, includes the administration of polluted sacraments, the sacrifice of animals, and of children, orgiastic rites and dances in circular formation.

Almost in the realm of black comedy is the ritual for making the witch invisible, for which the recipe was as follows: 'Make an unguent compounded from the incinerated bodies of new-born infants mixed with the blood of night-birds. Fast for fifteen days and then get drunk every fifth night on wine in which poppies and hemp have been seeped. The rite must be performed over candles made of fat from corpses and fashioned in the form of a cross; the bowls to be skulls; the fires must be fed with cypress branches, with wood of desecrated crucifixes; the ceremonial cloth woven by a prostitute . . .' and so it continued with other instructions too gruesome to mention. All are consulted, though I doubt they are ever performed.

It is easy to see how the Pagan Federation and other defenders of witchcraft and the occult, under attack from the Christian fundamentalists, have difficulty in explaining away some of the more socially unacceptable ceremonies available to renegades and rebels among their number who merely have to research the old archives and books for their instructions. And by and large, it is only the darker practices that receive attention.

The vigilance of the popular press in reporting any outbreaks has ensured a continuous supply of stories which contain all the usual ingredients of nakedness, sex, blood and desecration. More often than not these stories blame either witches or satanists for the 'perverted black magic rites', and though it is easy for the ill-informed to generalize and for local vicars to get excited at the discovery of occultism within their parish, what seems at first glance to be perverted activity to the uninitiated is quite 'normal' witch coven behaviour.

As an example, the following report appeared in a Sunday newspaper about a policeman who was also a witch.

A naked girl was led into the centre of a ring of chanting witches in an incense-filled basement. The high priest pointed a glisten-ing sword at her bare flesh. The girl was being initiated into the ancient religion of witchcraft but this was a ceremony with a difference. For the girl was the daughter of a police superintend-ent and the High Priest was another policeman. He admitted, 'Yes, I was the High Priest . . . I have been a white witch for eight years and I am not ashamed of what I do although some of my colleagues pull my leg. I have helped to initiate at least fifteen witches in the past three years.

The report went on to describe how the initiate was led before the altar for the ceremony at the home of a witch who lives in the south, and who is head of thirteen covens.

What happened in the basement of her home was neither unusual, illegal nor – in the eyes of the witch community – perverted. It was a classic initiation ceremony as described else-where in this book and universally used; what made it 'unusual' was that a police constable was the leading male participant, though even that is actually not as rare as it sounds. Everyone involved followed the Book of Shadows to the letter; what took place was the accepted form of witchcraft ritual performed by consenting adults in the privacy of their leader's home. There was nothing 'black' about it.

Similarly, the Isle of Man, where there have always been strong links with witchcraft, attracted a flurry of interest when traces of blood and candle wax were found in a little-used Anglican church and a young girl reported seeing lights late at night. A local lay preacher, Graham Elliott, who was also a policeman, warned his flock to beware and said that a disused airfield in a remote part of the island had become a centre for witch ceremonies. The island bishop, the Rt Revd Arthur Atwell, took up the cause and warned mothers to keep their children away from Hallowe'en celebrations. 'We know there are adults on the island who are trying to introduce children to witchcraft for their own demonic reasons,' he said.

There are said to be up to a dozen separate witch covens operating on the Isle of Man and if any one of them was a group that had gone 'black' and was resorting to sexual and blood rituals involving young women, then it could naturally be expected that the whole of the island's witches would be branded as black. And thus, witchcraft as a whole continues to be classed as bad, and the best hopes for members of the Pagan Federation who want to see their movement gain a better public image, take a further knock.

Maxine Sanders described scenes that she had personally witnessed and showed how 'corruption' in a coven could occur and how, as she put it, 'the lines between white and black can become blurred . . . and a coven can enter a shadowy no man's land.' She has witnessed the sacred initiation ceremony perverted to sexual extremes of the kind, she admits, that gets witchcraft a bad name.

She had been invited to an initiation ceremony at a house in London. The surroundings were no different from a thousand coven meetings she had attended. She knew the High Priest quite well, and he was known for his powers. The ceremony was already in progress when she arrived, and she put on her ceremonial robes and was shown into a second-floor room, where an overpoweringly beautiful crystal chandelier was the main feature. But it was not switched on, and glistened only from the light of candles on a large altar. There, straddled naked across the altar, she saw a young – 'very, very young' – girl who was made up to look like an ancient Egyptian. She was lying in the fivefold position for the Great Rite for Third Degree Initiation. She said,

> I was absolutely certain in my own mind that she was a virgin, she looked so young, but she was obviously a willing participant. She wasn't strapped down and made no move to get up. Somehow I feared the worst. I wanted to get out of that place but the doorway was guarded by two men holding ritual swords.

The Great Rite that was being performed has no place in white witchcraft. This was palpably a black imitation and the real purpose behind it was to raise power for the High Priest. He was calling upon dark forces. He began in what sounded like gibberish – but was Enochian texts. Then, standing close to the altar, he took the girl for brutal intercourse while the rest of his black flock watched. Finally, he led her away, tears streaming down her face. I got out as soon as I could.

Maxine recalled another scene in Epping Forest, a popular venue for black workings. This particular invitation concerned an experiment using a medium to contact non-human forces and her assistance in ritual magic was requested. She agreed because the details intrigued her, though she had no idea of the real experiment. It was a pitch black night, and there were eight of them taking part, five men and three women. Maxine was positioned in a triangle made of cords laid on the ground. She was naked, her hands were tied behind her back and she was blindfolded as her companions began the ritual of casting a magic circle. Then she heard a terrible scream, and another scream and she immediately thought that something had gone wrong with the experiment.

She pulled herself free from the binding cords and ripped off her blindfold.

Immediately, I wished I had not done so for there before me were four wooden stakes and upon each one had been impaled a dead cat. I had been tricked. I vomited. I was sick at heart, infuriated and fearful. I did not know where my clothes were so I grabbed a cloak which was lying on the ground and just ran through the forest never quite knowing whether they were still around and if they were following me.

She eventually reached the road and hitched a lift in a car away from the scenes of black magic.

Descriptions of such scenes are not uncommon and only go to reinforce the popular image of witches being involved in black sorcery. Thus it becomes increasingly difficult for observers to distinguish the difference between white witches 'cavorting naked under the stars around a bonfire' with the black workings which necessarily involve the worst kinds of extremist activity.

There are many case histories where it is easy to see how the white witch initiation ritual as invented by Gerald Gardner has become the model for black and even satanic ceremonies.

Nicky, an attractive blonde aged twenty-five, became involved with a black witch coven who wanted to make her their Witch Queen. Her initiation at midnight on a secluded beach in North Devon was on an altar set up in front of what was to become a gathering of 200 people, whom she assumed were all witches who had travelled from a considerable area to witness her initiation.

She said cocaine and cannabis were freely available; she herself was laid across the altar and was effectively raped by the High Priest for what would have been the Great Rite, though its existence as a ritual in witchcraft was totally unknown to her previously. She said she was also forced to drink the blood of a sacrificed cockerel, into which drops of her own blood had been mixed. The description fitted many similar 'ceremonies' I have come across during my conversations and is aimed at raising the power of those immediately involved in the rite within the magic circle, notably the High Priest who performs the sexual act.

The description sounded far more akin to the Black Mass performed by satanists and thus the ceremony was likely to have been performed by a coven that adhered to no particular tradition, and made up its own rules for a ceremony designed purely to provide the maximum possible excitement.

The arrival of these groups who have no particular affiliation is another problem that concerns the elders of witchcraft. As Lois Bourne pointed out, the revival of witchcraft in the twentieth century has meant the appearance of instant witches who do not appreciate the dangers, nor the damage they cause to witchcraft when they are caught – especially those who get involved in blood-lust activities and the ritual slaughter of animals.

A case in point occurred in the north of England not long ago when two young men in their early twenties, David Hughes and Derek Barnes, became interested in witchcraft. Books by Aleister Crowley and others were found in one of their homes. They performed blood rituals, slaughtering and decapitating a family's pet goat and torturing and skinning a cat. Both were sent to prison. Neither man had any previous contact with witchcraft and got all of their ritualistic workings from books. The very existence of a system of belief which allows such dabblers to be guided step by step through rituals of this nature is clearly dangerous.

Eventually it becomes increasingly difficult to rule out the possibility that there is a mass of practitioners who have bad intent. There are hundreds of books on witchcraft and the occult available through outlets like the Sorcerer's Apprentice, Astonishing Books and many other similar shops throughout the country. Many meticulously record the practices of the occult. It is not out of morbid curiosity that these books are acquired. They are largely bought as a manual for black and satanic workings and it surely follows that there are many practising black witches in the British Isles today.

It is in the exploration of this area of witchcraft and occultism that the stone descends deeper into the murky gloom of my pond. The reading matter available to the occult world is wide and varied, and it is not difficult to obtain guides to the highly explicit rites I have already mentioned earlier in this chapter, practices ranging from an abundance of witches' spellbooks to *Satanic Rituals* by Anton LaVey.

The latter, for those committed to the left-hand path of witchcraft, is among the more notorious reading matter on the subject. But even the simplest of spellbooks contain recommendations that prompt questions challenging the whole concept of witchcraft as portrayed by the pagan credo.

It may well be that the majority of witches will 'harm none', but how then is it possible to rationalize the ready demand for a plethora of books by authors such as Anna Riva, whose titles include *Spellcraft, Hexcraft and Witchcraft* and the *Modern Witchcraft Spellbook*? There are many such publications under similar titles and Ms Riva is careful to enter a disclaimer that all material contained in her own book is 'strictly legendary' and carries no claim of supernatural powers. But there are entries which must surely provide a source for some of the proliferation of stories in the latter part of this century concerning the tampering with graves by those indulging in black magic.

Under a chapter headed 'Graveyard Dirt' in Riva's book of spellcraft, there is a full description of the uses of soil taken from graves – 'one of the most forceful of all magical hexing elements', she writes. She goes on to describe how graveyard dirt is taken from specific graves and believers claim that each kind has its own subtle differences and attributes. For instance, dirt from a murderer's grave is carried to protect oneself, or scattered in a path of an enemy to place him in danger while dirt from an infant's grave carried by a pregnant woman will insure an easy and healthy birth. Yet, Ms Riva goes on, it can also be used to secure an abortion.

There are many other applications listed for the use of graveyard dirt – making an enemy ill by mixing it with bat's blood and smearing it on his doorstep, or smearing another graveyard dirt mixture on a black feather and hanging it near the enemy's house to effect a dangerous curse. Alternatively, a hexing bag can be sent to a foe who 'is sure to feel the effects of malicious intent' when he receives a red flannel pouch in which should be placed raw chicken livers mixed with graveyard dirt and asafoetida gum.

There is also a misfortune box described by Ms Riva as a small box inside which are placed three thorns, earth from a cemetery, a dead insect and a picture of the person for whom the spell-caster wants to bring misfortune. The box is sealed with black wax and by night placed close to the victim's home. And she adds that graveyard dirt, as with so many sorcery materials, can be used in any number of ways for varied objectives, 'help yourself or harm others, the choice is yours!'

The list of potions used in casting spells, curses and performing black witchcraft is equally disturbing. There are recipes to ward off curses, break spells and return the malice to the sender. She lists among her most popular and effective ingredients bats' eyes, bats' hearts, the eye and the bone of a black cat to bring luck, the eye or the heart of a swallow to ensure love and devotion from a partner, and a whole host of other concoctions.

Sorcery practised with the use of dolls and effigies, feared among the African and Carib nations in its voodoo form, has long been a popular aid to witchcraft. As we have seen from the descriptions of witch practices, wax models or dolls made from cloth or straw are used as part of healing rituals in modern witchcraft; they are also one of the prime tools of black magicians.

The doll is merely a symbol on which the magician will focus his magic and the effect can be strengthened by gluing a photograph of the subject to the doll, or attaching hair or fingernail clippings. This kind of imagery is used for casting love spells and for issuing curses, and in the latter the model is usually stuck with a pin through the area of the heart or the liver.

There is little point in discussing the belief or otherwise in these aspects of witchery, but let me say I could now go on to quote dozens of examples of the effects of curses, along with the recollections and testimony of witches who have seen the results. No witch I spoke to recoiled from the view that spells and curses *can* work; no witch denied having his or her own effective combatant to magical attacks if ever they arrived. The effects may be slight, or they may be catastrophic.

The Wicca movement in its entirety – good and bad – knows the secret of cursing; it exists as an intrinsic part of the craft and the faith and cannot be used lightly. Even the benign and white witch covens have a cursing rite – and they use it when the High Priest deems it necessary and they can overcome the governing creed of 'harming none' by the explanation that any action they take which may harm someone may be justified to stop that person harming others, thus the result is beneficial.

Cursing is one of the specialities featured by the most notorious practitioner of the darker arts, Anton Szandor LaVey, and recommended in his book, *The Satanic Witch*, first published under the title of *The Compleat Witch* and now widely available in its republished form with a foreword by his 'bewitching daughter' Zeena, the Queen of Satanic Witches. In the foreword Zeena discusses how the practical use of her father's advice has affected her own life from the moment when, at the age of three, she became the first child in history to be publicly baptized in a satanic ceremony before a sea of black-hooded celebrants in May 1967. I will deal more fully with LaVey and his life and times in the section on satanism. Meantime, more about his daughter . . .

In her teens, Zeena boasted that she was the personification of a woman with the ultimate carnal knowledge – a knowledge that she could put to good use through her father's teachings. She made herself 'versatile enough to attract different people for different purposes', her admirers ranging from married lawyers and policemen twenty years her senior to juvenile delinquents and bikers who volunteered to kill anyone who bothered her. But she claimed her main task in adulthood was to re-educate many a newcomer to the 'true meaning of witchcraft', a meaning which she said was opposed to the pervasive good witch syndrome emanating from the British Wiccan movement. The woman who grasped and fully understood LaVey's work would also understand true feminism, which meant the liberation of all women, his theory being that at the core of every human body is a demonic inner self waiting to be released.

LaVey then goes on to set out in 250 pages of what he describes as explicit instruction how modern witches should attune themselves to society, using every extrovert technique and hidden magic available, with an especial emphasis on the sexual, and bringing into play his own rules, such as the Laws of the Forbidden and the Virtues of Embarrassment; these, in effect, recommend the breach of most of the rules of life by which Christian society in general conforms; but then if it did not, his readers would presumably have been exceedingly disappointed.

His initial instruction is a basic one: to disregard the myth of the white witch. He says that regardless of what others may prefer to believe, a witch *does* have to make a pact with the devil himself, at least symbolically. Among his ten commandments is one that calls for confidence in the belief that a witch can destroy rivals through the use of curses thrown without mercy – 'the only way a curse can be thrown is without mercy, and the power of the curse is most effective.'

Spells and curses are his speciality and he insists that a witch 'cannot be half-hearted' in casting spells; the witch must be sure of the end in view and take full advantage of it when it arrives. LaVey's way is very similar to that used by the white witches in healing rituals – i.e. stirring up enough personal energy to 'send' a curse while focusing the mind on the photographic image of the person at whom it is aimed.

The method he particularly recommends is the using of a voodoo doll, to which a photograph or drawing of the individual to be attacked is attached, and then the curse can proceed. He warns that one of the most common causes of failure in a curse is guilt and advises that the person doing the cursing must have no guilty conscience at having performed the ceremony. White witches will say that if you curse a person it will return threefold but naturally, he points out, if you are so sanctimonious that you have to impress others that you are a white witch, it's certain that the curse would bounce back and harm you.

Another of his methods is the gingerbread technique which he believes to be the origin of the gingerbread man. It is to bake an effigy in dough or biscuit and when cooked, use ritual magic to pour out thoughts of disdain and contempt upon the poor unfortunate gingerbread man. It should be tormented and tortured, and the witch should allow herself to be overcome by trembling terror until finally 'with slow, fiendish delight, bite its head off. Chew it through, smacking your lips and swallow it . . . Gnaw off the arms, legs and finish up with the body . . .'

There is one more aspect of the LaVey guide to witchcraft that gives more than a passing hint as to the underlying black intent of his teaching. He is an advocate and tutor of a method of occult attacks by a witch on the man of her choice, whereby she becomes a succubus, an evil female demon that visits men in the night for the purpose of sexual activity. In fact, the definition of a succubus is exactly that – 'a spirit which is capable of acquiring or materializing a body for the purpose of having sexual relations with a human being.'

The belief in black magic circles is that it is possible for the magician to achieve a state of being verging on astral projection, whereby the spirit may travel to the 'victim', engage in sexual activity and return. The female attacking a male is known as a succubus; the male attacker is known as an incubus and both have their origins in the recorded witch trials of the sixteenth and seventeenth centuries. The object of LaVey's method is for the witch, by the use of magic, to force an image of herself into the mind of a man with whom she desires sexual relations. Then, she proceeds to achieve a sexual climax by either force of will or masturbation, and supposedly effects a coinciding reaction from her 'dream lover'.

Apparently this business of imagined or spiritual sexual intercourse is not as uncommon as it might seem and it can also be fraught with problems. Far from being a recommended source of occult activity, it is positively advised against in some quarters, especially if either party involved is in any way psychologically disturbed.

I noticed a mention of the activities of a particularly menacing succubus in an Agony column in the issue number 23 of Chris Bray's magazine, *Lamp of Thoth*, billed as 'Aunt Sally Answers . . . The world's first occult problem page . . .' S. K. from Torquay had written to say that he was worried about the visits he had been receiving from a dark-haired woman, a spirit travelling to him in the astral, attacking him physically and sexually. 'She has her fill and then subsides . . . the attacks come every four hours or so, and I am now constantly drained.'

The writer added that he had tried a number of methods for psychic self-defence but had been unable to stop the attacks. Aunt Sally explained that the visits were from a succubus which arrived in the night to feed off his own sexual energies. In a long and complicated letter of advice, Aunt Sally recommended a course of action to deter the succubus from appearing. It would take a monumental effort of mental ability to stop the attacks.

Again, it is impossible for anyone not associated with the occult to be impressed by such claims – other than a psychiatrist who might see another client appearing on the horizon with a rather more off-beat story to tell. But really that is the very point, and in summarizing the whole scene of witchcraft today I think it can be seen that it has a stopping-off point for virtually every level of interest, and accommodates every range of intent.

White witch with good intent or black witch with blood-curdling ambitions for excitement, there is a strong reliance on an historical tradition, even though its accuracy is questionable.

You can make of witchcraft what you will and, in short, all of the people who have climbed aboard the spiritual bandwagon in the past two or three decades have largely tended to follow the Elen Williams school of paganism – it is a kind of religion, invitingly tinged with mystery, superstition and legend but irrevocably damaged and distorted by evil.

But the writings of old are not necessarily the most surprising in content. Before leaving the darker elements of paganism, I must touch upon the activities of modern day vampires who, like those who practise necromancy, have always been associated with black magic. Many black witches believe that they will become vampires after their death. The use of blood in many occultist rituals is common; some forms of black magic and satanic ritual call for the drinking of blood mixed with other substances from a chalice, in blasphemous copy of the Communion wine.

Some of the most virulent types of ritual invented by Aleister Crowley, as we will discover, involved the draining of sacrificial animals of every drop of blood. This occurred again in satanic rituals performed in Britain and America in the sixties, and it still exists today in many forms of ritual for those with stomach enough to become involved – apparently these are not few in number.

The fear of vampires, famous since Bram Stoker's novel *Dracula* and the subject of many horror films, books and plays was strongly held in the eighteenth century, so much so that a law was passed in 1823 prohibiting the practice of burying unhallowed dead at a crossroads with a wooden stake driven through the heart of the corpse. History has its share of famous fictional vampires, usually portrayed as evil spirits who can be dispelled by the use of a stake and a cross; they are usually described as living corpses which sleep during the day and rise at night to go off in search of blood.

That is the fictional version. In real life, it is a different story. Psychotics like the murderer John George Haig drain the blood of their victims and drink it. In black magic, blood serves two purposes; firstly to add energy to the performance of the magic and secondly to give renewed vitality to the drinker.

To imagine it being drunk must, as I said, be a matter of revulsion for the layman. And yet it comes recommended by one of the more famous occult personalities, Mr Philip Hine, who explained the taste for blood in an article in the spring of 1992.

Mr Hine is well known as the editor of the magazine *Pagan News* and former editor of the magazine *Chaos International*. He lectures regularly to occult audiences and was the top-of-the-bill attraction among the personalities booked to appear at the UK Chaos Magick Convention, organized by the Magickal Pact of the Illuminates of Thanateros at the Conway Hall, Red Lion Square, London, on 1 July 1992.

In May 1991, he published a long article in his *Pagan News* on the satanic ritual abuse scare, under the headline: 'Satan: A moral panic exposed' in which he set out all the usual arguments as to why no one should believe the Christian fundamentalists and said that in reality it was the cry of people who could not look their own demons in the face.

No one in the occult world, however, seemed to find it strange that a year later he should be writing in *Chaos International* under a headline 'Droplets' in which he explained his apparent penchant for the taste of blood. He asked his readers to imagine discovering what gave them most pleasure; the one thing in the whole world . . . pure uncomplicated joy . . . and then to realize that if the pleasure was pursued it might kill. He knew that if he took a razor blade to his own veins there might, one day, be no turning back, and he would die. Although some called him a vampire he did not endanger others by bleeding them. He never took too much blood and if his donors demanded money, he gave them what they asked. If some expected sex for comfort, he indulged them 'but for their sake really'.

He said that withholding the 'pleasure' sharpened his appetite until the craving rose like bile in his throat and went on to say that his thoughts are 'all red' . . . that earlier in his life he thought that blood was just part of his sexual kicks but later he saw that it was the blood that mattered and the sex was ephemeral. He had no wish to play games of 'power and submission' he just wanted to see blood trickle and taste it. The blood itself was more important than penetration and the gender of the donor did not matter as he realized, for instance, that a thin scarlet thread wending its slow way across a woman's breast could be just as engrossing as slivers of red across a young man's shoulder.

Hine wrote that at one time he sought understanding for his

craving, not because he wished to be cured but to discover the origin. He said he then remembered the moment, as a child, when he was with a young friend who fell from the kerb in front of a lorry . . . 'Red droplets misted across my face and in the long, frozen moment that followed I licked a bright bead of blood from the back of my hand.'

Though the article was blurred by attempts at prose, Mr Hine was apparently telling his readers that he possessed an insatiable desire to drink blood, sometimes his own and sometimes that taken from a person he had taken back to his home.

Admittedly the motto for the magazine, printed on every page, is 'Nothing Is True. Everything Is Permitted'. However, the first-person account by Hine appears to be truthful – but whether we believe it or not is immaterial. He presents yet another account of an activity that someone, somewhere, might feel inclined to copy. And we stumble, once more, across the contradictory attitude of occultists, who on the one hand expect to be left in peace to do as they please, and do not seem either to anticipate or accept any criticism, and on the other condone practices that are surely dangerous. And so when Mr Hine writes an account of vampiric practices – admittedly in the privacy of a limited circulation magazine – that go completely against the grain of society, he also negates the trust any non-occultist might have for his views on such matters as the alleged satanic ritual abuse of a child.

Hine and his friends would argue that they are not interested in conforming to standards set by a largely Christian society; in fact they are not interested in conforming in any conventional sense, and thus they must be relegated to talking among themselves, because in the end their views have no value elsewhere.

PART TWO

RITUAL MAGIC

There are few major towns or cities in the British isles that do not harbour at least one – often several – secret societies whose purpose is the study and performance of esoteric religions or ritual magic. They are generally made up of small groups of people aligned to various separate organizations and beliefs whose proliferation in the twentieth century has continued apace in what Francis King, the acclaimed author on occult matters, described as an 'astonishing revival of medieval magic and alchemy'. King is right when he says that the newspaper stories of the desecration of some deserted country church for the purposes of black magic or the activities of some cult or secret society, illustrated by photographs of naked men and women dancing around a blazing fire, or standing rapt before a crude altar, are only the tip of the iceberg. As leaders of witchcraft recognize, students of ritual magic and the occult are on a higher plane of activity which has throughout history attracted many gifted minds. They scour antiquity for the roots of a particular persuasion in a constant search for the source, the Philosopher's Stone or such age-old secrets as turning common metals into gold. They seek and perform the old rituals of past and famous magicians; they try to define the question of being and, as the controversial nineteenth-century magician Eliphas Levi proclaimed, magic furnishes the human mind with an instrument of philosophical and religious certainty as exact as mathematics. He insisted that those who attained this knowledge and adopted it as a rule of life could make themselves masters of all inferior things.

151

Similarly, Paracelsus, the sixteenth-century magician, wrote, 'The magical is a great hidden wisdom . . . no armour can shield against it because it strikes at the the inward spirit of life. Of this we may rest assured . . .'

CHAPTER NINE

THE BEAST 666

Occultists draw on the past. Everything they do has some historical, sometimes religious, tie. Rumours, myths and superstitions surround almost every aspect of the secret societies of men and women who gather suspiciously – because of the secrecy – and perform their dark and dramatic rituals, formulated from old grimoires handed down and rewritten through the ages.

Personalities, too, figure predominantly. But there are very few forms of modern occultism that do not, at some time or other, rely upon the legacy – some would say lunacy – of Aleister Crowley, the self-styled Great Beast 666. At the pinnacle of his career he was renowned for a wild mix of debauchery, drug addiction and magic but today is revered by thousands the world over who are rereading the ramblings of this most unreliable of men who believed himself better than Shakespeare. Though almost forgotten at the time of his death in 1947, and only publicly noted for his huge and extrovert excesses, he was soon to be placed in the higher orders of magical remembrance and eventually became more important to the practitioners of many of the occult traditions than he had ever been in his lifetime.

He was in many ways the catalyst for the twentieth-century explosion of occult interest, moulding as he did many of the antiquities of ancient magic and Kabbalistic mysticism, the alchemy of the Middle Ages, the sorcery of the Renaissance, the latter-day psychological theories of Freud and Jung and the new theosophical expressions of the early twentieth century. Crowley was one of many mercurial figures wavering somewhere between

genius and madness who have become signposts in the development of the occult arts, and no less controversial than some of his
predecessors of whom he claimed to be the reincarnation.

It was a decade or more after his death before his writings were
rediscovered on a popular level, and they and his new disciples
can be held more or less responsible, for example, for the 1960s
upsurge of mysticism, experiments with psychedelic drugs and the
achievement of altered states of consciousness of which Dr Timothy
Leary and countless contemporary pop singers and writers
preached to the masses.

Below the level of popular inspiration was a heavy layer of
magical complication that was of interest only to his followers in
the occult. At this point in our journey, as we move on to this
'higher plane of discovery', it is necessary to refer to his work and
influences and his associations with such diverse contemporary
personalities as the Irish poet W. B. Yeats and L. Ron Hubbard,
the inventor of Scientology.

All bear a crucial significance in the expansion of esoteric
pursuits and the growth of interest in almost every aspect of the
occult. But before plunging the reader into this morass of cultism
that surrounds Crowley's life after death, it is perhaps advisable to
recall the path of magic through myth, legend and actual events
on which today's revival was based.

What has gone before in the antiquities of time is important;
names, places, methods all have a bearing and are easily recognizable. Back in the mists of the pre-Christian centuries is where the
modern occultists discover their starting-point – in a world thick
with more danger than they could ever have imagined possible.

The search by those who indulge is as daunting as life itself
and it is necessary to delve into the past to find at least some
reason, some explanation, as to why the pursuit of magic and
ceremonial ritual has sustained itself through to the present day
with such a large and continuous following, in spite of all the
attempts by the Vatican to obliterate it. Occult history is populated
with numerous figures whose hazy backgrounds lie partly in
mythology and partly in fact. Throughout, it comes down to a
question of belief because as always, though there is circumstantial
evidence in abundance of dramatic events brought about during

the rituals of this thing called magic, actual proof is a less tangible asset.

It is worth reminding ourselves before we proceed that apart from the search for the hidden powers of the human mind and body, the very essence of magic involves bringing about an altered state of consciousness, so that it becomes possible for the magician and those involved with him actually to have visions and believe in them, whether they take the form of invoked gods speaking through the magician or the actual manifestation of spirits.

Right up to the eighteenth and nineteenth centuries, the existence and manifestation of demons and devils was accepted without question; it still is by some. I would like to quote a classic description of one of the most controversial aspects – the manifestation of spirits which most magicians secretly yearn to achieve, and the more manic and devoted spend their lives in isolation attempting to fulfil. James Blish, author of *Black Easter*, describes the evocation of an evil spirit during a ritual of high magic:

The thing that dominated the room . . . [was] a vast double circle on the floor in what appeared to be whitewash; between the concentric circles were written innumerable words. Farthest away from all this, about two feet outside the circle and three feet over to the north, was a circle enclosed by a triangle, also much lettered inside and out. [The magician, named Ware] entered the circle and closed it with the point of his sword and proceeded to the centre where he laid the sword across the toes of his white shoes; then he drew a wand from his belt and unwrapped it, laying the red silk cloth across his shoulders. 'From now on,' he said, in a normal, even voice, 'no one is to move.' From somewhere inside his vestments he produced a small crucible which he set at his feet before the sword. Small blue flames promptly began to rise from the bowl and he cast incense into it. 'We are to call upon Marchosias, a great marquis of the Descending Hierarchy,' he said. 'Before he fell, he belonged to the Order of Dominations among the angels. His virtue is that he gives true answers. Stand fast all . . .' With a sudden motion, Ware thrust the end of his rod into the surging flames . . . at once the air of the hall rang with a long, frightful chain of woeful howls. Above the bestial clamour Ware shouted [his incantations to begin the ritual of evocation] 'I adjure thee, great Marchosias, the agent of the Emperor Lucifer and of his beloved son Lucifuge Rofocale by the power of the pact . . .' The noise rose higher and a green steam began to come off the brazier. But there was no other answer. His face white and cruel, Ware rasped over the tumult: 'I adjure thee, Marchosias, by the pact and by the names, appear instanter.' He plunged the rod a second time into the flames. The room screamed . . . but still there was no apparition.

The rod went back into the fire. Instantly the place rocked as though the earth moved under it. 'Stand fast,' Ware said hoarsely. Something else said, 'Hush, I am here. What dost thou seek of me? Why dost thou disturb my repose?' The building shuddered again . . . then from the middle of the triangle to the north west, a slow cloud of yellow fumes went up towards the ceiling, making them all cough, even Ware. As it spread and thinned [they] could see a shape forming under it . . . it was something like a she-wolf, grey and immense, with green glistening eyes. A wave of coldness was coming from it . . . the cloud continued to dissipate. The she-wolf glared at them, slowly spreading her griffin's wings. Her serpent's tail lashed gently, scalily . . .

As we have already noted in the historical backtracking of witch-craft, magic has been around since the beginning of time and was a fundamental ingredient of many cults and old religions. The medicine men of pre-historic tribes, the shamans, are claimed as the far-off ancestors of modern magicians, just as they are for witches. The shamans were supposed to possess incredible powers which enabled them to go into a trance when their spirits would leave their bodies. In this state they could see into the future; they could kill by sight; they could communicate with the spirit world; they could cast spells and they could heal. Apart from the basic work of tending the sick, this early magic was more widely applied to the well-being of life in general, to control the elements, bring rain to water the crops, to guide the hunters, ward off dangers from hostile tribes and bring fertility to all living things. As civilization developed, men who possessed special skills were themselves seen as minor magicians; craftsmen guarded their trade secrets as if they possessed supernatural powers.

The element of fertility/sex was important even then. Ishtar, the great goddess of love and the mother of all life, was worshipped at Babylon. The oldest profession began in harmony with the magical belief that all matters sexual enhanced fertility in all aspects of human nature. Thus sacred prostitutes filled the Eastern temples to serve as the goddesses and to provide the lifeblood to ritual. Magic was the underlying basis of all human life, and death. It was used to smooth the path to the other side and to ensure a happy existence thereafter.

Jewish magic, emanating from the Kabbalah and supposedly based upon texts provided by God to Adam, was an early influence on the creation of many beliefs and none more so than the rites of Solomon, son of David and the last king of a united Israel in the tenth century BC. Solomon is credited in many writings as being a master magician and who, according to the Old Testament, was endowed by God with brilliant powers of wisdom. He built the first Temple of Jerusalem and legends have surrounded it ever since. How could he have constructed it in seven years without superhuman assistance? How could the stones have been split into the desired size when, according to legend, God had forbidden the use of iron tools?

He is said to be the author of one of the earliest grimoires of spells and incantations in what became perhaps the most famous textbook for western magic, known as The Key of Solomon, whose authenticity is often challenged but which has been passed down through the centuries in many different forms. Efforts to disprove its authenticity are largely disregarded by those who seek to emulate its teachings and who, like many who engage in occult activity, are adept at ignoring the inconvenient.

Whether or not it is the work of Solomon now seems to matter little; more important is the fact that these writings have survived the centuries because it was thought that the text had to be copied out by hand for the magic to work for those who were to perform it, a belief that is still prevalent among occultists today.

The British Museum possesses a Greek version of the Key of

Solomon which has been dated to about the twelfth century AD and Vatican records show that in 1350 Pope Innocent VI ordered the burning of a work by Solomon which apparently described his rituals for calling down demons and offering sacrifice. The rituals attributed to Solomon provided the original basis for the casting of a magic circle. He described this as necessary to contain the demons and spirits who would tear the magician to pieces if the circle was broken before they were ritually banished.

The Key of Solomon also provides the basis of many of the rituals used today in higher magic. It gives instructions for the making of the robes, the knife, the sword, staff, wand and other instruments of magical art abundant in modern ritual. It explains how an adept should enter an abnormal plane and equip himself with the power to 'charge' with magical energy the pentacle and talismans – performed in the tenth century BC virtually as I had seen them performed in 1991.

Legend maintains that Solomon possessed a magic ring given to him by God with which he controlled all of nature and all spirits. There is another set of writings, known as the Lesser Key of Solomon, which gives details of incantations for summoning seventy-two principal demons, all named and their appearance and function described. These demons continue to intrigue modern day magicians.

The Queen of Sheba was so fascinated by the stories of Solomon that she travelled from her court in the ancient Kingdom of Arabia to challenge his wisdom. According to the Old Testament story in 1.Kings X, she put many hard questions to him and he answered everything, and gave her all that she asked of him. This is the only biblical authority for the mass of legend which has been collated around Solomon over the centuries, although the Koran does go somewhat further in admitting the existence of several books of magic.

The Muslims explain, however, that the books were written by evil spirits in an attempt to blacken Solomon's character. When he died, the spirits informed the Jewish elders to dig under his throne and they would discover the secrets of how Solomon had acquired absolute power over men and the elements. They did, and found books abounding with magic and superstition. It was believed that these were written by Solomon 'until Mohamet, by God's command, declared him to have been no idolater.'

Similarly, the Egyptian kings became symbolically associated with the ceremonies of magic and the invocations of Gods. The Pharaoh became the god Horus in his lifetime and was believed to be the son of the gods Osiris and Isis. The process was one of continual renewal and Osiris was the mythological source of Egypt's well-being. Around him grew mystical stories, making him the husband of Isis and the brother of Set, the god of darkness worshipped today, incidentally by a large following of satanists who operate under the name of the Temple of Set and whom I will visit in later chapters.

Osiris was anointed the judge of the dead and god of the afterlife, represented in mummified form with a plumed crown. The scribe to the Gods was Thoth (thus Chris Bray's magazine *Lamp of Thoth*) who alone, according to Egyptian legend, possessed knowledge both human and divine and was capable of continuing the will of the unseen and the unknown creative power. He instructed Osiris on how to reconstitute his body to become king of the underworld and god of the dead. These are the fundamentals of the higher forms of necromancy practised today.

To the Egyptians, the retention of the physical body was necessary for this transference and so their kings and their sacred cats were mummified to allow their continued earthly influence. And when, centuries later, the tombs were raided, the walls were found to be covered with magical symbols and paintings and the tombs themselves protected by spells and curses. The names of these Egyptian gods have been invoked throughout history, and are no less in use today.

Egypt became a receptacle for all the mystical and magical beliefs of the east and it all came flooding out when Alexander the Great conquered Persia, Asia Minor, Syria, Egypt itself and then India. The by-product of these conquests was the merging of magical traditions.

The Greeks had long been fascinated by magic. Pythagoras was said to have travelled to the east as a young man and became engrossed in the work of magicians. Later, he travelled to India and then to Britain to experience the master magicians of the

Celtic Druids. When he returned home he secretly began teaching his knowledge to others. Plato and other Greek philosophers were similarly intrigued, as indeed were the Romans who collated and adopted all kinds of magical beliefs as the boundaries of the empire expanded.

Never great originators of tradition themselves, they plundered and copied the eastern religions. No better example can be found than Bacchus, the Roman god of wine and fertility who was identical to the Greek God Dionysus, and can be identified with the Egyptian Osiris. Legend tells how Bacchus travelled and taught but came to be exiled for his evil. Soon the name Bacchus became associated with licentiousness and drunkenness – which naturally made him a popular figure of worship when he was enrolled among the gods.

Many festivals were held in his honour and a grand feature was the presence of the women called Bacchantes. Thousands of men, women and young people were initiated into what was a religio-magical cult dedicated to sexual perversion. Those who refused to submit to any of the sexual abuse would be sacrificed, according to historical records, and there is substantial evidence to support the allegations.

In Rome, where the festivals were called Bacchanalia, the celebrations grew more objectionable until in 186 BC they were banned; hundreds of initiates in virtually every province of Italy were rounded up and executed. In Greece, the festivals were called the Dionysia and were accompanied by similar orgiastic ritual.

To these emerging and consolidating traditions of myth and magic which crossed the boundaries of all the countries of the Mediterranean and the east, were added mystic elements from the Jewish Kabbalah and the controversial beliefs of the Gnostics, a rival to the advent of Christianity. Gnosticism was a spiritual and metaphysical system, combining oriental cults with Greek philosophy. A mystery religion which is experiencing a major upsurge of interest in the 1990s, gnostics believed that a spark of the divine exists in man, but could only be freed by the achievement of gnosis – the saving of knowledge gleaned from meditative visions. The gnosis was not intellectual knowledge but esoteric, attributing virtue to talismans and amulets.

It is, finally, the knowledge of one's true identity which, according to teaching in the second century AD, is revealed by one's guardian angel who accompanies each individual throughout their lives and who is really that person's true, divine self. But it is worth repeating again that magic is the combination of inner force, derived from the ability for self-discovery and to summon hidden powers, and the external elements with their vast cast of gods and goddesses, incantations, ritual and a plentiful supply of demons and spirits.

There were curses, too, prevalent in all early civilizations which, by the time of Christ, had virtually become part of the local religion and judiciary. They were taught with great precision, even down to the tone of voice which should be used during incantations.

Then, as now, certain magicians made money by writing curses for people who required ill to befall an enemy. A popular method was to write the curse on a piece of pottery or figurine which was then smashed; dolls of wax or straw were also used and burned. Religious cursing was almost as blood-curdling; in the Old Testament, Chapter 28 of Deuteronomy lists a whole array of curses which would be risked by all who failed to obey: 'the Lord shall smite thee with madness and blindness and astonishment of heart . . . and no man shall save thee.'

The Romans were particularly fearful of curses and when the Roman army attacked Wales in AD 61, it was confronted not just by local warriors but a line of women in jet-black robes with their hands raised to the heavens screaming foul curses at the invaders. Julius Caesar was told that the Celts believed that the only way of saving life was to give another life in its place, and held regular state sacrifices. When Gaul and Britain had been overpowered, he ruled that the Druids should be wiped out.

As these various ancient traditions came together to be transmitted in the form of legend and superstition, fact and fiction were intermingled into an emerging shape in the centuries immediately before and after the birth of Christ – who was himself considered to be something of a magician, as were the three wise men who came bearing gifts at his birth.

It was also around the time of the birth of Christ that the practice of alchemy came more fully into the equation. It was originally a mixture of religious fervour, astrology and newly acquired techniques of metallurgy that were blended together to form what was a forerunner to modern physics. The metal treasures of Solomon and Sheba were long ago recorded – 'now the weight of gold that came to Solomon in one year was six hundred three score and six talents . . . he made three hundred shields of beaten gold; three pounds of gold went into one shield', says 1.Kings X. And thus the alchemist of the early centuries AD sought the Philosopher's Stone which was believed to turn anything it touched into gold, cure all ills and keep its owner perpetually youthful.

Astrology, too, was highly popular around the time of Christ, and when he came along and began performing his various feats and miracles, the pagans were impressed and the converts began to flock towards Christianity, bringing with them many of their pagan ways, including some of their rituals and general interest in magic. In the hierarchy of the new Church, great suspicion and ill feeling were aroused towards some of the books of learning on alchemy, herbal medicines and potions, astrology and mathematics. Scholars surrounded their work with symbols and numerical inferences, so as to confound the ecclesiastical authorities who very soon began to regard these writings as heretical.

Though kings and noblemen continued to employ magicians and astrologers, there was mounting opposition to all forms of magic within the Christian Church. In medieval times successive popes announced their total objection to it. Witchcraft, as we have seen in earlier chapters, took the brunt of the attack, especially as the Church became possessed and obsessed by the fear that demonic magic and diabolical powers were abroad in Europe.

Satan became established as the arch-enemy of all Christians and the work of the devil was identified in almost everything that went against religious teaching. Gradually, a kind of definitive separation between witches and magicians emerged – witches were a lower caste, possessed innate powers and were in league with the devil, while magicians were generally more intellectually inclined and used technical terms and equipment, and so were more acceptable. Magicians, mostly posing as philosophers and alchemists, continued to be respected if not feared, members of society up to and including the years of the Inquisition.

Occasionally, there would be a sensational case of 'evil magic' which would highlight its continued existence. In 1441, for example, the Duchess of Gloucester was arrested for conspiring to murder Henry VI with three accomplices, Roger Bolingbroke, an astrologer and magician, a priest named Southwell and a witch called Margery Jourdemain. Bolingbroke was placed on public display at Paul's Cross in London, wearing his wizard's robe and sitting in his magician's chair with four swords attached to it, along with his tools and potions. Then he was hanged, drawn and quartered. Jourdemain was burned at Smithfield, while the priest died in prison. The Duchess of Gloucester was found guilty of treason by burning a wax image of the king and was imprisoned.

These cases were few and far between. Magicians by and large enjoyed a fairly charmed life compared with their witch counterparts. The same century that saw witches disposed of by the thousand was also the Hermetic century – producing some of the most famous names associated with the history of magic, including one whose works remain among the most widely read of the late twentieth century – Michael Nostradamus.

First, though, the life of Heinrich Cornelius offers a good springboard towards the present day; and it will be seen that there is a thread of similarity running through most of these stories, and a warning that those whose quest for greater knowledge of the occult takes them down the path to the darker arts, invariably end up in mortal danger themselves.

Cornelius, who was born in 1486, was a well-educated student of Greek philosophy who preferred Plato to Aristotle; he was a natural medium and mystic and after studies at the University of Cologne he went to the University of Paris where he met like-minded occultists.

At the age of twenty-four, Cornelius completed a three-volume tome entitled Occult Philosophy which was a compilation of the work of earlier magicians, moulded with his own thoughts. He changed his name to the grander Agrippa von Nettesheim and began to journey through the countries of Europe, gathering an ever-increasing knowledge as he indulged his fascination with the Kabbalah and astrology. His assertions regarding the performance of magic were forceful for the era in which he wrote them . . . 'he that works in magick must be of a constant belief, be credulous and not at all doubting of obtaining the effect.'

He studied at the University of Dole, won a Doctorate of Divinity, fell in love and settled down with the wealthy daughter of a local nobleman until his continuing activity in the occult was denounced by a Franciscan friar, and Agrippa was forced to leave for England. The wealth of stories about Agrippa began to pile up. He was said to pay for his food, drink and board at local hostelries in gold coins which turned into worthless metal when he left.

As the years passed, he descended more deeply into the darker realms of magic, summoning demons and spirits almost at will. Like many magicians obsessed by their craft, his quest for knowledge and power dragged him into the black abyss.

Perhaps the most famous story about Agrippa concerns the death of a student who was lodging at his house. While the master was away, the student persuaded Agrippa's wife to unlock her husband's workroom. He went inside and stood reading aloud from a book of spells that lay on the table; suddenly a demon appeared and demanded to know why he had been summoned. The student was so shocked he could not answer and the demon grabbed him by the throat and strangled him.

Agrippa returned to find the student lying dead on the floor of his laboratory, and realizing that this could mean trouble, he summoned the demon to return and bring the student to life long enough for him to be removed. This was done, and the student walked out of Agrippa's house into the market-place where he immediately collapsed and died. When the local doctor discovered the marks of strangulation, Agrippa and his wife were forced to beat a hasty retreat, and continue their restless wanderings through Europe.

Agrippa's reputation grew and went ahead of him; he was known wherever he travelled and the once-brilliant young scholar appeared now to have turned totally towards black workings. He was despised by the ecclesiastical hierarchy of Europe who pursued him with vigour and gaoled him twice for heresy. Two wives died of the plague and a third left him financially ruined. The pressure of it all slowly took its toll, and Agrippa died a shattered man in Grenoble, France, not long before his fiftieth birthday.

There were other master magicians travelling the same route at exactly the same time. The story of Faust is the most familiar through legend and literature and though he was a man of mystery, there is sound proof that he existed. He was Dr Johann Faust, a profligate necromancer and charlatan who travelled the continent professing his skills as a great doctor, magician, astrologer and alchemist.

As word of his miracles spread, so did the story that he had made a pact with the devil, written as usual in his own blood, in return for magical powers. When the given time of the pact had expired – five years after Agrippa's death – the Prince of Darkness arrived to claim his soul and there was 'a terrific din' at the house of Faust; according to some colourful reports, a wind howled and lightning struck and no one dared answer Faust's cries for help. In the morning, when all was silent, his crumpled body was found in the yard. His rooms were splattered with blood and his eyes were stuck to a wall.

The legend of Faust flourished. Christopher Marlowe wrote the *Tragicall History of Dr Faustus* and Lessing wrote a Faust play in the eighteenth century, though Goethe's great psychological drama remains unsurpassed, and it delivered to many thousands of people, perhaps, their first inkling of the power of medieval magic.

In England, meanwhile, a young scholar was emerging, whose work would also be added to the collections of writing on magic, and would eventually form a major part of the practical gospel for twentieth-century followers. Dr John Dee, born in 1527, was not an occultist and admitted he had no special psychic powers; yet he is recognized today as one of the founders of modern psychic research two centuries before it became a popular pursuit. Like his contemporaries, his career was colourful and laden with often dubious notoriety, especially when he was thrown into gaol accused of attempting to murder Mary Tudor by enchantment.

His career as a mystic and magician began when he had barely left his teens and his magical exploration proceeded through five reigns of English monarchs, Henry VIII, Edward VI, Mary

Tudor, Queen Elizabeth and James I, all of whom became involved with him, one way or another. His father was a member of Henry VIII's court, and after Chantry School in Chelmsford, Dee went on to St John's College, Cambridge, at the age of fifteen. There, he was regarded as something of a genius. He studied day and night and at the age of nineteen, he was made a Fellow of Trinity and an assistant professor of Greek. In search of broader experience and knowledge, he set off for Europe and spent time at the University of Louvain where, coincidentally, Agrippa had lectured some years earlier and where a copy of his book, *Occult Philosophy*, was to be found. In Paris, Rheims and back in London he became an acclaimed lecturer on Greek mathematicians. Henry VIII died in 1547 and was succeeded by Edward VI, then ten years old. Edward granted this impressive scholar a pension and the prospect of royal patronage augured well for the future.

Gradually, Dee's work veered towards the study of the occult and two years after his return to England, he met Jerome Cardan, a covert witch who proved himself to have considerable powers of second sight. His theories on astrology and other natural discussion points among occultists, such as astral projection, finally convinced Dee that his work should indeed be linked with occult studies. He was certain that Cardan's belief that the spirits could guide him towards significant discoveries was correct. He had in mind the age-old search for the Philosopher's Stone, or even knowledge of where secret hoards of treasure might be buried, knowledge which he intended to glean from his crystal ball or the summoning of spirits by necromancy.

Almost from the outset, he had embarked upon the dangerous course of seeking wealth. His expectations of royal favour seemed to assure his future – until Edward VI died at the age of sixteen and Dee's immediate patron, the Earl of Northumberland, declared that Lady Jane Grey, granddaughter of Henry VII, should be Queen. Henry VIII's eldest daughter Mary, naturally enough, did not agree, and had the lady and her sponsor beheaded.

One day Dee was asked to prepare Elizabeth's horoscope. While preparing one, he decided he might as well do two – and cast Mary's also. He foresaw that Mary would have a short life and that Elizabeth would assume the crown, and reign for many years. This, according to Mary's courtiers who gained knowledge of the horoscope, amounted to treason. Dee was thrown into gaol, accused of plotting the Queen's downfall, and there he remained for two years. His predictions, though, proved correct. Mary died three years later and Elizabeth immediately asked Dee to nominate the most favourable day for her coronation, when all the astrological influences would combine to ensure her of a long and successful reign. He chose 14 January 1559.

Dee was a prolific writer though, as with many of his contemporaries, little of his work was published during his lifetime and instead became the source of research and guidance for future generations of magicians. His interest in the occult continued to take him into deeper channels in his quest for knowledge, though his luck did not improve.

He married when he was almost fifty, and his wife died a year later of the plague. He married again two years later a woman very much his junior who soon produced the first of their eight children. Queen Elizabeth continued to favour him, though rarely paid him. He had become fascinated with a new interest, that of crystal gazing through which he believed he would make contacts with spirits who would inform him how to achieve great wealth.

Dee could see nothing in the crystal himself, and so sought out a 'scryer' – a person with occult powers who was capable of looking into the crystal and transcribing his visions. The man he chose was an unstable young Irishman named Edward Kelley who had trained as an apothecary's apprentice and had also served a prison sentence for forgery – for which crime he had also been punished by having his ears clipped. Dee hired him after giving him a test: Kelley gazed for a long time into Dee's crystal ball, and soon began describing the vision of an angel whom John Dee immediately identified as Uriel, the angel of light. And so began a magical partnership which was called upon by European monarchs for assistance. They held long sessions of contact with the spirits and eventually Kelley professed to have been given the secret of the Philosopher's Stone, having been led by his spiritual advisers to a place in Glastonbury where he discovered an ancient manuscript and powder for changing base metals into gold.

Kelley's new life of privilege led him into bad habits, however, and the two men quarrelled often. But word of their alleged abilities in communicating with the spirit world reached the continent and they were invited to travel to Prague to visit King Rudolf II. Going via France and Spain, the journey was to last four eventful years, though they apparently failed to produce gold for the continental nobleman and were eventually thrown out of Prague on the instructions of the Pope who branded Dee guilty of necromancy.

However, Queen Elizabeth still seemed convinced of Dee's powers. He was invited back to London with Kelley to make gold to help the British nation finance its defence against Spain. Not long afterwards, the magical partnership broke up, though not before Kelley had persuaded Dee that the angel Uriel had instructed them to share their respective wives, to the horror of Dee's wife Jane. Dee seemed convinced of the importance of the idea, and wrote 'There is no other remedy but as hath been said of our cross matching, so it must needs be done.'

Elizabeth continued her patronage and appointed Dee to the wardenship of Christ's College, Manchester, where he spent most of his declining years. His wife died of the plague, and then Elizabeth was succeeded by James I, whose opposition to witchcraft and sorcery was well known. Dee died in poverty at the age of eighty-one leaving behind many unpublished volumes of writing. Kelley fared no better; after some success in casting horoscopes, he returned to Prague where he was eventually thrown into gaol, and then killed trying to escape.

There were others who found similar fame in the sixteenth and early seventeenth centuries, but by then magicians, sorcerers and astrologers were temporarily going out of fashion partly because the purge against witchcraft was reaching its peak and partly because the future they foretold was laden with gloom and despair, especially for the nobility. The most gloomy prognosticator and last great seer of the Renaissance period was Nostradamus whose prophecies, made in hundreds of four-line stanzas, were to last to the end of the second millennium, at which point he vaguely suggested the world might end, or at the very least would be struck by a great catastrophe.

Nostradamus, who was born at St Remi in Provence, in 1503, remains a key figure in the history of magic and mysticism. His writings and predictions have fascinated occult believers, writers, poets, scientists, ecclesiastical scholars and statesmen through the centuries. He was a skilled exponent of not merely astrology and crystal-ball gazing, but of magical techniques, too, and this adds to the mystery surrounding him.

If the prophetic wisdom of Nostradamus was to be believed, or at least not discounted as just lucky imagination, then his supporters concluded that his predictions also gave credence to the belief of ancient mystics that the present was eternal, and the future already exists. And so we are plunged once again into the equally eternal and unanswerable debate as to whether man's future is pre-ordained – in which case is it feasible that Nostradamus could have glimpsed part of it? And thus we come back to one of the mysteries which has become no less insoluble than the Philosopher's Stone – except, that is, to the total disbelievers who are prepared to accept the bold and broad one-word description: fraud!

Influenced by the mysteries of the Kabbalah and Iamblichus's book *De Mysteriis Egyptorum*, Nostradamus worked from a room at the top of the house, where he gazed long and hard into a carafe of water balanced upon a brass tripod, as recommended by Iamblichus.

Over the next eight years, he began writing his predictions in four-line verses in which he used French and Latin words as well as anagrams and obscure phraseology, some of which might be recognized only by initiates of magic ritual; it was almost a code because he was still very aware that if his work fell foul of the Inquisition, he might be taken away and burned. This might well have been the case had it not been for the influence of one of his early patrons, Catherine de Medici, who became Queen of France.

The verses he wrote were not merely to apply to the immediate future, but onwards through the years to what he considered could be the end of time – somewhere around the year 2000. They were in no particular order, many did not have dates or geographical locations, and most would be identifiable only to the believer.

Nostradamus made it easy to imagine him sitting alone with his forbidden books in what he called 'secret study', dressed in his robes and waving his wizard's wand over his bowl of water used for scrying – for his own description of his method of divination seems to confirm that his basic motivation was magical. The first stanza of Century ɪ reads:

Estant assis de nuict estude,	Sitting alone at night in secret study;
Seul repose sur la selle de'aerin;	it is placed on the brass tripod.
Flambe exigue sortant de solititude	A slight flame comes out of the emptiness
Fait prosperer qui n'est a croire vain	and makes successful that which not be believed in vain . . .

The next stanza confirmed an almost ritualistic approach: he touched the middle of his tripod with his wand – which presumably he had energized through ritual ceremony beforehand – and sprinkled water on the hem of his robe and at his feet, another known part of magical rite. He noted that he was scared and trembled as his power came to him, but then the fear subsided with what he called 'divine splendour; the gods sit nearby' and he went into a trance-like state of peace as he wrote down his descriptions of his vision.

The content of his verses, liberally populated with blood and gore, flood and plague, death and destruction, fired the imagination of those anxious times, when people were desperate for news of what the future held. Many of the stanzas are vague and without affiliation to time and place. There have been many arguments, of course, for and against the various interpretations and in the end, the reader must make up his own mind whether to believe them or not.

Nostradamus's predictions contained too many uncannily correct descriptions of events far in the future to be easily dismissed – or did they? Some now believe that his stanzas might actually have been coded 'news' about events in the past which had been censored. And so with all things magical, you believe what you will. And of all the doomsday prophecies, perhaps the most chilling is one which does have a date attached and is translated as follows: 'In the year 1999, and seven months, from the sky will come the great King of Terror. He will bring back to life the great king of the Mongols. Before and after war reigns . . .' It is difficult to imagine or believe that this ageing old doctor could sit in his study having misty visions in a bowl of water of Edward and Mrs Simpson, or John Kennedy being shot in Dallas or of the world facing calamitous and horrendous happenings in the seventh month of 1999.

Nostradamus was the last great prophet cum magician of the Renaissance age. After him, sorcery and astrology began to vanish off the face of Europe. The persecution of witches had become a daily event and it was a courageous magician who continued his craft openly; the terror of the sixteenth and seventeenth centuries virtually put the professional sorcerers out of business and drove the rest underground.

The result was a proliferation of secret societies whose clandestine object was the study of magic. There were a number of cover organizations which were used and infiltrated – such as the eighteenth-century Egyptian Society founded in 1741 to discover the mysteries and wisdoms of the Nile regions. The Royal Society had some hidden occultists and in 1782, one of its fellows, James Price, claimed to have turned mercury into gold. The news naturally created something of a stir; he was invited to give a personal demonstration before the society. Unfortunately, he committed suicide instead.

But apart from the impostors and charlatans who dotted the occult landscape with occasional outbreaks of madness, the real fear among the hierarchy of society was the upsurge in interest in the secret societies. The Inquisition had instilled a certain fear in the community of all kinds of supernatural activity. Whereas demons and spirits were once accepted, now they were feared. The secret societies were also feared; members of these secret groups were rumoured to cloak their activities to hide widespread depravity, sexual misbehaviour and crime, just as they were in the 1980s. There were some who were seeking ancient mysteries, such as the true origins of the Rosicrucian legend which many writers believed was the basis of Freemasonry itself. One who lectured at Masonic lodges all over Europe was Count Cagliostro – an eighteenth-century nobleman who had a colourful past and a chequered future. In his early days, he had teamed up with the infamous Italian adventurer Giovanni Casanova and together they charmed a regular and tidy income from the pockets of wealthy women through magic and astrology. There is little point in discussing the 'magic' performed by these two men since it is wrapped in the fraudulent, verging on the farcical with all the usual tactics – such as the ability to make gold, conversations with a spirit who would lead them to buried treasure and so on.

Casanova's magic was often linked with amorous ambitions. Among his more famous exploits was his involvement with the eccentric widow Marquise d'Urfe who possessed her own alchemy laboratory and a large occult library. She wished to be reborn as a man. Casanova set up a ritual for spiritual contact; she wrote a letter to Selenis, spirit of the moon, and burned it in an alabaster cup. Shortly afterwards a reply from Selenis appeared, written in silver ink on green paper, floating in the madame's bath – which Casanova just happened to be sharing at the time. The letter said that a spirit would appear in human form who would impregnate the marquise with a son who would have all her personality traits. Unfortunately, the messenger from the spirit world was discovered to have syphilis and Casanova had to make a hasty exit.

However, Goethe and others took an interest in Cagliostro and he is important in the development of magic, since he was part of the stirrings of a revival in the eighteenth century. Furthermore, in spite of the accusations of cheating laid against him by many writers, some did consider him to be a magical genius, with real power and an enthralling mind.

Goethe's friend, the Swiss scientist and philosopher Johann Lavater, who wrote many books on mysticism, became one of Cagliostro's supporters. He was also spectacularly successful in terms of wealth – until he had an unfortunate run in with Marie Antionette over some expensive jewels and was temporarily incarcerated in the Bastille. His career went into rapid decline and ended when he tried to form a Masonic lodge in Rome. The Pope thought this to be something of a cheek and had him arrested amid accusations that he was involved in plotting the French Revolution.

He was locked away in a prison at the Castel San Leo where he died aged fifty-two.

The key event which put the revival firmly on its way was the publication in 1856 of a book entitled *The Ritual of Transcendental Magic*. The author was Alphonse Louis Constant who, for literary and magical purposes, used the alias of Eliphas Levi. Born in 1810 in poverty, he was the son of a French cobbler. Like many of his predecessors who were significant figures in magical history, he had an unusual background, and was of an unreliable nature. He first joined the priesthood and took a vow of celibacy but, like many priests of his era, he secretly took an interest in occultism. Discovery of this interest led to his expulsion from the Church.

Levi was by no means a scholar, though he had studied with a French philosopher and prophet and this grounding gave him confidence enough to begin writing. One of his early efforts, a pamphlet entitled *The Gospel of Liberty*, was so reactionary he was imprisoned for six months. Soon after his release he shocked his friends and associates by marrying a girl aged sixteen – in spite of his vow of celibacy.

The girl bore him two children, but then she discovered that Levi secretly dabbled in black magic and left him. He began studying the past works of great magicians and produced a series of books on high magic, which though suspect because of his lack of experience, established him with the reputation of being a master magician. His writings became especially noteworthy to those who were anxious to follow his supposed skill in making personal contact with demons and spirits.

Actually, it was surprising that he established such a reputation; though his writings were rediscovered and translated into English for twentieth-century occultists, who read them avidly, his techniques were said to be suspect and descriptions of manifestations were thought by many to be the result of a very active imagination or drink. Regardless of these considerable flaws, Levi became a famous magician and the publication of his books was undoubtedly responsible for a sudden upsurge in interest in magic in nineteenth-century Europe. History records only one serious example of outstanding success and this happened before he achieved fame through his writing.

In 1854, Levi travelled to England hoping to give lessons in occultism, but could find very few who were prepared to pay him money for such studies. Most wanted him to do tricks, like making demons appear before them. Among those who contacted him was the English novelist and politician Edward Bulwer-Lytton who was the author of *Zanoni*, a novel about a master magician with which he had had moderate success in 1842.

Lytton himself was a member of a number of secret societies, and was an initiate of a group who described themselves as Rosicrucians. He was a model of the type of people who were said to be involved in the 'secret society' conspiracies, a high-ranking member of society who moved in political circles and was able to wield some influence among his fellows.

While Levi refused point blank to perform the public evocation of spirits, he did agree to make private contact with the spirit world on Lytton's behalf, to discover the answers to two questions. He performed twelve hours of continual incantation and described the ritual in his book, *Transcendental Magic*. He claimed that at the end of it, the spirit Apollonius appeared in a grey shroud. It wafted in and out, objecting to Levi's magical sword. During conversation about this, Apollonius touched Levi's arm, and he wrote that it remained numb for several days afterwards. Finally, he was able to put Lytton's questions to the spirit, who told him the answer to both was 'death'. Lytton was a devotee of Levi's work and clearly the Frenchman was the inspiration for his writing on the supernatural. It was Lytton's own interest in Levi and the occult in general that truly began the revival – and this time it gained a new kind of respectability because of the interest it attracted from the literati.

There was another reason. In 1875, the year in which Eliphas Levi died and the young occultist Helene Petrovna Blavatsky founded the Theosophical Society, Emily Bertha Crowley gave birth to a boy. This, according to the boy's own testimony in later life, was his fifth incarnation – previously he had been Eliphas Levi himself, Cagliostro, Dr Dee's scryer John Kelley and the hedonist Pope Alexander VI.

On the infant boy's body were, unknown to his mother or his father (an evangelist living on the profits of the family brewery) the three most important distinguishing marks of a buddha. He was tongue-tied, until the fraenum linguae was cut; he had the characteristic membrane which 'necessitated an operation for phimosis some three lustres later'. Lastly, he had upon the centre of his heart four hairs curling from left to right in the exact form of a Swastika.

Aleister Crowley, the Great Beast, to be self-styled 666, had arrived . . .

CHAPTER TEN

THE EMBODIMENT
OF EVIL

When children between the ages of five and eight were being interviewed by social workers investigating claims of ritual abuse in 1988, they described ceremonies which might well have come from the diaries of Aleister Crowley, of whom one of his biographers said 'he provided the key to the occult mysteries of the present age.' As we have already seen, there is a good deal of hand-me-down in occultism.

Just how, eighty years after he created his original rituals, they were transferred into the arena of child welfare in America, Britain and Holland is open to debate, and I will discuss this in my final section. But the remarkable similarity between these recent cases and Crowley's records of depravity surprised those who could indentify them. His ritual involved elements of blood and excrement consumption that featured regularly in child abuse interviews, along with descriptions of sexual and sacrificial rites which both formed part of Crowley's early rituals and are described in detail in notes of his workings in the first decade of this century. They were part of Crowley's personal depraved preferences.

As I write in 1992, the OTO, as it is universally known, is reckoned to have become the largest occult order in existence with lodges throughout England, Europe and America, some officially sanctioned by the masters of the OTO to whom the lodges pay royalties. Some of the lodges run unofficially, though not for long, being either discovered and closed down or, lacking the will to become official, they fade away. The OTO is linked, according to some occult commentators, with some of the oldest medieval secret societies and has connections with the fringes of Freemasonry though Freemasons would deny it, having no wish at all to be associated with the taint of Crowley – indeed some of the OTO lodges think Crowley's past association is a cross they have to bear.

The common thread running through the whole pattern of modern occultism is the overbearing influence of the man dubbed the wickedest on earth. His basis for ceremonial ritual was sex magic; his speciality was *coitus reservatus*, often aided by drugs, practised until the participants had extended their lovemaking to such a degree that they were in a virtual trance. He was obsessed by images of the vagina and the penis. To study Crowley, his work and his life, is to realize and appreciate what is possible within the world of the occult and what is passed off as being essential to the quest for esoteric knowledge when in truth it is a whole range of sexually based ideas that can barely be put in the context of normal life. But normality and conformity were not words that the man recognized, and neither do his successors in the variety of lodges, secret societies and orders that followed in his wake. Many, it must be recognized, are no more harmful to society than the average Friday night Masonic lodge meeting where a few men and women dress up in their hooded robes and perform their rituals. Others are deeply sinister.

Aleister Crowley was the creature of a bizarre legend, and today is revered and idolized by followers around the world who strive to re-enact his ritual and teachings. Even occultists who disliked him praise him as the greatest magician of the twentieth century and instantly defend him against accusations of satanism and other terrible deeds, such as sacrificing children. But those who are more honest with themselves, and about their traditions, will admit that Crowley was a second-hand magician who stole his ideas from older writings; he was a charlatan – and also the nearest any living person could become to evil personified. Around his memory now revolves a vast and enthusiastic occult movement.

He laid the ground rules for modern magic in a single sentence, 'Do What Thou Wilt' – misunderstood and misrepresented though it has become. He apparently meant it to mean something deep and philosophical, that every person should find his own true will and exert it, just as he tried to do by making his own image disappear from the mirror. Everyone was a star, he proclaimed.

Instead, that sentence provided occultists of an extreme nature with the excuse to do just as they pleased, to be as nonconformist as possible, to shun the requirements of modern society, to be as vile as they wished and to stop at nothing if they were so moved.

He was a cheat and a fraud, and a genius and master. He wrote gifted prose and spoiled it with pornography which so disgusted 1920s Britain as to be left unread because it was unreadable. He was a rampant womanizer and a brutal homosexual who used his phallus as his prime tool in magical pursuits and the debauchery on which he thrived; he also signed the initial A in the form of a phallus, just to make sure that everyone knew his intent; he was utterly and totally obsessed by sex.

He destroyed people with his magic and his overbearing personality; they went mad, or fell into dissolute habits or committed suicide trying to please him. And like all great magicians, he thrived temporarily on the legend that he became in his own lifetime, only to lose it all and die in the most humble of surroundings in a boarding house in Hastings, alone, hated and injecting enough heroin into his veins to meet an addiction that would kill several normal men.

Today, Crowley experts such as the Cambridge graduate, author and public schoolmaster Gerald Suster criticize the 'gutter press' for making 'idiotic' claims about Crowley – which were merely repeats, he says, of libels made against him in a series of articles in *John Bull* in 1923, appearing under the headlines 'King of Depravity', 'A Cannibal At Large' and 'A Man We'd Like to Hang', which Crowley did not answer, much less fight. So let us first look at the man, and how he became such an overbearing influence on the world of darkness as it exists in 1992 and the writings that eventually found their way into the allegations of satanic ritual abuse.

Crowley was born Alexander Edward, just as occultism and theosophy were becoming popular again. He changed his name to Aleister; it was only the first of many aliases, social and magical, including Count Vladimir Svareff, Lord Boleskine, Baphomet, Frater Perdurabo, the Beast 666 and, on his attainment of the

The more attractive face of occultism, displayed here by a witches' coven practising an age-old form of pagan ritual worship of the sea gods Neptune and Poseidon at Beachy Head in Sussex. (*John Drysdale/Camera Press*)

Right: High priestess Morganna Le Fey illustrates the witches' magic symbols, including knife, broomstick and horn — all implements used to raise power. (*John Drysdale/Camera Press*)

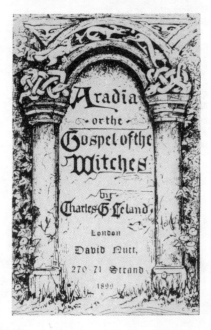

Three of Britain's most famous and influential witches who were among the creators of today's worldwide witchcraft movement. *Above left*: Alex Sanders, founder of the Alexandrian movement and King of Witches until his death in 1988. (*Tom King/Daily Mirror*). *Above right*: His former wife, Maxine Sanders, now spiritual head of the movement and Witch Queen emeritus. *Left*: Gerald Gardner, recognized today as the founder of modern witchcraft. *Right*: The title page of the book that started the witch craze of the twentieth century – *Aradia or The Gospel of the Witches*.

Pagan ritual is followed to the letter by witch covens everywhere and though some practices vary, the general pattern is the same : (*left*) a high priest portraying the Horned God will observe the correctness of every ceremony ; (*above*) the initiate is led blindfold and usually naked into the magic circle ; (*below*) the final stage of initiation, when a witch becomes a high priestess, is the Great Rite, in which the sex act may be performed in actuality or in token.
(*Left, below* : *John Moss/Camera Press.*
Above : *Universal Pictorial Press*)

Above: A typical witch coven meeting around a bonfire in a secluded woodland; the High Priest conducts the ceremonies and the witches begin to charge themselves with their magical forces by a circular dance to drumming music.
(*John Moss/Camera Press*).

Left: A witch wedding, when Grenville Russell Gough married his bride, Celia, leaping over the flames from a cauldron and the traditional broomstick. There are between two and three dozen witch weddings every year.
(*John Drysdale/Camera Press*)

Above: Two of Britain's leading witches today, former Fleet Street journalist Stewart Farrar and his wife Janet, who give lecture tours in Europe and America. (*News of the World*)

Right: Witch trick: the pentagram is the central symbol of a witches' altar and represents the five elements — water, fire, earth, air and akasha, the witches' spirit. (*John Drysdale/Camera Press*)

Below: A typical witches' altar which would be at the centre of an indoor coven meeting for a fertility rite, with a statue of the horned god of Pan.

In the 1990s few parents would risk allowing their children to be publicly involved in witchcraft but at the time, High Priestess Marion Unsworth was happy to allow six-year-old Adrian into some of the secrets of the craft. Today the Pagan Federation does not ban children from witchcraft ritual and positively encourages the family group at pagan festivals.
(*John Drysdale/Camera Press*)

The two extremes of children's involvement in the occult: *above*: leading Satanist Anton LaVey places his own daughter Zeena on the living altar and calls upon 'the Prince of Darkness, Ruler of the World' to observe her initiation into his Church of Satan. (*United Press International*) In contrast (*left*) the London white witches, Selidy and Nigel Bourne, who run the Wiccan magazine *Ace of Rods*, are happy to allow their five-year-old to observe minor ceremonies.
(*Peter Macdiarmid/Independent*)

Chris Bray, one of the most influential and powerful members of the British occult scene, at his shop and mail order distribution centre, known as the Sorcerer's Apprentice, in Leeds. He has one of the world's largest collections of occult paraphernalia, equipment and books. (*Asadour Guzelian*)

Myth and legend provide colourful ingredients from which today's Satanic worshippers often draw their inspiration. This scene showing newly appointed disciples at the court of Satan is from Gerard d'Euphrates's *Livre de l'Histoire et Ancienne Cronique*, printed in Paris in 1549.

The weird world of Aleister Crowley, self-styled Great Beast 666, the man who unquestionably had the greatest influence on every aspect of the occult this century. He is pictured above in his robes. *Above*: Now in his early thirties, Crowley was at the height of his powers. *Above right*: In typical phallic pose. *Bottom left*: The official seal of the Ordo Templi Orientis, the occult organization he headed.

Michael Aquino and his wife Lilith are rulers of the Satanic
organization The Temple of Set. (*Central Independent Television*)

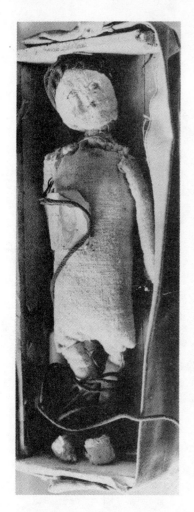

A symbol of Satanic worship, the statue of Baphomet (*above right*) is part man, part woman, part goat and signifies the devil incarnate. This lifesize statue is part of the collection at the Gardner Museum of Witchcraft, San Francisco. (*Ray Hamilton/Camera Press*)

Above left: A typical effigy in a coffin, often bearing a photograph of the victim of a spell or curse, over which the Satanic ritual is performed. (*Camera Press*)

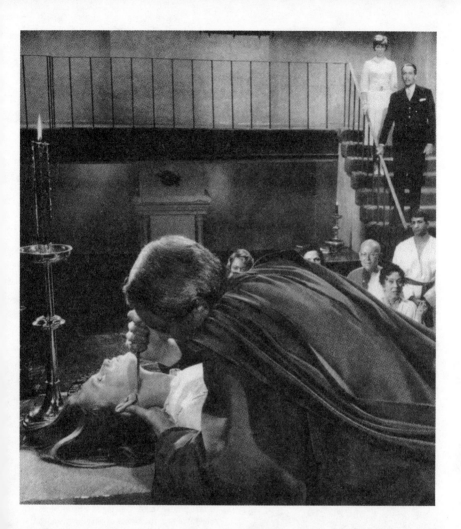

True Satanists often claim they are defamed by the colourful descriptions of their activities given by novelists and Hollywood, though the less discerning of their number have been known to use them as a reference point. This scene from the 1967 film *The Devil Rides Out*, based on a Denis Wheatley novel, starred Christopher Lee and Patrick Mower and depicts a human sacrifice.

History provides a unique reference point for those investigating the allegations of Satanic ritual abuse in the 1980s. The most notorious example was the seventeenth-century French case involving Catherine Monvoisin, occult adviser to Louis XIV's mistress Madame de Montespan and a priest turned sorcerer named Guiborg. They were alleged to have plotted to kill the king by a Black Mass, celebrated over the bodies of naked women, and to have sacrificed newborn children, as depicted in the picture above.

In England in the eighteenth century Sir Francis Dashwood (*left*) one-time Chancellor of the Exchequer, led the satanic revelry of the Hellfire Club, which has also since become an oft-exaggerated but well-used basis for twentieth-century mimicry.

Anton LaVey (*left*) is the founder of modern Satanic worship and author of *The Satanic Bible*. His Church of Satan has become the largest occult group in the world devoted to the furtherance of satanism. (*UPI*).

LaVey is shown below holding a chalice of bourbon and mandrake root wine.
(*Harold Painter/Camera Press*)

Anton LaVey in classic pose with horned hood, standing before his living
altar with a naked disciple. (*Harold Painter*/*Camera Press*)

godhead, Ipsissimus. These were additional to the names which he claimed he had borne in previous incarnations, like Eliphas Levi, Cagliostro, Dr John Dee's scryer Edward Kelley, and the Borgia Pope Alexander VI from whom he inherited his insatiable sexual desires. He also quickly began to display the main characteristic of all of these men – unreliability.

His childhood was as narrow as his adult life was diffuse. His father, a retired brewer of Crowleys Ales, was a fanatical follower of a Christian fundamentalist who insisted upon the literal acceptance of the Bible. Aleister Crowley's only inspiration from his father's inflexible religious bullying was a contemplation of the Hereafter, and especially the intriguing aspects of the Hereunder.

Crowley, with fundamentalism drummed into him until the age of twelve when his father had the decency – in his son's eyes – to die, had become obsessively fascinated by what he termed the most interesting characters of the Holy Bible, and by that he meant the evil ones. His literary executor, who was joint editor of his memoirs, John Symonds, made the point that Crowley, in his revolt against Christianity 'set himself up in God's place. It was not a temporary attitude, it stayed with him and set the course of his whole life.'

Directing his adolescent rebellion towards his relatives, he turned against Christianity so completely that he eventually sought to destroy it; one day his mother plucked up the courage to inform her son that he had become the Great Beast 666 of Revelation, an identity which he was more than happy to accept in perpetuity. She realized at that moment she had spawned a small monster. At the age of eleven he had dedicated himself to a life of evil which was later to embrace every excess, from sexual perversions to sacrificing living creatures, even, according to some, children. His first victim was the family cat. He was eager to discover whether it had nine lives and administered a large dose of arsenic then chloroformed it, hanged it above the gas jet, stabbed it, cut its throat, smashed its skull and, after it had been thoroughly burnt, drowned it and threw it out of the window so that the fall would remove its ninth life. He added, 'I was genuinely sorry for the animal; I simply forced myself to carry out the experiment in the interest of pure science.'

His voracious appetite for women started when he was fourteen, when he seduced the kitchen-maid on his mother's bed while
the family were at church. From then on, he enjoyed an endless
succession of whores and mistresses. Women were fascinated by
his vitality and hypnotic eyes. A titled woman who stopped to look
in a shop window in Piccadilly was overcome by the reflection of
his eyes as he stood behind her.

They had never met before, yet the woman immediately booked
into a hotel with him for ten days. In later life, Crowley claimed to
wear a secret aphrodisiac called 'The Perfume of Immortality',
which he rubbed into his scalp. It was made up of musk, ambergris
and civet, and women found it irresistible, as did horses; they
whinnied after him in the street.

He treated women in a despicable fashion. They should, he
said, be 'brought round to the back door like the milk'. And when
he had had his fill, he discarded them like empty cartons; he drove
both his wives into lunatic asylums and abandoned every one of his
mistresses to either the bottle, the hypodermic syringe or the streets.

Sex was always to be the most powerful element in Crowley's
form of black magic, and too much attention to this and not enough
to his studying cost him his degree at Cambridge University. He
had become obsessed with the occult and moved to Paris to join
the Hermetic Order of the Golden Dawn in 1898 when he was
renamed Frater Perdurabo (meaning I will Endure).

His achievements and the pretensions which followed were
founded on a fortune which he inherited at the age of twenty-one
from his father's trust fund, a sum of £40,000 which then seemed
so vast that it could never run out, and he spent madly. He bought
Boleskine House on Loch Ness at twice what it was worth, in order
to perform magic rituals there. He began commuting between
England and Paris where he became the devoted pupil of Mac-
Gregor Mathers, Grand Master of the Hermetic Order of the
Golden Dawn, whose basis was a system of magic derived from the
ancient Kabbalah and distorted to fit the needs of this popular
secret society whose numbers included many politicians, writers
and artists of the day. However, Crowley's scandalous private life
was frowned upon by the London luminaries of the order, including
the poet W. B. Yeats who hated Crowley and all that he stood for;

the London order refused to grant Crowley the initiation into Adeptship and so he travelled to Paris to enlist the aid of his former master.

Mathers was initially on Crowley's side, but later there was a row and a battle commenced with Yeats in the forefront, leading magical attacks to which Crowley responded in kind. According to one of the Golden Dawn's diarists, a beautiful vampire was sent to seduce Crowley and reduce him to inconsequence. He realized this before she could attack, and turned her magical current against herself – with the result that the girl of twenty disappeared, and before him stood a decrepit hag of sixty. Next, they attacked his pack of bloodhounds and finally Crowley responded 'by summoning up the great demon Beelzebub and forty-nine attendant demons'. It was a colourful description of a battle which may well have been waged in the drug-induced state that Crowley increasingly found himself in; opium, cocaine, hashish and peyote were drugs he considered necessary for contentment and the illumination of mystic pleasures.

In the meantime, he married Rose, sister of the painter Gerald Kelly, who was later knighted and made president of the Royal Academy. Crowley took his new wife on an extended honeymoon, travelling through Italy, India and Egypt. It was in Egypt that his life was to change dramatically – more precisely, in the Cairo Museum on 18 March 1904 where he underwent a revelation.

This is his own account of what happened and it can be viewed now as either one of the most enduring confidence tricks of the twentieth century or, as his followers everywhere prefer to believe, the arrival of the Prophet of the New Aeon. While walking through the museum, Rose had spoken in a ghostly voice as if in a trance, 'Horus is waiting for you'. Crowley maintained that until that day he had never heard of Horus and Rose certainly had not, since she knew nothing about the occult or Egyptian mythology. As they were walking through one of the museum galleries, she stopped and called Crowley over saying, 'There he is!'

He peered inside a glass case where he saw the image of the falcon-headed god Horus, painted on an ancient wooden obelisk. What shook Crowley was the number on the exhibit label; it was 666, his number, the number of the Beast of Revelations.

That night, he performed some tests on his wife and claimed that she gave answers to his questions that she could not possibly have known herself. In a state of high expectation, Crowley began performing rituals in his hotel room to invoke the spirit of Horus and followed his wife's instruction to sit at a desk in their room at a specified time on three days. According to Crowley, Horus sent a spirit-guide named Aiwass who appeared at his shoulder and began to dictate a series of precepts and prophecies.

Then, over several weeks, Crowley incorporated the supernatural messages into a volume called *The Book of the Law* which subsequently became the bible of the New Aeon and, if widely adopted, would be the new bible to end Christianity for all time. Non-occultists have been known to dismiss this work as an unreadable and unreliable collection of meaningless mysticism and poetic predictions. However, the ultimate meaning was clearly spelled out: that mankind was on the brink of a New Dawn, and the prophet selected to lead the way was Aleister Crowley. Gerald Suster goes deeper:

> It proclaimed nothing less than that an Age had come to an end
> . . . Crowley was hailed as The Beast 666, Prophet of the New
> Aeon in which the supreme commandment would be: Do What
> Thou Wilt Shall Be The Whole Of The Law.

Suster maintained that initially Crowley rejected the fact that he had been chosen as the Great Prophet 'come to destroy Christianity and liberate Mankind'; in fact he misplaced the manuscript which he was directed to write in that Egyptian hotel room and it did not surface again for another five years.

In the meantime, he continued his alternative calling as an adventurer and a philanderer, and believed he had the wherewithal to prove that he was a genius, and a better poet than Shakespeare. He travelled frequently and was a great walker and mountaineer. He strolled across China, Spain and the Sahara desert; he climbed cliffs at Beachy Head and rocks at Wastdale, mountains in Switzerland, Mexico and the Himalayas. He financed two disastrous mountaineering expeditions, one climbing the infamous K2, the other an assault on Kanchenjunga with a subsequent tragic loss of lives. He never did explain what went wrong.

He was a prolific writer, dashing off verse, sonnets, plays, pornographic novels, macabre short stories, magic invocations, Kabbalistic and gnostic rituals – all published so lavishly, at his own expense, that they could never make a profit.

He was dazzled by what he regarded as his own multifaceted brilliance. He was a traveller in the physical and spiritual worlds as adventurous as Sir Richard Burton, a psychologist more profound than his coeval Freud, a scientific magician in the tradition of the greatest masters but their superior because he had been chosen by the gods to initiate the New Aeon of God the Child. This is what he truly believed.

In 1909, for example, he began publication of *The Equinox*, weighing 3.5 lb per volume and as large as London telephone directories; he claimed they were priced deliberately to make a loss. They were the journals of his newly formed Order of the Silver Star, which was going to be his own replacement for the Hermetic Order of the Golden Dawn whose members he found boring and uninteresting.

The true magician, he reckoned, should not make money by the publication of his esoteric doctrine but that was of course just a blind, to cover the fact that no one wanted to buy it, and instead it would lie dormant to be rediscovered in the second half of the twentieth century. There were those among his circle who believed him then, and even more who believe it today. True, he had an outstanding mind, and his knowledge of witchcraft, black magic, the occult and the ancient mysteries was unquestionably vast.

There was apparently something compelling about him, and also something appealingly dangerous. He threw himself into his new mission with manic fervour, marching backwards to the Dark Ages of cruelty, superstition and diabolism. This quest was further enhanced in 1912 when he became head of a German group specializing in erotic sex magic, known as the Ordo Templi Orientis. He made this society his own and today, in 1992, it is the largest of all the secret societies operating throughout the world. The order had been founded eight years before by a German master Karl Kellner, who was said to have bought it from a group which had direct links with the medieval Knights Templar. Crowley very quickly established himself as the OTO's leading international figure, though some German initiates were reluctant to accept him in view of the gossip and rumour concerning his private life.

Crowley then gathered around him a gullible retinue of disciples with whom he travelled the world and led into some horrific situations. He impelled everyone to study the *Book of Law* which he maintained to his death was the product of his contact with the gods. His followers still insist this is the case, though anyone with half an eye for the ancient ritual of pre-Christian cults will see that, stripped of his exotic and poetic prose, it was nothing more than an elaboration of old pagan mysteries and Kabbalistic teachings. But no one dared say it then, and no one in his extensive circle of disciples today will admit the truth, either.

Gerald Suster recalled that one writer described the *Book of Law*, with complimentary ardour, as 'an intensely beautiful but often cryptic prose-poem . . .'

But then beauty is in the eye of the beholder. And physical beauty was not one of Crowley's attributes, especially as his behaviour grew more and more erratic. He had two of his teeth filed into a point, so he could give women the 'Serpent's Kiss' when introduced. One woman, bitten on the arm, contracted blood poisoning; another had her left nipple bitten off and almost died from the resultant infection. He was prone to the most unsocial of habits, evacuating his bowels on drawing-room carpets, and when his hosts protested, he claimed his excreta was sacred. Like the old black magicians of the Middle Ages whom we have already visited, he believed he could make himself invisible at will. Diners at the Café Royal in London were astonished when Crowley appeared one evening, dressed in a wizard's robes and wearing a conical hat. He strode among the tables and left without saying a word. 'There you are,' he said afterwards, 'that proves I can make myself invisible! Nobody spoke to me, therefore they couldn't have seen me.'

His cavalier expenditure continued unabated and at the outset of the First World War, he discovered that his massive fortune had all but gone and his cash richness had been replaced by the nonnegotiable paper wealth of piles of unsold books, and manuscripts, published and unpublished. With the war a reality, he went to the United States, hoping to sell to John Quinn, the book-collector, Crowleyana to the tune of $5,000. He failed and was forced temporarily to seek gainful employment.

He later insisted that he was employed by the British Secret Service though was never able to confirm this with evidence of a discernible nature; Gerald Suster and other supporters today believed his version. More correctly, he decided that the only way he could serve his country was by pretending to be a German agent and writing such violently anti-British propaganda that the United States was brought in on the Allied side. Some said he was a paid German agent.

After the war, he returned to Europe. His wife had taken to drink to block out the horror of his magical rituals all of which centred round sex. 'I rave, I rape, I rip and I rend,' he said in his Hymn to Pan. His ceremonial sexual acts with his followers were usually perverted and frequently with several partners at the same time. Apart from Rose, there was always a 'permanent mistress' in tow to act as his scribe and to assist with his rituals. Each one bore the name 'The Scarlet Woman'. The first was a neurotic New York singing teacher named Leah Faesi, whom he met in 1918. Crowley branded her on the breast with 'The mark of the Beast' – a cross within a circle – using a dagger heated in the fire.

Though his followers today deny he was a satanist, evidence of his early infatuation with the medieval followers of the blood-lust cult had already appeared. As Blanche Barton points out in her history of the Church of Satan, Crowley had obviously noted the earlier fictional and factual enclaves of satanism, in Rabelais's utopian Abbey of Thelema as described in *Gargantua and Pantagruel*, a palace of perpetual indulgence. And then Besant and Rice fuelled belief in the reality of the fictional abbey in the 1878 novel, *The Monks of Thelema*, in which the hero tries to establish a nineteenth-century Abbey of Thelema in England.

Crowley was taken by the idea of owning a temple of black magic where he could practise his rites undisturbed. His dream came true in March 1920, when he located an isolated villa, hidden among olive groves near the fishing village of Cefalu, on the northern shore of Sicily. 'My house is going to be the Whore's Hell,' he said, 'a secret place of the quenchless fire of lust and the eternal torment of Love.' Like many occultists, then and now, much of Crowley's inspiration came from books and he was to call his new pleasure palace 'The Sacred Abbey of the Thelemic Mysteries'.

On the floor of the inner temple was a magic circle, with an altar in its centre. A copy of the *Book of Law* was placed on the altar, surrounded by 'Cakes of Light', a mockery of the consecrated wafer made of oatmeal, honey, red wine and animal or menstrual blood. Outside the circle were the thrones of the Beast and the Scarlet Woman, and the walls of the temple were covered in Crowley's own paintings, depicting every kind of sexual act possible.

It was here in the Abbey of Thelema that Crowley could act out the many roles he had chosen for himself – the latest being a flash of light which informed him he had become a god, Ipsissimus – and it was clear he had taken his precept of Do What Thou Wilt quite literally. He used the poet Victor Neuberg and others as mediums through whom to invoke the gods and to participate in homosexual magic, in which Neuberg was the catamite.

Neuburg, at his initiation into the OTO, had to do what Crowley willed, which included sleeping naked for seven nights on a bed of gorse. Another penance was scarring the body with a knife while thinking distracting thoughts. He could have refused to do as Crowley willed but in that case he would have faced expulsion from the Abbey. Neuberg had long been the subject of Crowley's depraved rituals, which involved work within the magic circle, a considerable amount of scourging, brutal and disgusting sado-masochistic pleasures, which drew blood in profusion, and various sexual and bestial acts. Neuberg became so ashamed he refused to describe his involvement with Crowley when questioned about his past by his young poets' group – which included Dylan Thomas and Pamela Hansford Johnson.

Crowley entertained any women who cared to join him, and many did. Though he made much of the fact that he did not receive money for his magical services, such as casting horoscopes and so on, he was only too willing to accept donations from well-wishers. Many of them were neurotic women to whom Crowley's magical practices were undoubtedly extremely dangerous. One of the reasons which Victor Neuburg gave for deserting Crowley, whose invocations he continued to believe in with terror in his soul, was that Crowley used magic not for the attainment of esoteric knowledge but in order to raise money to recoup his fortunes.

The perverted ceremonies performed inside the Abbey soon became notorious. During one drug-induced ritual, the Scarlet Woman committed bestiality with a goat, after which its throat was cut by Crowley, allowing the blood to flow over another woman's back. The superstitious Sicilian peasants, terrified of the evil aura of the Abbey and of the screams, the shrieks and the wailing that floated from the building after dark, crossed themselves every time they passed.

There was never a shortage of disciples who flocked to the Abbey to take part in the orgies. Among them was a twenty-three-year-old Oxford University undergraduate named Raoul Loveday, and his wife Betty May, an artist's model. Loveday became the first of Crowley's victims. Crowley found Loveday such a promising pupil that he renamed him 'Aud', meaning 'magical light'. Betty May was less enthusiastic. She detested Crowley and his horrific sex orgies, which were frequently watched by Crowley's own children.

Loveday became a mass of self-inflicted wounds, caused by the need to scar his body for ritualistic purposes and drain blood for the chalice, as well as from injecting drugs into his arms and legs. Betty May could see him growing physically weaker from loss of blood and dissipation.

One night, during a black magic ceremony which was being performed inside their magic circle, Crowley forced Loveday to sacrifice a live cat. This was not an uncommon practice; any passing animal, or birds which landed in his trees, were liable to be trapped and used for sacrificial purposes. Scarlet Woman held up the screaming, petrified creature over 'The Cup of Abominations' to catch the blood, while Loveday flailed at the cat with his knife. The first wound was insufficient to kill the animal outright and the cat escaped his grasp and raced round the room, blood streaming from its neck. Trembling and emotional, Loveday managed to catch it and kill it with a second blow, although doing so meant leaving the 'protection' of the magic circle. Scarlet Woman handed him the cup and he drank the blood.

Shortly afterwards, Loveday fell ill and deteriorated rapidly, despite the use of mystic spells and incantations and the attention of a conventional doctor. Crowley believed Loveday had fallen victim to an evil spell after breaking the magic circle. Raoul Loveday died two days later.

The newspapers surrounded Betty May the instant she returned to Britain. The *Sunday Express*, which had continued its relentless pursuit of Crowley, described the whole scenario as 'A maelstrom of filth and obscenity' which was not far off the mark. It said that this time, Crowley had sunk to the depths of depravity. Reporters descending on the Abbey of Thelema noted the inscription over the door 'Do What Thou Wilt' and that the Scarlet Woman's solemn oath, as inscribed in the Abbey's Record, was bold and clear: 'I will work the work of wickedness. I will be loud and adulterous. I will freely prostitute my body to the lusts of each and every living creature that shall desire it. I claim the title Mystery of Mysteries, Babylon the Great and the Number 156 and the Robe of the woman of Whoredoms and the Cup of Abominations.'

Another of Crowley's faithful disciples also died an unnatural death. Norman Mudd, a professor of mathematics who gave up his life and career to follow Crowley and who looked after the running of the abbey, was eventually rejected and cursed by the Beast during one of his tantrums. A few years later, Mudd committed suicide.

All of this was sufficient to send Mussolini into a rage as he surveyed the international publicity which Crowley achieved. In May 1923, the Beast was expelled from the country, complete with all the accoutrements of his ritual magic – the bell, the *Book of Law*, the black candles and Cup of Abominations. He drifted through Africa, where he claimed to have caused the manifestation of the demon Choronzon, the epitome of all disharmony and confusion, whom he conjured up in the form of a naked savage. Then he moved into France and was promptly deported after allegations that he was a German spy. For a time, even his home country refused him entry and in the eyes of the newspapers he had become a Satan without a hell to go to.

Crowley went to ground and wrote six volumes of *The Confessions of Aleister Crowley*, during the 1920s, of which only two volumes were published (in 1929, by the Mandrake Press, after Collins had refused to publish any more of his works, in spite of the fact that they had already paid him an advance). The remainder did not appear until 1969, over twenty years after his death. When he presented his final manuscripts to his literary executor in 1945, he said, 'I have no motive for deception, because I don't give a damn for the whole human race; you're nothing but a pack of cards.'

His route since the mid-thirties had been downhill for Crowley who scraped a living with his pornographic novels, and by borrowing and selling charters of the OTO. It was hardly surprising that the creator of such malice should be attacked by accusations of equal weight, starting with Somerset Maugham's novel *The Magician* which accuses him of being thoroughly disreputable and evil and whose publication came when every Christian person viewed Crowley with great distrust and disgust, such was his infamy. Yet as the Prophet New Aeon, he sincerely believed that, having crossed the Abyss, none of it mattered and the human race could go to hell, or worse, heaven.

Undoubtedly the pinnacle of his notoriety, from which there could only be rapid decline and obscurity, came in 1934 when as one writer so colourfully described it, the nation suddenly came face to face with 'a man who had stared into the very abyss of Hell and seen its abominations'. And a High Court judge, Mr Justice Swift, proclaimed: 'I have been over forty years engaged in the administration of the law in one capacity or another. I thought that everything which was vicious and bad had been produced at one time or another before me. Yet, I have never heard such dreadful, horrible, blasphemous and abominable stuff as that which has been produced by the man who describes himself to you as the greatest living poet . . .'

This attack was rained down upon Crowley as he made his last futile attempt at re-establishing his position. He was sixty years old, balding and thickset. Apart from the heavily ringed and puffy eyes which still pierced like a cutting edge, he looked something of an English gent until he boasted, 'I have exposed myself to every form of disease, accident and violence. I have driven myself to delight in dirty and disgusting debauches, and to devour human excrement and flesh.'

And on 14 April 1934, he stood awaiting the verdict of a court hearing, expecting a jury to find in his favour. Aleister Crowley had been on trial, yet he was not the accused. He had sued for damages for libel. Desperately short of money, he sought to ease his problems with a lawsuit against Constable and Co, publishers of a book written in 1932 by Crowley's former friend, authoress Nina Hammett.

It was her autobiography, *Laughing Torso*, in which she wrote, 'Crowley had a temple in Cefalu in Sicily. He was supposed to practise Black Magic there, and one day a baby was said to have disappeared mysteriously. There was also a goat there. This all pointed to Black Magic, so people said, and the inhabitants of the village were frightened of him.' Crowley saw the defamatory reference as an opportunity to seek damages, spurred on by an earlier claim, in which he had succeeded in obtaining damages from a bookseller. He would regret it for the rest of his life.

It was in his book *Magick in Theory and Practice*, under the heading 'Of Bloody Sacrifice', that Crowley wrote that the

> bloody sacrifice had from time immemorial been the most 'considered part of magick'. The ethics of the thing did not appear to have concerned anyone nor need they do so, [he went on]. The animal should be killed within the circle so that its energy cannot escape and should be selected so that its nature accorded with that of the ceremony. For the highest spiritual working, one must therefore choose 'that victim which contains the great and purest force; a male child of perfect innocence and high intelligence is the most satisfactory and suitable victim.'

He gave a footnote which added, 'It appears from the magical Records of Frater Perdurabo [alias Crowley] that He made this particular sacrifice on an average about 150 times every year between 1912 and 1928.' The reference was said to be sick humour on Crowley's part but many people took it seriously, and the rumour spread that Crowley had admitted sacrificing 1,500 children in his magical circle and had practised cannibalism.

As the libel action neared, Crowley solicited the aid of friends to come to court and give reference to his good character, and help him project the image of being an ageing author and poet who, though slightly eccentric, had been grossly misunderstood. None was prepared to come and indeed the novelist J. D. Beresford wrote to Crowley urging him to drop the action, saying 'I haven't the least doubt that some very extraordinary damaging charges will be made against you if you come to court, the kind of charges that would spoil any chance you might have with a judge, who is a kind of professional moralist.'

Even his own lawyers urged him to drop the case. After reading a copy of the immensely pornographic *White Stains*, his lawyer wrote, 'I have no hesitation in saying that if the defendants are in possession of that book your chances of winning this action are negligible.'

Crowley persisted and sat back with a smug smile on his face as he listened to his counsel, Mr J. P. Eddy, KC, describe him as an 'altruist, a white magician, whose life has been a crusade against black magic'. How his friends must have chuckled at that lie; even the notorious Abbey of Thelema at Cefalu was described as 'a little community for the purpose of studying white magic'.

Mr Malcolm Hilbery, KC, counsel for the defence, knew differently. He had a pile of Crowley's privately printed books on his table, and the top one was *White Stains* which he flicked through and then banged shut.

HE ASKED: Are you asking for damages because your reputation has suffered?

CROWLEY: Yes.

COUNSEL: For many years you have been publicly denounced as the worst man in the world?

CROWLEY: Only by the lowest kind of newspaper.

COUNSEL: Did any paper call you 'The Monster of Wickedness'?

CROWLEY: I can't remember.

COUNSEL: Have you, from the time of your adolescence, openly defied all moral conventions?

CROWLEY: No.

COUNSEL: And proclaimed your contempt for all the doctrines of Christianity?

CROWLEY: Not all the doctrines.

COUNSEL: Did you take to yourself the designation of The Beast 666?

CROWLEY: Yes.

COUNSEL: Do you call yourself The Master Therion?

CROWLEY: Yes.

COUNSEL: What does Therion mean?

CROWLEY: Great Wild Beast.

COUNSEL: Have you not built a reputation on books which are indecent?

CROWLEY: It has long been laid down that art has nothing to do with morals.

COUNSEL: Decency and indecency have nothing to do with it?

CROWLEY: I do not think they have. You can find indecency in Shakespeare, Sterne, Swift, and every other English writer, if you try . . . I should like to be universally hailed as the greatest living poet. Truth will out.

Mr Hilbery then began to question Crowley on his magical experiments, turning immediately to quotations from his own book on magic and the occult and challenging the magician on an aspect that he knew referred to necromancy, and the art of raising the dead.

COUNSEL: You say here, 'I had two temples; one white, the walls being lined with six mirrors, each six feet in height; the other black, a mere cupboard, in which stood an altar, supported by the figure of a Negro standing on his hands. The presiding genius of the place was a human skeleton . . .'

CROWLEY: Yes, the skeleton was from Millikin and Lawley's, the medical shop.

COUNSEL: '. . . which I fed from time to time with blood, small birds, and the like . . .' Was that true?

CROWLEY: Yes.

COUNSEL: That was white magic, was it?

CROWLEY: It was a very scientific experiment.

COUNSEL: '. . . the idea was to give it life, but I never got further than causing the bones to become covered with viscous slime . . .'

CROWLEY: I expect that was the soot of London.

The defending counsel then turned to other of Crowley's books, quoting and requoting references to sacrifices, human and animal, and to the corruption of the consecration of bread and wine. Members of the jury noticeably leaned foward in their seats when he was asked about his ability to invoke evil spirits and summon up supernatural darkness during daylight hours. Crowley said he had done all of those things in the cause of experimentation.

Then an article Crowley had written for the *Sunday Dispatch* was read aloud, in which he admitted: 'They have called me the worst man in the world. They have accused me of doing everything from murdering women and throwing their bodies in the Seine to drug peddling.'

COUNSEL: Is that, then, your general reputation?

CROWLEY: Any man of distinction has rumour about him.

COUNSEL: You wrote, '. . . James Douglas described me as a monster of wickedness. Horatio Bottomley branded me as a monster of wickedness. Horatio Bottomley branded me as a dirty, degenerate cannibal . . .' You never took any action against any of the persons who wrote and published those things about you, did you?

CROWLEY: No.

COUNSEL: And then comes this silly little paragraph in this book, and you run to your lawyer with it, according to you, to bring an action for injury to this reputation of being the worst man in the world. Is that the case?

CROWLEY: I also have the reputation of being the best man in the world.

Crowley's case had fallen apart and Betty May Loveday, whose husband died at the Abbey of Thelema, added the final words to destroy him as she gave evidence concerning the blood rituals which Crowley had performed at the Abbey, his heavy use of drugs, the blasphemies and obscenities, the animal sacrifices, the pornographic paintings round Crowley's room, known as 'The Chamber of Nightmares'.

It was just too much for the jury. Counsel's closing speeches had yet to be completed when the judge noticed that members of the jury were talking amongst themselves. He asked them if they were speaking to each other. The foreman said the jury wished to stop the case there and then. The judge explained that as counsel had already begun their speeches it was necessary for them to hear both sides, and the final plea on Crowley's behalf. The jury listened as instructed but their minds were already made up.

The judge made his summing up, stating that never in his forty years had he heard such terrible things and ended by asking the jury, 'Do you want the case to go on?' The foreman replied emphatically: 'No.'

Crowley looked shocked; the case had ruined him and he was done for financially and socially. He became a total outcast. A few friends rallied round and assisted him in his last years, but he drifted out of the limelight and into apparent obscurity. He ended his days in a seaside boarding-house at Hastings, a complete wreck injecting himself with heroin until the day he died.

Unknown to the outside world, however, Crowley continued to be the most influential figure in one of the largest worldwide secret societies, outside the Masons. From his room in that Hastings boarding-house, he remained the international head of OTO which provided him with a source of money, not least through the sale of charters to aspirants wishing to set up new OTO lodges in various parts of the world. The lingering strength of his influence on the occult world was displayed by the number of friends and associates who came to Brighton Crematorium in December 1947 to listen to the Black Mass he had prepared for his own funeral. It included a prayer to Satan which outraged the people of Brighton.

The fact that he still had worldwide authority up to the time of his death was revealed in the battle for the leadership of the Agape Lodge of the OTO in California in the mid-1940s; investigation of this and subsequent events also reveals the extent to which the

OTO had penetrated the higher orders of society and the type of people who were being recruited – and, of course, who were to set the pattern for the future.

In the last months of his life Crowley took charge of the developing situation of conflict in the Californian lodge and by letter persuaded a wealthy young scientist, Jack Parsons from Pasadena, to become head of the lodge. Parsons was working on top-secret government projects at the Hughes Aircraft Corporation at the time and carried high level security clearance.

Even so, by then Parsons was deeply involved with the OTO and had been since 1938 when he was visiting Los Angeles for a conference and was introduced to the Agape lodge by fellow scientists who were already members. At the time, members of the Agape lodge used to give weekly public performances of a Gnostic Catholic Mass – which Crowley had also created – to attract potential OTO members.

When Parsons joined, his entry in the lodge magical records read: '26 years of age; 6′2″; vital, potentially bi-sexual at the very least; University of the State of California; now engaged in Cal. Tech. chemical laboratories developing bigger and better explosives. Travels under sealed orders from US government; writes poetry; has had mystical experiences . . .'

Parsons progressed through the order and followed Crowley's teachings to the letter. Crowley was pleased with reports of the man though he had reservations: 'Jack's trouble is his weakness, the romantic side . . . he gets a kick from some magazine trash or an occult novel (if only he knew how they were concocted!) and dashes off in wild pursuit,' Crowley wrote to a fellow member. However, he was sufficiently confident about Parsons' abilities to appoint him head of the Californian OTO in place of William T. Smith who was having an affair with Parsons' wife Helen.

Meanwhile, Parsons had taken a new magical assistant who was to be his scryer and scribe. The man's name was Ron Hubbard, the future founder of the Church of Scientology who was then a writer of pulp fiction and regarded by all who knew him as something of an eccentric.

Parsons expounded his qualities in a letter to Crowley in 1946, '. . . he has no formal training in magick . . . but I deduce that he is in direct contact with some higher intelligence, possibly his Guardian Angel. He is the most Thelemic man I have ever met and in complete accord with our own principles. I think I have made a great gain.'

Hubbard joined Parsons in his new obsession, which eventually became known as the Babalon Working – an attempt to invoke the Goddess of Babalon in a series of rituals during the early months of 1946, for which he also recruited Betty, the younger sister of his wife Helen.

The whole scenario is a complicated morass of magical workings, far from the understanding of those who have not experienced the rituals of the OTO. In short, Parsons was pursuing the original pompous Crowley theories and believed that the Second World War and the invention of the atomic bomb were part of the beginning of the new Age of Horus heralding confusion and terror. It would be manifested, he believed, by the destruction of old institutions and ideas, the discovery and liberation of new energies, and a trend towards power governments, war, homosexuality, infantilism and schizophrenia.

The Babalon Workings, which were aimed at invoking a god to show him the light, consumed Parsons and his assistant Hubbard for weeks on end. Descriptions of their rituals in Parsons' magical diaries shows them to have been long and complex, lasting for days at a time. The final stages of the Babalon Workings contained the necessary blood element in the instructions for three rituals which were apparently dictated by some non-human entity, and written down by Hubbard as a means of achieving an apparition of the Goddess of Babalon:

'Wear black. Cut from thy breast the red star. Renew the blood. Lay out white sheet. Place upon it the blood of birth, since She is born of flesh and by thy immortal power upon earth. Thou shalt recognize by the sign. Babalon is born. It is a new birth . . .'

It is not recorded how the blood of birth was to be obtained but one can imagine, and the rituals – farcical to the uninitiated – continued in this fashion as Parsons and Hubbard tried to reach the goddess. Hubbard appears to have become bored with the proceedings however and left, taking a large amount of Parsons' money, said to amount to $17,000, which had been deposited in a joint bank account in which Hubbard had placed only $1,000.

Crowley, angered by these developments and the running of the Californian lodge, washed his hands of Parsons, saying that he had fine ideas but was led astray, then robbed of his last penny by 'this confidence man named Hubbard . . . I have no further interest in Jack and his adventures. He is a weak-minded fool and must go to the devil in his own way.'

Parsons, meanwhile, sued Hubbard for the return of his money and eventually they settled out of court. When Hubbard's involvement with Parsons was rumoured as he founded his new Church of Scientology in Britain and America, the church put out a statement saying that Hubbard had been sent in as a secret agent of the FBI to break up a dangerous black magic ring which included several prominent US scientists of the age, all said to be working on highly secret government projects.

If the story had broken then, there would have been a worldwide scandal of major proportions in the US defence industry; as it was the whole thing was covered up. Clearly, the US authorities were aware of Parsons' strange pastime and that he was one of many personalities in sensitive jobs involved. The US government withdrew his security clearance in 1948. A report on his activities stated that 'he is a known member of a religious cult believed to advocate sexual perversion, organized from the subject's home.'

Parsons was brought before a closed court to face charges that he was, among other things, a member of a secret organization, namely the OTO. He successfully appealed against the loss of his security clearance on the grounds that membership of a religious order was not a criminal offence but two years later, in 1950, he lost it again when he was sacked from his job at the Hughes Aircraft Corporation after being found in possession of a number of classified documents. Other papers in his possession showed that he was in the process of building a larger mystical order, with links to paganism, witchcraft in Britain and other occult orders. He did not survive to complete the task.

Having sold his Pasadena mansion to set up a chemicals

business, he was preparing to move his whole operation to Mexico when on the afternoon of 17 June 1952, he was blown up in a mysterious explosion at his house. He had reportedly dropped a container of fulminate mercury which completely wrecked his laboratory and his house, and he was so badly injured that he died before reaching hospital. There was considerable speculation among his friends over his death, and whether it had been inspired by security-linked killers. More mysterious, though, was a reference in his Book of Babalon which was among his papers, which seemed to forecast his own death in exactly the manner it happened once he had achieved the manifestation of the goddess – '. . . blown away in the Breath of the Father'.

CHAPTER ELEVEN

THE CROWLEY REVIVAL

Aleister Crowley left behind him the organization of the OTO and enough written material to inspire the formation of the Cult of Thelema and a formidable industry in what has become known as Crowleyana. By 1992 the cult had proliferated worldwide in a way he could never have imagined as he neared the end of his life, although he had taken steps to ensure its survival. Immediately after his death, one of the German members of the OTO who had followed Crowley, Karl Germer, who was by then in America, took over as head of the order and was responsible for getting a number of previously unpublished Crowley books into print. Since then there has been a massive upsurge in the publication and sale of most of Crowley's titles. There were also other valuable copyrights which Crowley willed to the OTO, such as his work on tarot cards and the Thoth Tarot Deck which became a best seller.

There were others in America also working to preserve Crowley's memory. Shortly before his death, he had become closely associated with one of his earlier pupils and devoted disciple, a US Army Major named Grady McMurtry who later claimed that Crowley had given him the caliphate powers for the future operation of the OTO if ever it was in danger of dying out.

In the sixties, with the revival of interest in the occult, there seemed little prospect of that happening, especially when new editions of his 'autohagiography', *The Confessions of Aleister Crowley*, appeared, along with the republication of some of his earlier works. By then, the British writer Kenneth Grant, one of the two joint editors of Crowley's papers, was described in the jacket notes to the *Confessions* as head of the OTO.

Activity flourished with this revival of the occult, especially on the west coast of America, where Dr Timothy Leary began his own experiments in social behaviour (before the CIA began taking an interest in him). Interest slipped again in the seventies, however, and McMurtry contacted two other elders and former Crowley associates, Israel Regardie who lived in California and Gerald Yorke in London, to point out that Crowley had charged him with the task of ensuring the OTO's survival.

This he did, against competition from other OTO personalities who believed that they had rights to the Charter. McMurtry pursued what he saw as his last remaining mission in life and from his base in Berkeley, California, began to push the extension of the OTO throughout America and Europe. A rival group also claimed ownership of the OTO Charter, and announced that it formally recognized Kenneth Grant as its official head.

A long battle ensued over who was the legal custodian of the charter and in 1985, a US Federal court judge finally ruled that the OTO copyright was owned by McMurtry's Californian Agape Lodge, which – unknown to the judge but certainly known to the CIA and the FBI – had drawn members from many scientific and academic circles in America.

After the court hearing, the satanist Michael Aquino – head of his own officially recognized satanic church, the Temple of Set – wrote in his magazine *Scroll of Set* Vol. XII no. 5 in October 1986: 'While sitting in the courtroom watching Judge Legge preside sternly over the slug-out, I couldn't help wondering if he had any idea he was ruling on which group had legal claim to anal sex as the supreme religious sacrament in the United States.'

In January 1992, I met one of the OTO's English masters. He refused to describe any of the ritual, although these days much of it is available in books for those who really wish to discover it. Other than that which I have already mentioned, there seems little point in repeating what to the lay reader is a meaningless ramble of chants and varied sexual rituals. However, though reluctant to discuss either the identity of himself and others, or the 'secrets' of their lodges, he did mention a few interesting facts:

Membership of the OTO in the mundane sense – i.e. at grass roots level – has reached its highest levels in 1991 with lodges throughout the United States, Britain and Europe, notably in Germany, Switzerland and Yugoslavia, with a few in Holland and France. There was especially renewed interest in Germany and Switzerland of late. By 1987, the international organization of Ordo Templi Orientis had undoubtedly infiltrated many levels of modern society. The most senior members who had achieved the highest degrees of knowledge were once also known as the Hermetic Brotherhood of Light. They were men and women drawn largely from academic, scientific and political circles or the leading professions. Today, there is a similar group representing the higher echelons of international occultism way above OTO and unconnected with it. Members – by invitation only – of a higher order, the ultimate secret society involves famous names in international politics and with members of European royalty among their membership. They in turn are associated with the infamous P2 Masonic Lodge which has undoubtedly taken, and accepted, some of the blame for activities originally inspired by this high-ranking occult fraternity based in Europe, simply so that the order would never be identified as all of the scandals broke involving Calvi and the death of Pope John Paul I. They are the inheritors of an occult order which goes back several hundred years and had to be protected. Two very senior European royal figures are said to be among the leading group because of ancestral connections, as was a member of the Reagan administration who was a direct contact between this group and the CIA. The object appears to be to quell the political power and influence of the Vatican.

To prove such statements is virtually impossible and conspiracy theorists could have a field day; the more one trawls through this maze of possibilities, the more one realizes that nothing can be ruled out. Below this level of hierarchy, who might be the Illuminati, and back at the normal functional level, are the many lodges whose activities are centred around lesser degrees of the order, in towns and cities throughout America, Britain and Europe.

Today, Crowley's own manifesto, first drawn up in 1910, is largely followed by those who are officially chartered groups:

> The OTO is a body of initiates in whose hands are concentrated the secret knowledge of all Oriental Orders ... Its chiefs are initiates of the highest rank and recognized as such by all capable of such recognition in every country in the world. The Order is international and has existing connections in every civilized country in the world.

There are now many official chartered lodges which conform to a central international organization whose Sovereign Sanctuary, or headquarters, is given as London and Miami.

The OTO is distinct from the Cult of Thelema, now similarly worldwide in its appeal and based upon the studies of Crowley's *Book of Law* and Thelemic ritual writings. Oxford has one of the largest followings of Crowleyana and Thelemic study groups – especially among the academia – and the city is also the home of a glossy occult magazine, available only on subscription, called *Nuit Isis* – which quotes Crowley's 'Do as thou wilt' slogan and describes itself as 'a Journal of the Nu Equinox'. It consistently drums home the message that Christian society has projected its own repressed dark side on the minority groups and religions and declares 'now more than at any time in recent history is there an urgent need for magicians everywhere to resist, or face the prospect of hiding in the shadows for another three hundred years.'

Many satanists say they are entirely justified in recognizing Crowley and his movement because of one of the names he used, Baphomet, which is the symbol adopted by the Church of Satan in 1967. And indeed, one offshoot organization which uses the OTO as a basis for its charter is the Ordo Templi Satanis.

America has by far the largest proliferation of OTO lodges spread right across the country. In Britain, I estimate that there is a membership of 7000 people involved in OTO lodges, though the number of temples, official and unofficial, can never be known because they operate in such strict secrecy. The rituals and temple practices vary. As I have said, many are no more harmful or important than a Friday night masonic meeting but as is the norm right through the occult traditions, there are no limits for those who wish to explore the dark and sexual–magical depths of Crowley-inspired rituals.

The great secrecy which surrounds the higher echelons of the order makes it virtually impossible to penetrate any senior lodge meeting, and indeed no person who has not been initiated into the OTO would be allowed to observe even the most simple of rituals.

Because of this secrecy, which is seldom broken – even by a deserter – it is virtually impossible to identify those at the top, although there are numerous worldwide camps or lodges which make no secret of their existence in magazines dealing with the occult. There remains, apparently, some competition for leadership of the OTO between Europe and America. In 1992, it was in the hands of a group of senior adepts in Britain including the author and public schoolmaster Gerald Suster, who by then had already attracted some of the media attention that has been the lot of his predecessors.

Suster is the author of *The Legacy of the Beast* on Crowley and more recently *Crowley's Apprentice*, on Israel Regardie whom Suster first met in 1966 at the age of fifteen.

Regardie contributed to the strong revival of the occult with his huge history of the Hermetic Order of the Golden Dawn, which today is selling for hundreds of pounds a copy. His friend Gerald Suster, author of nine novels, a study of Hitler's occult ideas and a practising occultist since he was at Trinity Hall, Cambridge, found himself in the headlines during a series of misadventures in the late 1980s. First, he had travelled to the Turkish sector of Cyprus to visit a friend who was subsequently found dead. Police at first believed foul play might be involved, but this was eventually ruled out.

Suster, shocked by the circumstances of his friend's death, returned to England to take up a teaching post at the exclusive Boarzell Tutorial College in Sussex, where he spent a mere three months before his association with the OTO was brought to the attention of the school governors and he was removed from his job. The *News of the World,* reporting this development, made much of Suster's interest in the occult.

In Chris Bray's *Lamp of Thoth* magazine, the following tribute was paid to Mr Suster who was recognized as the head of OTO: 'His knowledge of the Golden Dawn system of magic is immense and his stewardship of OTO is underpinned by several excellent and studious books on occultism.'

In a 1991 issue of another occult magazine, *Chaos International,* produced by Temple Misanthropy, London Pact of the Illuminates of Thanateros, an example of Mr Suster's interests was highlighted. Magazine editor Ian Read included a long article by Suster centred around his review of a book entitled *The Correct Sadist,* by Terence Sellers (in spite of her name, Sellers is a female). The article was a long discourse on a subject in which he clearly had a considerable fascination and was written with a use of expletives and graphic descriptions that certainly would not be permissible in the halls of Boarzell Tutorial.

He ends the article reaffirming his own personal commitment to the doctrines of Aleister Crowley, by quoting another of his most famous statements. Suster declares that he is going to read more of Terence Sellers' work and would try to get her novels, *The Obsession* and *The Degenerate.* Although he intends to read them with his 'finest attention', his greatest hope is 'that she realizes the basic truth Love Is Law, Love Under Will.' (The latter phrase comes from the Crowley writings.)

Meanwhile, the Cult of Thelema – described by another of my interviewees as 'sometimes a pain in the ass, often literally' – inspired by Crowley, continues to grow with a similar worldwide interest. It is a body of mystical and magical doctrine that is separate from all other Crowley-associated groups because it was not his creation. He merely gave it shape through his *Book of Law* for which the two key phrases for the Cult of Thelema remain: 'Do What Thou Wilt shall be the whole of the law' and the one above used by Suster to sign off his article on sado-masochism, 'Love is Law, Love Under Will.' It is a high-blown set of deep and complicated theories concerning man's hidden psychological and mystical powers, much of which can be released by ritual sex.

So the tradition lingers on. To this day, anything that bears traces of the Crowley stamp of invention will be liberally applied with what the Thelemics might describe as 'phallic consciousness' and which, in Crowley's case, could be summed up in one word: Depravity.

CHAPTER TWELVE

SECRET SOCIETIES

The mystery of secret societies has long been a part of man's total fascination with the occult and it would indeed be wrong to give the impression that all forms of magical and mystical endeavour follow the extremes of the dubious doctrines of Aleister Crowley. They do not. There are many other pursuits and secret organizations which are more correctly described as mystical or esoterical, embracing a wide variety of students and scholars seeking the knowledge of Western inner traditions. Then, more in tune with popular suspicions about secret societies, there are also occult groups whose object is clearly to influence the world order, by infiltrating the Church, politics, pressure groups and the business community. If the latter sounds more akin to the beliefs of a rampant conspiracy theorist, it is only necessary to scratch gently below the surface of many events in recent times to discover some link with secret societies.

They fall largely into two categories which we will examine more fully in the narrative of this chapter.

The first is almost impossible to penetrate but evidence gleaned from occasional defectors and mishaps suggests the existence of an international brotherhood whose members and agents are operating in the upper echelons of the world establishment circles. This brotherhood is not of a sensational or world-threatening order, far from it; but it exists, has a voice among powerful bodies in international politics and is strong enough, too, to have become deeply involved in the various scandals that have enveloped the Vatican these past two decades. Its aims have been varied and covert, ranging from utopian dreams to profound reactionary intent, and historically their importance to the destiny of European courts and governments, and in the foundation of the United States of America, is often overlooked.

The second level of secret societies is pure occult, based on old traditions, with meetings of like-minded individuals who are moved by the romanticism of gathering for the purpose of divine illumination and reaching out for contact with non-human entities, either in their spiritual or physical manifestation. The idea of these groups of men and women meeting secretly for mystical or occult pursuits, adorning themselves in their expensive robes and calling themselves by obscure titles lends itself to colourful theories about what they actually do before their secret altars. Fuelled by images from Denis Wheatley's imagination and novels and a few indifferent movies, it is easy to conjure up the view that all that is secret must be evil. This is not the case, yet activities of these occult groups are fascinatingly sinister.

The basis for much of the ritual secrecy and traditions of occult societies invariably leads us back to the famous Order of the Knights Templar, formed initially in 1119 for the purpose of protecting pilgrims travelling to the Holy Land and which subsequently became noted both for its military prowess against the Saracens and the immense wealth of those who joined. Baldwin I, King of Jerusalem, provided them with headquarters in his palace, which was said to be part of the Temple of Solomon.

Much of the modern ceremonial ritual in a variety of secret lodges goes back to the Knights Templar. The OTO, as we have already discussed, can be traced in part to the Templars. And yet, the Knights Templar are also the claimed ancestors of modern satanists, a fact which is decidedly hard to prove, though within an organization so large there may well have been diverse groups who followed their own calling. The knights, largely from France and England, joined the order over a period of many years. They had a system of leadership with a Grand Master, knights, chaplains, sergeants, craftsmen, seneschals and commanders. The order had its own clergy and its meetings were held in the strictest secrecy. Unmarried knights wore a white mantle with a red cross while others wore a black mantle with a red cross.

The brotherhood established orders in virtually every Latin country, drawing membership from all over Europe. It also became a great trading agency and though originally the Roman Catholic Church actually supported a number of secret societies who were Christian-based, the power that the Templars began to wield became the fear of successive popes and of European noblemen. Philip IV of France began a series of attacks against the Knights Templar and his campaign was given official blessing by the election of Pope Clement V (1305–1314) who renounced the Templars as immoral heretics.

Stories were already circulating that the Templars, behind the closely guarded doors of their temples and meeting places, indulged in the most offensively blasphemous rituals said to be directed totally towards the reversal of Christianity itself. They were said to worship a goat-like idol, the Baphomet, anointing it with the fat of murdered children, roasting children and eating them, laying women across their altars for the most violent forms of indecencies to satisfy their lust for life-blood especially at times of menstruation; they were said to have indulged in homosexual rites and other various claims alleged they stamped the Holy Cross under foot, spat and urinated upon it and used the Mass as the basis for their own worship – later to be known universally as the Black Mass.

Actual proof of these events is largely contained in the confessions received under torture which followed the arrest of the Templars' Grand Master Jacques de Molay on the orders of Philip IV. He and 140 of his brethren were imprisoned in Paris, tortured and then executed en masse. De Molay, under extreme torture, confessed to speaking against Christianity but denied depravity. In 1314, he was brought out on to a scaffold in front of Notre Dame cathedral and ordered to repeat his confession in front of the crowds and accept a sentence of life imprisonment. On the scaffold, he burst into a rage of anger and protested innocence of all charges and thus signed his own death warrant.

The order was given that he should be burned at the stake and as the flames licked his body he summoned the King of France and the Pope in his dying breath to meet him at the Bar of Heaven. Since both of these men died a matter of months afterwards, some writers have used that to show Jacques de Molay's innocence.

Pope Clement V, a Frenchman and the only Pope to live at Avignon, sent orders to every country where the Templars operated, instructing that they should be arrested and charges of heresy and sorcery brought against them. The process continued long after Clement's death and hundreds of knights were brought to trial, tortured and executed. The vast wealth of the Templars went largely into the hands of the French royal family and to the coffers of the other crowned heads of Europe. Hundreds of subsequent books on the subject of the Templars have yet failed to unravel the truth of its ritual, though many writers seem to agree that the Templars had rejected Christianity in favour of at best the dualistic teaching of Gnosticism, and at worst were indulging in devil worship. What remained to be handed down and revived, especially in the twentieth century, were the *rumours* of ritual and dastardly happenings which many of today's extremist followers of the Knights Templar seem prepared to believe and accept with some enthusiasm.

One of the more important traditions handed down by the Knights Templar concerns an instruction for future secret societies. On the day of the burning to death of the Grand Master Jacques de Molay a pact was made and communicated to all surviving Templars who had now gone to ground. The instruction was clear – that the Order of the Knights Templar should be continued in perpetuity. It said simply that surviving Templars should thereafter fight for the destruction of the papacy and certain kingdoms of Europe whose monarchs stripped the order of its wealth and murdered its members.

This tradition, it was said, should be handed on to descendants of the order, who at various points in history have included satanists and a diverse calling of occultists. What remained of the Templars went into limbo and the deepest secrecy, surfacing occasionally and surrounded constantly by rumour, but little discernible fact. The most secret of all secret societies, the Illuminati, is known to have existed in the fifteenth century when the title is first recorded to indicate an organization of people who 'possessed the light' or were in contact with the most supreme force. The Illuminati came to the fore again during the French Revolution when a group of subversives were discovered to be using the cloak of Freemasonry for occult practices and rituals to attack the monarchy and the Church. They were said to have been given favourable shelter in Austria, in particular, and according to Maynard Solomon's biography, *Beethoven*, the Illuminati paid Ludwig to write an appreciation for the Emperor Joseph von Habsburg entitled 'Illuminated Monarch'.

Throughout the last three centuries, Illuminati agents were said to be operating at every level of European politics, and drove Pope Leo XIII in the last years of the nineteenth century to proclaim that secret societies were working to 'establish Satan's kingdom on earth', an accusation which was a direct throw-back to the age of the Knights Templar; and that dictum still exists today. The Roman Church continues its virulent outspokenness against the secret societies it has blacklisted, such as the Illuminati, the OTO, the Golden Dawn, the Rosicrucians and others whose intent was to infiltrate and influence the running of the Roman Church and assert its own ideals. The Illuminati have travelled through various groups and in many guises, and it is virtually impossible to identify membership or the controlling organization, if indeed one exists.

One known group adhering to the 'old Templar traditions' is the child of the Psychosophical Society which claimed to be the true successor of the Illuminati. It was founded in Switzerland in 1950 by Herman Joseph Metzger, who was also a member of the OTO. Metzger anounced the reconstitution of Ordo Illuminatorum, the World League of Illuminati which originally came into being in Berlin in 1893 and was a forerunner to the OTO, the latter having been formed as a rival faction by Theodore Reuss after a split among the leaders. It was Reuss, it will be recalled, who later approached Crowley. The OI continued until it was disbanded on the orders of the Gestapo in 1934, and was revived in Switzerland and Austria after the war. The links with the OTO were healed, and in October 1973 an edict by the Psychosophical Society stated that the OI had existed since the sixteenth century and today comprises the World League of Illuminati, the OTO, the Gnostic-Catholic Church and the Fraternis Rosicrucian Antiqua . . . 'and the task we have undertaken is to transfer the Order on to the next generation in all its purity . . . thus it is authenticated that the OI unites all three named branches within itself . . .'

There are, however, other even more clandestine groups who claim heritage from the original Illuminati whose influence, experienced particularly in the eighteenth and nineteenth centuries, has certainly not been confined to the dustbins of history. Piers Compton, a former editor of the Catholic newspaper *The Universe*, quite recently alleged that the infiltration of the Roman Catholic Church by the Illuminati remains and points to the link of the Illuminatist symbol of an eye in a triangle which was used on the personal cross of Pope John XXIII. Compton had also alleged that dozens of leading clerics are members of secret societies, and as recently as 1976, seventy-five leading members of the Catholic hierarchy were said to belong to clandestine organizations. The controversial and right-wing Archbishop Lefebvre, one of the leaders of the Catholic traditionalist movement, has long proclaimed that secret societies operate within the Vatican.

The hotbed of intrigue, rumour and gossip at the Vatican which over the past few years has involved the death/assassination of Pope John Paul I, the suicide/murder of Robert Calvi over the scandal of the Banco Ambrosiana and the assassination attempt on John Paul II, invariably links the Propaganda 2 (P2) Lodge and various Intelligence agencies like the KGB and the CIA with a scandal which is too immense to expound here, nor is it suitably part of this book. What can be said, however, is that occult groups working within the traditions of the Illuminati represent a definite consideration which is quite often overlooked by historians of these events.

As to its base of operations today, these are as secret as the society itself but I am assured they are widespread and as active as ever.

Another of the most mysterious of orders with lingering connections in today's occult world is the elusive yet often mentioned Fraternity of the Rosy Cross, the Order of Rosicrucians – a sideshoot of which was named by the Psychosophical Society as being a sponsor of the OI. The Rosicrucians are even more secretive than the Illuminati and their existence was first noted with the publication of a pamphlet published in Kassel, Germany, in 1614. Entitled *Fama fraternitatis*, the unsigned tract which became widely circulated told the curious story of Christian Rosenkreuz, a pious and educated young man born in 1378, who spent his early adult life on journeys to the east and returned to Germany as a master of mathematics and the possessor of certain secret occult knowledge. He gathered seven disciples around him; his brotherhood went into the world to perform good works – one of them came to England and cured the Duke of Norfolk of leprosy – and to spread the word among communities. They pledged to reunite annually, to elect worthy successors and to maintain secrecy. The *Fama* went on to describe the discovery, 120 years after Christian Rosenkreuz's death at the age of 106, of his perfectly preserved corpse in the building the fraternity had used as its headquarters. A second pamphlet, *Confessio fraternitatis* appeared in 1615, explaining the purpose of the brotherhood, and one year after that, a third was published, telling of a mysterious allegory with an occult overlay. The pamphlets were thought to have been the work of a well-known German theologian of the period, Johann Valentin Andreä and the effect on seventeenth-century Europe was incredible. Because of the secrecy and the mystery, thousands wanted to know more and were desperate to join, though they did not know what they were joining. The Order of the Rosy Cross was so élitist that no one could actually find it, and people even began advertising their willingness to be contacted by bona fide members, so that they might join. This enthusiasm reached such hysterical proportions that the authorities banned the order, even though they could not prove that it even existed.

And yet, interest in the Rosicrucians and the Order of the Rosy Cross is as widespread as it has ever been. Rosicrucian Orders have sprouted all over the world, but no one really knows their true basis. Some modern members regard the story of Rosenkreuz as a fable which was invented to reveal the existence of the Rosicrucians, arguing that they date back to the era of the Templars and gleaned their esoteric knowledge from the same eastern schools of mystery and mysticism. Alleged Grand Masters of secret Rosicrucian Orders are said to have included the magician Agrippa, Paracelsus and Dr John Dee, the Italian writer Dante, Sir Francis Bacon, Sir Christopher Wren, Benjamin Franklin and

Lord Bulwer-Lytton, the nineteenth-century statesman and novelist. In fact, the Rosicrucians were said to have collected members, through the ages, in positions of far greater power and influence than the Illuminati. Today's inheritors of the Rosicrucian legend who claim specific descent from their founding fathers of the Middle Ages are complemented by a large and diverse number of non-affiliated groups. The official organizations who are made up of secret societies adhering to the traditional rosicrucianism include Rosicrucian Fellowship, the Fraternity of the Rosy Cross, the Ancient and Mystical Order of the Rosy Cross and the Lectorium Rosicrucianum.

Most have connections throughout Europe and latterly in the United States and one, the Fraternity of the Rosy Cross, claimed descent from a member of the OTO. No such connection is claimed by the most public of these normally very secret groups, the Ancient and Mystical Order of the Rosy Cross whose membership is an indication of the current revival in these mystery religions and semi-secret societies. In 1992, AMORC alone boasted some 60,000 members and operates from its headquarters in San Jose, California, with affiliated lodges in Britain, France, Germany, Australia and South Africa.

A similar revival has been experienced in the Golden Dawn occult traditions, another of the late nineteenth-century arrivals, born out of a mixture of Templar ritual and Kabbalistic beliefs. Today, there are several groups who are preserving the traditional beliefs of the Hermetic Order of the Golden Dawn which was founded in 1887 by three British Freemasons, Dr William Wynn Westcott, a coroner, S. L. MacGregor Mathers, a translator of occult texts, and William Robert Woodman, a physician, who were also members of the Rosicrucian Society of England.

The Golden Dawn's traditions and rituals were naturally based upon Masonic tradition and Rosicrucian legend. The three founders claimed it was based primarily upon another mysterious document, a cipher manuscript found in a second-hand bookstall. The author of the manuscript was not identified but it was obviously someone with a very intense knowledge of the Kabbalah, alchemy, astrology and the magical theories of Eliphas Levi. This document provided the basic rudiments for the Hermetic Order of the Golden Dawn, and the founders were allegedly aided by another occultist named Fräulein Anna Sprengel, a resident of Germany who claimed to be the only surviving holder of the true secrets of the Order of the Rosy Cross.

Out of this was founded Britain's first real occult order of the Golden Dawn, and it immediately attracted some of London's sophisticates, writers and poets who were to immerse themselves in the discovery and in what was called rejected knowledge – that based on superstition or magic and held in contempt by the establishment. The Golden Dawn had colourful and ornate rituals and its purpose was 'to obtain control of the nature and power of my own being'. Its prominent membership included the poet William Butler Yeats and the actress Florence Farr, who were at one in objecting to the initiation of Aleister Crowley, who eventually entered through the Paris lodge, then headed by MacGregor Mathers. These internal disputes and feuds eventually brought about its destruction in the early twenties and it was not until the revival in occult interest in the second half of the century that the Golden Dawn became the subject of renewed interest. Aleister Crowley's former secretary, Israel Regardie, wrote a massive four-volume account of the Golden Dawn's aims and rituals for which there is a steady sale today at well over £100 a set. Though the existence of a Golden Dawn operating charter is disputed, there is a number of groups which claim to be preserving its traditions, with lodges in America and Europe.

What is common to all, however, is the suspicion of badness whenever secret societies are discussed, a generalization not always justified but almost inescapable.

CHAPTER THIRTEEN

THE MYSTICAL QABALAH

The Jewish mystical Kabbalah is at the heart of virtually every system of magical belief, corrupted and distorted though it may have been to make it fit a variety of applications. In its occult form – known as the Qabalah – it exists as one of the major secret societies with temples worldwide.

Legend has it that the Kabbalah originated as the secret wisdom God gave to Adam and Moses and it was passed orally from one generation to another through the ages, added to by scholastic writings and practices and repackaged at the start of the 1900s for present-day seekers of the tradition and its occult offshoot. It survived in spite of comparatively little early documentary evidence to confirm even its existence, and it has been criticized and attacked by many Christian and Jewish scholars alike for its secrecy and complexity, and in particular for claiming its original source is God.

The first known written work is the 'Sepher Yetzirah', an account of the creation of the Universe, which legend attributes to Abraham. But the first known work of substance did not appear until the thirteenth century when Rabbi Moses de Leon wrote a thirteen-volume work entitled the Zohar – the Book of Splendour – which was supposed to be a sort of biblical commentary about the teachings of a Kabbalistic rabbi in the second century, though now generally accepted as having been the work of de Leon himself.

Anyway, this veritable goldmine of stories, poems, anecdotes and visions that made up the Zohar became central to the whole future of cabbalistic teachings. It was embraced by the Jewish Kabbalists in Spain, and then Northern Italy. Hasidics in eastern Europe used it as the original basis for their system of prayers, meditation, chants and dances. For centuries, the key texts of the Kabbalah have been used by seekers of the meaning of such intriguing mystical experiences as dreams, visions, altered states of awareness, spiritual ecstasy and prophecies.

All of these attributes ensured that the Kabbalah would also become central to magical study and it was developed in the occult world by devotees like Agrippa, Paracelsus, Nostradamus, Levi and then recently by twentieth-century occultists. As a result, the Qabalah is no longer in any way the preserve of orthodox Jewry, nor is it Christian in any regularly accepted sense, but belongs more to the magical system which evolved during the last two hundred years.

Before we go any further, perhaps I should explain for those who, like myself initially, are confused by the various spellings of the word itself – and the different meaning of each spelling. The original word is 'Kabbalah' which usually refers to the Jewish mystical tradition of prayer and the study of esoteric teachings on the whole body of Jewish sacred writings and other scriptures. The spelling 'cabbala' is generally applied when discussing the spread of this knowledge into Christian circles during the Renaissance period.

The word 'Qabalah' is applied to the occult traditions of the Kabbalah, which began to emerge as a specific path at the beginning of the nineteenth century when practising magicians brought the various elements together – kabbalah, gnostism, alchemy – for what many occultists now consider to be the purest form of magical working. The ancient traditions of the Kabbalah have expanded into the occult subculture over the centuries, becoming established as the backbone of genuine magic as performed by the true devotees of the so-called magical arts. Such is its fundamental importance to many occult traditions that without the powerful psychological system of the Kabbalah, the very concept of ritual magic would collapse.

Today there are literally dozens of scholarly books by renowned authors and rabbis in a variety of languages, offering the student of the Kabbalah every conceivable type of reading matter, from translations of the original text through to psychological principles for the application of its mysteries. The majority have been published in the past twenty years when interest in the esoteric mysteries began to increase rapidly, especially in America, and was spurred on again, more recently, by the advent of New Age thinking.

In popular occult terms, the British author Dion Fortune wrote the simplest and most famous guide to the traditions with her book, *The Mystical Qabalah*, published in 1938. This and Crowley's *Magick in Theory and Practice*, became two of the major signposts for modern magicians. Today's intelligentsia of the occult or the intellectual students of the Kabbalah may regard Dion Fortune's book with some derision, since it simplified matters so much that her version of the Qabalah did not bear a huge resemblance to the original form.

However, she had modernized the whole proceedings to match the latest occult ideas, and with the lack of any other explicit and easy to follow ritualistic work on the market, the book became a best seller in occult terms. By 1971 alone, it had been reprinted thirteen times and has gone into many editions since.

In many respects, Dion Fortune was as important to the occult world as Aleister Crowley – and for different reasons and qualities. Her work and her writings, especially her novel, *Priestess*, were influential in the moulding of new pagan witch covens.

In the world of the magician, she was best known for the formation of the Fraternity of the Inner Light which practised very much on the lines of the lesser mysteries of the Golden Dawn, with some elements of the Qabalah mixed in, and which still exists today though in altered form.

She had many theories about the abilities of powerful minds. Everyone, she once wrote, possessed magical capabilities but, fortunately, most were not aware of them; more fortunately those that were did not delve deeply enough to discover their true potential.

In bringing the Fraternity to life, she herself was subjected to what she described as 'magical attacks' by an opponent and eventually she was to accuse her attacker of murder by magic.

It was an interesting coincidence, therefore, that when I began researching the occult Qabalah I came across a reference to the following entry in an old copy of the *Occult Review*:

> The mysterious death of a student of occultism, Miss N. Fornario, is receiving the attention of the authorities at the present time. Miss Fornario was found lying nude on a bleak hillside in the lonely island of Iona. Round her neck was a cross secured by a silver chain and near at hand lay a large knife which had been used to cut a large cross in the turf. On this cross the body was lying. A resident of London, Miss Fornario seems to have made her way to Iona for some purpose connected with occultism . . . one newspaper report alludes to mysterious stories on the island about blue lights having been seen in the vicinity where her body was found and there is also the story of a cloaked man . . .

Miss Fornario was a very close friend of Dion Fortune and behind this brief note in the *Occult Review* in January 1930 lay another of those fascinating stories of the occult that are barely believable, yet seem to have no explanation other than the magical. Dion Fortune, whose real name was the less romantic Violet Firth, had been a prominent member of the occult scene from her early twenties when she studied for a while with Crowley. In 1920, she joined the Alpha Omega Lodge of the Order of the Golden Dawn which was mushrooming, with temples being formed throughout the United Kingdom and America. The lodge had been founded by Moina Mathers, who collected royalties from each charter; she was the widow of the former head of the Golden Dawn MacGregor Mathers, who was carried off by the influenza epidemic in 1918.

The two women fell out and Fortune went off to form her own group, the Fraternity of the Inner Light, using some of the Golden Dawn rituals.

Very soon, she claimed to be under attack from Moina Mathers who, according to Dion Fortune, was using black magic to launch a psychic attack upon her. She described the attacks in articles in the *Occult Review* though she did not name Mrs Mathers, merely describing her as a person she once considered a friend. She wrote: '. . . some very curious things began to happen. We became most desperately afflicted with black cats. They were not hallucinatory cats for our neighbours shared in the affliction, and we exchanged commiserations with the caretaker next door who was engaged in pushing bunches of black cats off the doorstep and windowsill with a broom, and declared that he had never seen so many or such dreadful specimens. The whole house filled with the horrible stench of the brutes. Two members of our community at that time went out to business every day and at their offices in different parts of London, they found the same penetrating reek of the tom-cat.'

Dion wrote that at first she attributed the plague of black cats to natural causes and concluded that some local female cat was the attraction, until one morning when she was going upstairs after breakfast she saw a 'gigantic tabby cat twice the size of a tiger coming towards me . . . it appeared absolutely solid and tangible; I stared at it petrified for a second and then it vanished.' She realized it was a simulacrum – a thought form that was being projected by someone with strong occult powers, and being picked up by her own sensitive reception. Fortune went on: 'Feeling decidedly uncomfortable, I asked one of the household to join me and as we sat in my room meditating we heard the cry of a cat. It was answered by another and another and another. We looked out of the window and the street as far as we could see was dotted with black cats waiting and howling in broad daylight. I rose up, gathered my paraphernalia and did an exorcism, then and there. At the end we looked out of the window again. The visitation was at an end.'

It was a temporary respite. The battle of wills between the two women occultists continued for many months, and on one occasion, as she retired to bed, Dion Fortune discovered claw marks all over her back. She wrote that Mrs Mathers was 'well known for her astral attacks' and several other opponents had suffered similar discomfort.

Later Dion Fortune stated categorically that Mrs Mathers was responsible for the murder of a young woman member of the Alpha Omega Lodge, on whom she unleashed her psychic attacks. The victim was thirty-five-year-old Netta Fornario, who was deeply committed to the search for inner fulfilment. She was one of the twenties freedom girls who felt they could do anything. In October of 1929, she decided she was going to travel to the spiritual island of Iona, off the west coast of Scotland, where she stayed at a local boarding house run by a Mrs Effie MacRae. It is believed she was trying to escape psychological attacks.

Initially she went out walking among the heather, but then she remained in her room for some days. Mrs MacRae suspected that her lodger was carrying out mystical practices and this was confirmed one day when Miss Fornario confided that she had fallen into a deep trance which had lasted some considerable time, and if it happened again Mrs MacRae should summon the local doctor.

Netta remained on the island for two months where she was soon a familiar wandering figure. But as the days passed she became increasingly agitated and one Sunday morning, she rose early and seemed to be in a state of panic. She informed Mrs MacRae that she would be returning to London as soon as possible as she was convinced that certain people were intending to do her harm telepathically.

Later in the day, Netta had calmed down and announced that she had decided to cancel her departure and stay on for a while. The following Monday morning, Mrs MacRae discovered that Netta was missing from her room and later that day the villagers began searching for her. It wasn't until the following day that her body was found close to the remains of an ancient village. She had obviously been running frantically, because the soles of her feet were torn and bleeding. She lay face upwards on the cross that had been carved in the turf, and her right hand still held a large steel knife with which she had apparently carved the cross on which she lay; and there, according to the local doctor, she died of a heart attack.

Dion Fortune had no doubt that Netta's death was due to astral attacks; she claimed that there were scratch marks on the woman's body that were similar to those she had received herself and she was not backward in pointing the finger at Mrs Mathers, whom she believed had long ago stumbled towards the 'left-hand path' of occultism and was using black magic for vengeful and malicious purposes.

The point of this story is that in any of the occult traditions, the temptation towards the left-hand path, the weird science of black magic, is ever present, yet to the uninitiated like myself it seems unthinkable that a woman with occult powers can, as Fortune suggested, be sitting miles away sending telepathically controlled disturbances to the mind of another person.

The question came up when I interviewed Canon Dominic Walker, vicar of Brighton, who is one of the Church of England's leading authorities on the occult. Unlike the more high-profile Christian fundamentalists who lead a very public campaign against the occult, he positively shuns popular publicity and never reveals the details of the many case histories of those who have suffered occult disorders. He quoted cases he has known where it was possible to activate some deep trauma locked away in the human subconscious by the arrival of a postcard with perhaps symbols or a specific picture printed on it, or even by a telephone call from the initiator of ill-will.

We will meet Canon Walker later on, but I mention him now to demonstrate that such matters cannot be dismissed out of hand, especially today when witches and occultists intent on bad behaviour are quite likely to utilize their powers of hypnosis. The point that Dion Fortune often made was that all magicians at some time or other faced the temptation of the left-hand path, and they could be dragged further under the influence of bad forces almost before they were aware of what was happening. Her books are packed with material which she details in a straightforward, matter-of-fact way, without colourful language, as if there could be no question of disbelieving her accounts of occult happenings.

She thought it quite possible, for example, that creations in the imagination of strong-minded occultists could actually take on a life form of their own. She called these apparitions 'elementals' and quoted her own experience of how she lay on her bed one day thinking unpleasant thoughts of a person who had done her a disservice. Suddenly, a large wolf-like form materialized in the half-light of the room, sitting on the hearth rug waiting to do her bidding. She realized that she was 'at the dividing of the ways and if I were not careful would take the first step on the left-hand path.' The apparition remained with her for twenty-four hours and presented what she described as the 'opportunity for an effectual vengeance'. Instead, she decided to banish the manifestation and forgive the woman who had been in her thoughts. As far as is known, Miss Fortune was not given to drinking to excess.

The point that she made was that in the Qabalah, the intellect and imagination were placed on a higher level than the supposed magical abilities of the human mind and those who allowed the latter to control the negative aspects of their lives were eventually likely to succumb to character disintegration – a fact which has all too often become apparent in the various stories recounted so far in this volume.

That point is not lost among many of those who follow cabbalistic teachings today, and their search seems largely to be for an expansion of knowledge. As ever, there are those who treat the ritual meetings in a Qabalah temple as a continuing quest to contact non-human elements or achieve an actual manifestation of a spirit. Qabalistic practices, in the occult sense, are not for everyone; they occupy a twilight area between mainstream religious beliefs. They are neither Jewish in the orthodox sense nor in any way Christian and belong more to the alternatives which had grown out of the old traditions of the Kabbalah, the training of the higher will.

There are many advanced and almost scholastic practising temples in the Western world today. But because there is no hierarchical system which links the orders, it is simply impossible to estimate how many actual followers there are today – probably tens of thousands in the United Kingdom and a very considerable number in North America.

It was however something of a surprise to discover while researching the recent history of the Qabalah that there was an active group of Qabalists on my own doorstep in Northampton. And in a way, having its activities explained to me by a mature, quietly spoken electronics engineer and Open University student in his carpet slippers was a rather unexpected development.

The mystical calling that has been the source of so many of the occult traditions and taxing Israelite mythology seemed, in view of its vast history and biblical connections, oddly out of place in a semi-industrial town in the heart of England. But then why should it be? It is practised by thousands of people who gather in their temples for occult festivals and can be seen, in comparison to the Crowley offshoots, as something more akin to white magic, though again there are no clear-cut boundaries.

The Northampton group, I discovered, had among it members Ted Bray (no relation to Chris Bray, mentioned earlier) who was also a leading light in the Open University Occult Group. When I interviewed him at his home in Corby, Northamptonshire, in 1991, he told me he had been a member of the Northampton Qabalistic Order of the Golden Cross for a number of years:

I have a developing interest in the esoteric side of religion, an interest which was curiously enough inspired by the study of physics. That is not surprising, I suppose, because a lot of academics in physics are now writing books on mysticism, and the forerunner of physics, alchemy, as a source of magical power. At an Open University summer school, when we were chatting about it over coffee, a group of interested people just agreed that we should get together and form a study group. It developed into a society and that's how it got off the ground. The idea was to have a society which was not purely an academic study group. We would generalize and we were not a practising group. The whole idea is that there are innumerable paths to go along and it is up to the individual to choose. Tolerance to others' views is, I suppose, a cornerstone of our own beliefs. The Qabalah is my preference but the study group looks at Wicca, paganism and occult in general. I began studying the Qabalah some years ago, though it was through an English group that I became interested. More recently I have also been attending meetings and weekend courses run by a Jewish group. My order in Northampton consists of a collection of people who do not conform to any sort of dogma which sets down rules and regulations that say what I can and cannot do. One of the oaths taken within the order has a rider which says that I would be asked to make no obligations to the order which conflict with my own conscience. In other words, you determine your actions according to your own conscience.

We meet as a family, really. We do not do an enormous amount of ritual work together; we have a form of work – worship I suppose in laymen's terms – in which everyone is involved. There is no lay community, every member participates in the workings of the group. We believe that as a group we can acquire power and energy through ritual working, though we tend to do it only when there is a very good reason for doing so.

When the ritual is used to generate power within our circle, it is usually for healing purposes, or perhaps for the benefit of the group as a whole if things seem to be going through a difficult patch within the group itself. You have to be very careful not to try to determine how things should be done. The common error, whether in the mystic esoteric religions or the mainstream ones, is for people to say, 'Oh God! I'm broke. I need money.' They do not ask for gentle movement one way or another; the general request is for someone to go and do something for them while they sit on their backsides. That's why we tend to avoid that kind of power-linked ritual.

We celebrate eight main festivals each year. There are four quarter-days which we recognize, the two solstices and the two equinoxes. These are Hermetic or Qabalistic in nature; the festivals which the Hermetic magician would be more likely to use for acquiring power. The four cross quarter-days are Candlemas, May eve, Lammas and Hallowe'en and we would celebrate those in a similar way to Wiccan or pagan ways. We follow a very similar pattern of work, opening a magic circle and so on. You can see immediate similarities within a working – after all, most of the magical workings are based on the same source. I know everyone claims that their system goes back to a particular antiquity, but I rather feel that they are a couple of hundreds years old at the most.

Personally, I feel that this need for pagans and others to reach back into pre-Christian times and beyond for their roots actually demonstrates an unsureness, a lack of confidence in what they are doing. They seem to have a need to get a status for what they are doing by going back in time, and going further back gives further status to their form of worship.

The Qabalah is talked of as being quite ancient. Most people think of it as being derived from ancient times. Present-day Qabalah is nothing like that; it may well be based on the study of the Bible – which it is; the first five books of the Bible form the basis of the Qabalah.

The way of the Qabalah is not a strict terminology handed down from the times of Adam or Moses. The Qabalah was first taught by God to a company of angels and when man fell from grace then it was taught by God to an Archangel; then it was taught to Adam, Eliza, Moses, David and Solomon. I subscribe quite happily to that theory, the overriding mythology, if you like, which explains the origins of Qabalah. But the modern-day Qabalah has taken on board various beliefs from Islam, Christianity and other religions; it is a living tradition.

The Qabalah is not aligned to Christianity or paganism. Within the Qabalah, we have the Tree of Life which begins with the basic belief 'I am that I am'. Creation is a mirror by which God sees itself and we are divine agents whose job it is to work towards and achieve perfection so that the image in the mirror has become perfected and the end creation will be reversed. It's expressed very nicely in a couple of lines which say 'Creation was the voice of God' and we must all find our way back before the echo dies away. To do that I don't need to have a tag of Christian, pagan or Jewish.

The Jews will argue, of course, that I cannot claim the Qabalah to be my religion; to most Jews it is not a religion but the mystical element to their religion. We would say it can exist on its own. It is also true that many claim the Qabalah has no basis, challenging the very fact that Adam was taught it by God. We would say that it doesn't matter, now, even if the Qabalah was founded on a total misunderstanding; any religion exists from what people put into it. When we converge our energies on to some form of belief, which in my case is the Qabalah, then we invest that power to work.

I believe the same of any religion. I believe that Christianity is based on a false premise. It was just something that was worked out by Paul and given its structure by the Emperor Constantine.

I do believe that the actual power which is invested in the

symbol of the cross with a crucified figure in on it, by millions of people who have a true faith makes a true faith – true Christianity – and I respect that, as I do any other religion. I have a lot of criticism for many of the establishment within the Church who are behaving in much the same way as big business, utilizing their power for very selective interests. True Christianity lies with the genuine, faithful people who are investing in that symbol of power, the cross, which doesn't need to have any true historical facts proven.

That is where we stand; ultimately there is a divine force that we reach out for. We have a massive amount of symbolism; the thought of worshipping some idol is a total anathema. We have a lot of symbols because the human mind is totally incapable of understanding what God is; so that is the difference – ours is a mystical journey of discovery.

Our temple, within which one would work, is an ordinary room converted for the purpose; the building isn't of material importance. The floor of the temple is covered in black and white squares, representing the kingdom and the Temple of Solomon.

We use a simple table with a cloth over it, candles and incense. The whole idea of magic is to shift consciousness. A ritual is just a way of doing that, to get oneself on a higher plane, another sphere, and with a small number of us working together, it all helps to get on to that higher plane.

When you say you are calling down power, and enter a magic circle and say 'Lord, I need so and so . . .' it tends to give the impression of superatural abilities. I don't believe in the supernatural. What we are about is entirely focused on the divine source and I would treat as pure symbolism the saying that the air is filled with spirits and demons waiting to be called down into our circle. The reality is that very few people have the ability or magical skills to achieve this. However, it is not uncommon for the group to try to tap the energy source and look for help in our own problems but invariably that help comes from within oneself, the energy and the power are self-created.

That is not to say that I would dismiss as total myth and legend stories of manifestations and the like. There is generally a basis of underlying truth. I would not dismiss the story of the

magician Agrippa having a genie in his laboratory which strangled his assistant. It's a wild and wonderful story and you believe
it or not; I am not convinced, yet I would not dismiss it out of
hand. I do believe that a magician who is particularly adept is
capable of producing a manifestation but whether that manifestation would continue to exist in the material world when the
magician was not present is unlikely. There are few people in the
Western world today who could achieve that kind of power. It
requires a lifetime of practice and study.

In general, though, the slide towards seeking this kind of
power, and it is black magic really, is the preserve of very few
people indeed. Those who pursue it do so with the deepest of
commitment and become so involved in it that they have little
time or thought for anything else. There are those people around,
but at the more general level of magical operation the pursuit of
what we would term black magic tends to come from one of two
situations: firstly magicians develop what general occultists who
have been working for years on the true course of magic would
regard as an unhealthy interest in the darker arts, or secondly,
through a change in personal circumstances, perhaps redun-
dancy or whatever, they try to operate their magical powers for
the benefit of material wealth and position.

It is very, very easy for someone in that situation to switch
to these dangerous endeavours.

It is easy to justify doing something; by going in little stages
to a degree whereby suddenly an upright member of society
becomes a criminal. The same thing can happen in magic. It is
not easy to say there is white magic and black magic; there are
shades of grey and believe me it is not easy for anyone to claim
they operate solely in white magic. There comes a time, maybe
for a very good reason, that you are moving into grey areas and
if you are not careful, on into black. You need constantly to look
at what you are doing. I think it is reasonable to assume there
are a goodly number of black magicians in a world where there
are constant problems.

That brings us back to one aspect a lot of people will admit
to in esoteric religions, which is the seeking of power; it remains
a fundamental reason why a lot of people join societies. After

they become involved, they discover that it is just a means to an end which has to be used with extreme caution. But there are people to whom power is everything, just as there are in everyday life.

Evil is not a word which can be defined on its own, nor is the use of the word devil. It should be added that there is a function for Satan on the Qabalistic Tree of Life.

Satan is the tester; he has a pretty awful job to do which is not as the evil devil figure portrayed in the Christian religion. Satan within Judaism is not the devil; his job is to operate on the Tree to make sure that people do not progress through the stages towards perfection until they have managed to purify themselves, to make sure that nobody gatecrashes until they have worked hard enough and developed their life, that they do not get up the Tree until they have achieved total purification. The Christian definition of the devil sometimes amuses me, sometimes confuses me. I sometimes think that Christians invented the devil to impose it upon other religions.

That is not to say that evil entities do not exist. They can exist in the same way that any spiritual entities exist; they are a projection of the course a person's superconsciousness or subconsciousness takes. Evil and good are two forces bearing down but I don't like the idea of personifying either of them as being separate outside influences; they are a whole, a question of balance.

The idea of the Qabalah is an extended one because basically there are four worlds; there is the divine world, an archangelic world, an angelic world and a mundane world. From the divine world, we exist as a divine spark which is enclosed within a spiritual covering which takes on the cloak of the soul and the soul then is born into a body. The soul continues to permeate between the material world and the divine world until perfection has been achieved, returning each time to a new body. The whole idea of creation is that God wished to perceive God, creation is the voice of God or a mirror; when God has seen himself and perfection, the soul is returned to the divine source. That is why, to me, it is so easy to accept Christ, Muhammad, Buddha; they are souls who have taken on physical life and got to the point where they have achieved all they possibly can in the physical world and their ultimate existence in a physical form, their spirit and soul became so highly developed, and shines out, so that they are returned to source.

Most established religions have worked for hundreds of years by removing the necessity and the initiative for people actually to think. If you have a religion which says you must come to church, make a donation, here's a book which you must abide by and at the end of your time, you will be cared for, you are removing all incentive for people to look any further. Christianity works very well for those who are prepared to move through life without challenging the basic Christian principles they were brought up to follow; there is a rule that covers virtually every aspect of their lives.

Once you move away from that premise, and begin to look beyond those rules and the basic premise of conformity, then you have constantly to debate with yourself and prod yourself into discussion. For the masses, therefore, Christianity or one of the other mass religions, is perfect.

I must admit that the Qabalah, Wicca, paganism or any of the esoteric religions, are no substitute. These are all pursued by people in small groups. It is impossible for this type of activity to be transposed on to community life as a whole, and because of that it perhaps follows that those of us who do pursue it will be viewed as secret societies, apart from the rest.

It would be too demanding for the mass population. Whatever consensus of morality that exists in the population would also take a knock because there would be no justification for it. If Christianity has one great asset in its proliferation of dogma, it is that it provides a reason, a justification for morality in society. If you think in terms of the numbers of the population, it has achieved tremendous stability, and if you took any of the major religions away, the effect would be to undermine society as a whole. But that does not stop smaller groups discovering their own way.

To a mass public, all of those who deal in the occult are seen as one and the same, which of course we are not. When the issue of satanic ritual abuse became feverishly debated in the news-

papers, everyone who was a member of any occult organization
suddenly fell victim to the possibility of accusation – simply
because of fear and ignorance of what we do, simply because our
form of worship is not known.

I feel quite strongly on that subject. The publicity that a
certain small group has achieved has detracted from the work of
the social services and the police. Once you instil in the minds of
the public that child abuse stems from satanic rituals you create
a situation whereby no one looks at other parts of society, so that
if you find that a family goes to church, you tend to say 'Oh,
there can't be any problem there . . .' and everybody concentrates
their efforts on looking for satanic ritual abuse and that allows
other children to suffer whose cases might have been investigated.

As far as the question of whether or not satanic ritual abuse
exists, it seems fairly obvious to me that it would exist. After all,
if you think of people who are going to set out to abuse children
or anyone, what better way than under cover of a satanic group;
not only does it help them to help justify their actions because
they can put it down to being part of necessary rituals, but also
it creates fear in the minds of children – scares them into not
saying anything. It instils this fear into them that there is
someone watching them all the time, and you have got to use the
fear of the supernatural to get that reaction in children.

Therefore, it seems probable to me that anyone who would
want to do that would find a pseudo black magic circle the ideal
cover. It seems reasonable to me to believe that this must exist.
Paedophile groups are said to have done exactly that; but these
cases are not widespread. They exist. We all know they exist but
not on the scale mentioned.

The following description is of a portion of a typical meeting of a
well-established Qabalistic order, one involving the evocation of
spirits on which its members place great reliance. What I now
describe is a ceremony recently performed inside a Temple of the
Qabalah, exactly as it happened, and for as long as the Qabalists
would allow it to be observed by an outsider.

The setting was dark, and the robes were black. To those
ignorant of the rites of evocation, this might have been regarded as

classic black magic. In fact, it was one of the highest forms of Qabalistic ceremony demanding enhanced psychological insight. Its leaders warned categorically that this should not be attempted unless 'group members are skilfully led and adequately prepared by training, study and practice . . . and, finally, long and extensive preparation and purification for the ritual itself . . .' There was no blood or sacrificial rites, no naked women or vestal virgins, just ritualistically induced energy.

Yet the very atmosphere was one which provided hair-raising possibilities: the room was dim and murky, with a chill air, and the men in black robes moved like shadows, silhouetted against the flickering light of a single bluish flame from a wick in tallow and the glowing embers of a small heap of charcoal in an incense brazier. The walls were draped in black cloth with no accoutrements whatsoever. Barely visible on the floor was the magic circle, nine feet in diameter, and facing directly to the north and fixed firmly to the wall was a large silver triangle with a mirror in its centre. All objects and tools used by the magician had been the subject of purification and energizing in readiness for the ceremony.

The brazier was set on the floor immediately in front of the triangle; from somewhere, a handful of an unknown substance was thrown on the brazier and a pungent multicoloured cloud rose upwards to the ceiling, a thin pall of smoke continuing in its wake. In the mirror was a dim reflection of one of the three figures in the circle; the large hoods of their robes hung loose, caught in a certain half-light. No face, no form was visible, just darkness so that one could easily believe whoever was inside was invisible.

They stood one behind the other; the first was gazing into the mirror with an intensity that might crack the glass; his eyes were not visible under the hood, but the gaze came piercing through regardless. He was The Receiver, and held two large silver candlesticks with red coloured candles which he lit from the small blue flame in the tallow. He held the candlesticks so that they were positioned one on either side of the triangle, and the smoke and the glow from the candles cast an eerie, ghostly reflection in the mirror.

Immediately behind the first man, two feet back, was the

second man, The Magus, who stood with his arms aloft, holding his wand. As he began to speak in a deep voice, the third man behind him crouched down on the floor near the blue flame. He produced from within his robes a pen and pad and by the light of the flame he prepared to take notes. He was The Scribe, and was required to take down every word that was spoken by The Magus, who was leading the rite of evocation to bring the spirit into the body of The Receiver who would then speak its words.

The bold voice of The Magus began the incantation, calling: 'A mighty prince but of good nature who is able to declare things past and to state things to come; to tell of things lost and to guide our hand to things hid . . .' The spirit they sought was Vassago, one of the seventy-two mentioned in the Lesser Key of Solomon.

The Magus spoke again, directly to the spirit; the spirit did not reply immediately and the Magus continued, twice, three times before Vassago responded, speaking through The Receiver . . . and The Scribe wrote furiously; not just as a reporter but an interpreter, too, transcribing ancient words that to the uninitiated ear may have no meaning, and recognizing old Hebrew names. But it is not gibberish – The Scribe has learned the meanings and he began to write . . .

And that is as far as I can take you on this particular ceremony; what was said remained within the walls of the temple. And if, as many disbelievers and sceptics are apt to do, one is tempted again to dismiss this as ridiculous mumbo-jumbo, it is worth considering for a moment that modern psychological research increasingly supports the view first propounded by Jung that there are autonomous powers within the human psyche capable of attracting and manifesting archetypes through their human soul; the boldest of modern psychoanalysts have even been brave enough to suggest that through their ritual, skilled magicians are capable of giving these entities a life form, either through The Receiver or by a total manifestation.

This extract from the higher forms of magic practised by the experienced Qabalah groups owes more to the occult and more recently acquired knowledge of magic and alchemy, as written in the grimoires of Renaissance magicians, than to the original cabbalistic traditions of orthodox Judaism, who view the Qabalah in the same way that Christians view paganism and witchcraft.

It is, however, untainted by some of the more extreme blood rites and attracts a high proportion of intellectuals among its practitioners who go in search of the inner mysteries of life, rather than the more colourful schemes of other extrovert magical traditions.

So that is the mystical Qabalah, a following which demonstrates that not all occult pursuits need to have connotations more akin to the extrovert rituals as devised by Aleister Crowley, who stole much from the cabbalists for his own purposes. There is one other thing that he stole, and which had also been taken up by the satanists, and that is the system for tarot cards.

These mysterious cards are used by occultists of virtually every persuasion, yet the origins are probably cabbalistic and the meanings of the symbols were kept a secret for centuries – even today the occult association of the pictures on these cards is not generally known. The tarot can be arranged to form the Qabalah Tree of Life and the existence of the tarot goes back into the mists of time, though the earliest packs date from around the fourteenth century when they were known to have been used by gypsies and aristocrats alike in France.

The tarot has also been found in Eastern civilizations, including India and China. They blossomed into popularity with the Swinging Sixties, after the publication of an explanation of their full and accurate meanings by Israel Regardie, in his examination of The Hermetic Order of the Golden Dawn which also had Qabalistic origins. Crowley's version was also published, though as usual he adapted old designs to suit his own magical and sexual tendencies.

In the eighties, the tarot became perhaps the most popular form of divination; literally hundreds of books have been written on the meanings of the cards. Witches especially identify with some of the characterizations, such as the Hangman, and the Horned God who is shown as the devil.

The Qabalah and the tarot have played their part in the

occult revival, though less spectacularly than some of the more virulent strains of esoteric and magical beliefs. Still denigrated by the Church, they nevertheless present a more acceptable face of occultism – but set against the activities outlined in the last section of this book, which now follows, the quiet students of the Qabalah and other esoteric lodges may be fighting a losing battle.

PART THREE

SATANISM

I have fourteen separate folders of documents, interview transcripts, articles on satanism, speeches by international psychologists, social workers and police specialists, over 2,300 pages from worldwide sources – mostly alleging or reporting on some form of satanic abuse, ritual, orgy, murder, sacrifice, genocide – or the denial of same. I have read pages and pages of material dealing with allegations of unspeakable acts, which have been relayed in the most horrific detail by the enemies of satanic worshippers, to which Satan's disciples have responded in vitriolic kind.

Satanism as it exists today is a modern invention, linking darkest witchcraft mythology to the magic of Aleister Crowley and others and tacking them on to historical examples of the black arts from which the extremist orders and devil cults have discovered a voluminous supply of inspirational detail and often despicable description. Theirs is a religion of self indulgence; never take stances, never get involved, work only for the benefit of oneself . . . and to hell with the rest.

CHAPTER FOURTEEN

THE RISE OF THE BLACK POPE

The stone has hit the bottom of my pond, deep in the murky, muddy waters of satanism and be warned – what follows now, without doubt, goes against almost every moral principle of modern Christian society. But then, that is the whole object of it. Leaders of Satan's various cults boast about that and what you have read so far in this book could, according to some satanic priests, be classed Sunday school material.

In Britain, I have located six established satanic orders whose activities and membership I will examine in this section; there are many other pseudo-satanic groups and a number of renegade covens and small groups which conform to no structure other than their own. Some are more likely to be paedophiles operating under the cloak of the occult.

Satanism proper is a stronger meat than any other occult pursuit and, according to true practitioners, a more honest code which eliminates the theory that there is a distinction between white and black magic and derides the apologists of the occult and most great works on the subject of magic which the Black Pope, Anton LaVey, claims are 'the by-product of brains festering with fear and defeat, written unknowingly for the assistance of those who really rule the earth and who, from their Hellish thrones, laugh with noisome mirth.'

LaVey, founder of the notorious Church of Satan, largely dismisses the majority of occult writings as 'guilt-ridden ramblings and esoteric gibberish by chroniclers of magical law'. As one of the key originators of modern satanism, he took out the darker texts of history, utilized some of the magic of the Qabalah, fed in some of the thoughts of Aleister Crowley and rearranged and repackaged them into a vehemently anti-Christian, anti-authority, anti-science, anti-society set of doctrines that can best be summed up by literally applying Crowley's 'Do what thou wilt' to which might be added 'but understand what you are doing'.

The last line I have personally attached and it is vital to all who enter the Temple of Satan, to regard this not merely as a warning about the very secret activity in which they will find themselves embroiled; it also applies to their eventual attempts to escape. Though it is denied by most satanists, a pact with the devil is clearly sought in this, one of the prime invocations:

In nomine Dei nostri Satanas Luciferi excelsi!

In the name of Satan, the Ruler of the earth, the King of the world, I command the forces of darkness to bestow their Infernal power upon me!

'Open wide the gates of Hell and come forth from the abyss to greet me as your brother/sister and friend!

Grant me the indulgence of which I speak!

I have taken thy name as part of myself! I live as the beasts of the field, rejoicing in the fleshly life! I favour the just curse of the rotten!

By all the Gods of the Pit, I command that these things of which I speak shall come to pass!

Come forth and answer your names by manifesting my desires!

Hail Satan!

Hail Satan! That is the cry of those in the Church dedicated to the Prince of Darkness. Let us peer further inside the temple as we follow the beginnings of an evening's ritual and magic at a meeting of the Black Pope at his temple in San Francisco:

There were eighteen or more people moving down a dark corridor to the ritual room, a black-painted chapel with a red ceiling, and the door banged shut behind them, and two hooded guards stood to attention; no one could enter, no one could leave. It was pitch black and there was an uneasy silence. Suddenly their ears were alerted by the sound of curious organ music which was a preamble to a loud cacophony of instruments and sound effects that shattered the consciousness. The music stopped and somewhere a gong was struck three times, and the room was lit by black candles giving sufficient glow to reveal the black-robed figure of the High Priest, Anton LaVey, and his eyes peering, scowling down at them. Off to the side of him was another startling feature, a coffin standing upright and lined with black silk and it was just possible to catch sight of an owl, its eyes glinting, perched inside. Was it stuffed or alive? The eyes of the congregation wandered back to the High Priest and on the wall behind him it was possible to make out the image of the Baphomet, of the same design as that supposedly used by the fourteenth-century Knights Templar, that of a goat's head inside an inverted pentagram and surrounded by five Hebrew letters. Below this, in the darkness and gloom and the half-light of the candles, the body of a naked, nubile young woman came into view. She moved slightly and, unlike the owl, was not dead. She was also wearing the Sigil of the Baphomet which dangled on a chain and lodged between her breasts; beside her were two naked female acolytes and in front of her was a priestess, covered in a black velvet robe but with her long golden hair flowing over the lowered hood; she was holding her arms outstretched, clasping a sword pointing down in front of her.

The organ played again, a Hymn to Satan, and the naked girl lying across a stone mantle representing the living altar in the Church of Satan, stretched full length and became the focal point of all that proceeded, and for all the concentration of the congregation. And over her body they spoke their words, these priests and disciples in their jet-black robes and drank their Elixir of Life from a silver chalice . . . *In nomine Dei nostri Satanas Luciferi excelsi* . . . The ritual was about to begin . . .

I offer this brief taste of an actual satanic ceremony described just as it happened, as a preamble to the much more detailed descriptions of satanic ritual to follow, because once again it is necessary to resort to the historical aspects of devil worship to achieve a clearer understanding of all that is done in the name of Satan today.

This very aspect of occultism has experienced the most rapid growth of all the traditions, especially among young people, so that worldwide there are dozens of active and well-organized satanic groups. While the mainstream and 'official' cults deny the charges of sacrificial ritual and blood-lust, there are many less formal covens of worshippers and pseudo-satanic sects, some resorting to a kind of ritual – as I will show – that provides the blood, sex and disgust that the detractors of satanic worship insist is prevalent; and on that point alone I must agree with the opposers. There is a lot of it about!

Conversely, it would clearly be very wrong to indicate that satanists are all bloodthirsty, child-molesting monsters.

The key to the absolute abhorrence with which Christians hold their satanic counterparts lies in the Christian religion itself, and indeed in most of the single-deity religions. Whereas the witches of the world and the occult fraternity at large regard themselves as inheritors of traditions based on the pre-Christian beliefs of the ancient pagans and Eastern mysticism and magic, satanists are basically the creation of the Bible; they originally acknowledged the Christian God, even if they do challenge his existence in biblical terms. They are united only in their contemptuous regard for Gardnerian and Alexandrian witchcraft.

Furthermore, it was the Christians themselves who were originally accused of killing babies for sacrificial rites – a charge which has been renewed in the twentieth century against the satanists.

In the earlier days of Christianity, when worshippers gathered in secret for fear of reprisal by the pagan communities, Christian groups were rumoured to be performing horrendous and licentious cannibalistic ceremonies. In Rome, when the early Christians met in secret, their churches were said to be filled with the aroma of blood from sacrificed animals and babies. They were said to worship the horrific head of a donkey, pay homage to the genitals of a priest and to have indulged in incestuous sexual practices.

There was apparently no evidence for these accusations, yet very soon after Christianity had become established exactly the same allegations reappeared – this time against the heretics,

THE RISE OF THE BLACK POPE

pagans and so-called devil worshippers. This has been the pattern throughout history, down to the present day when it exploded once again with the usual vehemence.

Throughout history, the worship of Satan has ranged from spasmodic to epidemic proportions, and it has remained one of the prime tasks of successive Popes to crusade against any form of devil worship. Satanism derives from early forms of gnostic dualism – the idea that the world was the creation and the sphere of the devil while God was left to rule heaven – and accusations of satanism were laid at the door of a fairly mixed bag of groups who were considered to be heretics, often consisting of those who had first accepted the true faith of Christianity and later rejected it to form their own version of non-Christian activity which was neither pagan nor magical in its roots.

These groups were made up of those whom the Roman Church believed had turned against Christianity and worked to a constitution that was nothing less than a complete reversal of everything that Christianity stood for – leading subsequently to the worship of the devil.

Satanism was not a form of witchcraft; the two were totally separate though they became confusingly combined during the years of the Inquisition and the hammering of witches. But out of this moulding of the two quite different pursuits came the modern-day satanic witches who use the fundamentals of witchcraft aligned to satanism rather than to pagan beliefs.

Anti-Christian sects, or at least those identified by the Roman Church as being anti-Christian, appeared under such names as the Waldensians in France and Switzerland, the Cathars and the Luciferians. They were variously accused of holding orgies of sex and blood-lust at their secret meetings and feasts, to celebrate the devil, and of trying to harm Christianity in any way that they could, by defilement, obscenity and even murder.

Word of these activities spread across Europe through the twelfth and thirteenth centuries until the arrival of the Inquisition and the onset of mass arrests for sorcery, heresy and devil worship that we have examined in earlier chapters. But many of the accusations were politically inspired and were used to depose power figures in the community; we have largely to rely upon descriptions extracted under torture and written up by ecclesiastical scholars, which eventually created a pattern of repression applied wholesale to witchcraft.

The Bishop of Troyes was among the earlier of the more famous cases, when in 1308 he was charged with satanic acts and of murdering Jeanne de Navarre, wife of Philip IV, by black sorcery. He was said to have enlisted the magical powers of a Jewish sorcerer and a witch to conjure up the devil and kill the queen by use of a wax effigy.

The Knights Templar, as we have seen, were also accused of satanism and after their destruction stories of what they were said to have done inspired the acts of others. It is easy to see the progression of claim and counter-claim throughout the ages, and the descriptions hardly varied. The earliest known satanist, following the destruction of the Templars, also lived in France. His name was Gilles de Rais, bodyguard of Joan of Arc, who admitted involvement in satanic ritual. He procured children aged between six and twelve and, according to his confession after he was arrested, he and his occult colleagues murdered more than 800 children in the name of Satan. But it was the sensational case involving Louis XIV that brought satanism – or at least, the seventeenth-century version of it – to public attention and from France, the true home of modern satanism, it transferred via the aristocracy into the rakish life of the English landed gentry.

The story began in 1648 when Louis XIV's chief of police arrested a large number of sorcerers, fortune-tellers, witches and black magicians. Among them was Catherine Deshayes – known as La Voisin (the widow) – a notorious sorceress who advised Madame de Montespan, and a renegade priest aged sixty-seven named L'Abbé Guibourg. The police statement against Guibourg, now available for consultation in the French archives, reads as follows:

A libertine who has travelled a great deal and is at present attached to the Church of Saint Marcel; for twenty years he has engaged continually in the practice of poison, sacrilege and every evil business. He has cut the throats and sacrificed uncounted

numbers of children on his infernal altar. He has a mistress . . .
by whom he has had several children, one or two of whom he has
sacrificed. It is no ordinary man who thinks it a natural thing to
sacrifice infants by slitting their throats and to say Mass upon
the bodies of naked women.

There were further details from which parallels to modern-day
accusations can be drawn. Guibourg's Black Masses were conducted over a stone draped in black silk on which a naked woman
served as the living altar, over which was read the totally blasphemous rite which was a reversal and deformation of the central
feature of Christian mass. The most ardent participant of this rite,
and the one who lay naked across the silk drapes, was Madame de
Montespan herself – the same mistress who produced three illegit-
imate offspring for Louis XIV. With Guibourg's assistance, she
had been mixing aphrodisiac potions whose ingredients included
the dried testicles of cockerels and the poisonous cantharides,
Spanish fly, which she had been secretly adding to the king's food.

As the months passed and Louis began to lose interest in
Madame de Montespan, stronger rites were required. According
to the police evidence, which was regarded as reasonably reliable,
La Voisin and Guibourg devised a more sinister rite over the
naked, living altar of Madame de Montespan herself which
involved the combination of sexual orgasm with the consecration
of bread and the drinking of wine from a chalice into which the
blood from a child's throat was drained; at the same time a prayer
was recited to the demons Ashtaroth and Asmodeus . . . 'Prince of
Love, I beseech you to accept the sacrifice of this child . . . that the
love of the King may be continued.'

Madame de Montespan was eventually banished from court as
rumours of her sorcery reached the king's ears. At this, she ordered
Guibourg to concoct a death potion which apparently contained
menstrual blood, semen and dried, powdered bat's blood, all of
which was mixed with other more palatable substances to be added
to the king's food. He lasted many more years, though it was little
wonder that he suffered various undefined illnesses in the later
stages of his life.

With their protector banished, La Voisin and Guibourg were

arrested along with some 220 courtiers connected with de Montes-pan. Only half that number were brought before the judiciary; the king ordered the trials to be halted before any further damaging details were made public. Even so, La Voisin boasted of how extensively satanism had extended through French society, especially in the upper classes, and she claimed – again according to the records of the Bibliothèque Nationale – that she had personally been concerned with the ritual killing of 2500 children over a period of thirteen years. Among them were children born to herself, and induced prematurely, as noted here in the Paris record: '. . . Guibourg put the baby into a basin, cut its throat, poured blood into a chalice and consecrated it with the host, finished the host, then took out the child's entrails . . . which were distilled and put in a glass phial which Madame de Montespan took away. The child's body was burnt in a stove . . .'

Once again, these case histories of the day provided the research material which could form a basis of future rituals, and though modern-day occultists still attempt to discount these instances as either freak happenings or exaggerated nonsense dreamt up during the Inquisition, the evidence of horrific acts in the name of Satan becomes, in the end, all too similar and emphatic to be dismissed. The case of Madame de Montespan and her friends was reliably recorded by a diligent policeman under royal instruction, and can be taken as a factual account of what happened, and what the key players in this horror story confessed to, without resort to torture.

La Voisin and Guibourg were executed in February 1680 but their brand of black magic with satanic overtones intrigued the rich young men of the European capitals in the early eighteenth century, and what soon became known as the Hell-Fire Clubs quickly established themselves, with sex, Satan and living danger-ously as the prime objectives.

There was little or no religious or historical connection in their ritualistic ceremonies, with the exception of using Christianity as the focus of their blasphemy and young girls as objects of abuse and mutilation on their black altars. The Hell-Fire Clubs were rife in every city of Europe, and none more so than in London. In England, their occurrence among courtiers, the gentry and young socialites reached such proportions that George I decreed by Order in Council in 1721 that their horrible impieties should cease – which of course they did not.

The *London Gazette*, reporting on the king's concern on 29 April, wrote, '. . . members of these clubs meet in the most impious and blasphemous manner . . . insult the most sacred principles of our Holy Religion and affront Almighty God Himself . . . His Majesty the King will make use of the authority committed to him by the Almighty God to punish such enormous offenders and to crush such shocking impieties before they increase and draw down the Vengeance of God upon this nation.'

There were numerous key centres for the activities of these hellraisers. One of the most well known was in Conduit Street, London, where the 'King of Hell', otherwise known as Philip, Lord Wharton, held court and apparently presided over all manner of alarming acts of competitive bravado and sexual depravity which matched the stories related a few centuries earlier about the Knights Templar. But the most famous of all the Hell-Fire Clubs was that which met at Medmenham Abbey on the banks of the River Thames at West Wycombe. It was centred around Sir Francis Dashwood, Chancellor of the Exchequer, who took delight in dressing up in monk's habit and hiring defrocked priests to perform the Black Mass and supervise the general proceedings of debauchery.

Dashwood's reign as the Mad Monk of Medmenham ran for fifteen years, and was the talk of the élite, though written word of these events did not surface until ten years after his death. Even so, the Hell-Fire Clubs were themselves something of a parody, a creation for wealthy pleasure-seeking men of position, while authentic satanism was still the preserve of the committed in secret places and where no secrets were revealed through pain of death itself – and in some satanic orders that threat exists today.

The foregoing gives a taste of past history of satanic ritual which has been constantly scoured and researched by occultists and writers. It will now be a simple matter for the reader to indentify the origin of some of the modern-day allegations of child sacrifice. Much can be dismissed as being derived from creative mythology from the past four or five centuries and from the mud-slinging between the rival religious factions. But there was sufficient evidence, however slender, to form the basis of a belief system that has built up in the twentieth century, sufficient for the upsurge of Christian fundamentalism to draw on, and enough historical case histories upon which the extremists and dangerous dabblers in satanism could found their activities.

Apart from the accusations of satanism and child sacrifice laid at the door of Aleister Crowley, modern groups did not really begin to appear in any number until the sixties, when occultism became the rage with films like *Rosemary's Baby* and the likes of Dr Timothy Leary were suggesting various social and psychological experiments which involved extensive use of marijuana and LSD.

It was at the onset of this new age of permissiveness that satanic theology simultaneously gained new popularity in Europe, England and America, emerging partly out of the new witch craze and partly out of the Swinging Sixties era when famous pop stars and showbusiness personalities were seeking gurus and new mystical experiences.

As already discussed, the occult in general experienced a sudden gust of new interest. Crowley's work was rediscovered and republished in the late sixties. Until that time, it had been virtually impossible to find any copies of his past writings, but suddenly a new demand opened up, as indeed it did for all kinds of occult literature. And among the hundreds of reviewers of *Crowley's Confessions, Life* magazine determined that his edict 'Do what thou wilt' was the superior equivalent of the 'mindless cultists' of the sixties whose law was 'Do your own thing'.

Additional light on the sixties scene may be gleaned from the former Witch Queen Maxine Sanders:

> The world, it seemed, had been waiting for us. When Alex and I arrived in London we were caught on the crest of a heady wave of mysticism. The young, already high on Flower Power and hallucinatory drugs, were seeking an extension of mystical experience, and they turned to Alex and myself. It was as if we were being transported back three thousand years into the days of the old religion . . . young people would just turn up . . . they were also be-

coming aware that there were different ways of progressing spirit-ually, apart from the hand-me-down conventions of conventional religion. All this was behind the great new wave of occult interest.

Among those visitors anxious to discover the knowledge of witch-craft and the occult, Alex and Maxine Sanders drew the interest of a group who were members of a cult centred around Charles Manson, leader of the 'family' which called itself Satan's Slaves. Manson is still in prison for the infamous Sharon Tate murders.

The Sanders knew Sharon from a year or so earlier when they had been approached to act as consultants on a film called *Eye of the Devil*, an odd story of a French nobleman's obsession with a family tradition of pagan self-sacrifice. It starred David Niven, Deborah Kerr, Emlyn Williams, Flora Robson, Donald Pleasence and, in a lesser role, Sharon Tate. It was during the making of that film that Sharon met her husband-to-be, Roman Polanski, in London. He was about to begin filming what became the most sensational film about satanism of its age, *Rosemary's Baby*, with Mia Farrow.

Around that time, Alex Sanders had been invited to lecture what Maxine can now only identify as a fairly new occult order whose members had given up everything to join. Sanders gave two lectures and after the second members of the group arrived at their home in Clanricarde Gardens one day asking to borrow some books, including one by Aleister Crowley, relating to ritual magic he had performed in Egypt; it was then a very rare book. The rite was, according to Maxine, a blood ritual and the group, she had no doubt, was blood-obsessed. When the books were eventually returned, she discovered that one single phrase in one of the rituals had been underlined; it read 'kill the pig . . .'

A line very similar was scrawled in Sharon Tate's blood on the wall of her home after the slaughter by Manson's disciples. The link between London and the Californian occult scene in which Manson became involved was an organization called The Process, the Church of the Final Judgement, some of whose members evacuated to the Haight-Ashbury district of San Francisco in the late sixties to set up a branch of their organization in the midst of hippiedom, at 407 Cole Street. Just down the road, at number 636, lived Manson.

The aims and objects of the Process Church are set out in an article which appeared in the summer 1988 issue of Chris Bray's *Lamp of Thoth* magazine under the heading of 'The Process – What It Means'. More surprisingly, the article acknowledged publicly that Charles Manson had been among its early members but he had 'gone astray where others in The Process have succeeded.' The item went on to claim that The Process is the true penultimate world movement, the ultimate fusion of all religious, political, and magical beliefs. In The Process the dichotomy of good and evil dies. The article explains that we live in fear of what we despise because we fear what we cannot be. For Christians, this fear is symbolized by Satan; for satanists, it is symbolized by Christ. By seeking out fears in living experience we become fear itself. The 'ultimate aim' is out of the hands of The Process (at the moment) and rests in the hands of the gods, Jehovah-Lucifer-Satan – the symbols of Process as 'the triadic expression of Final Judgement'. The Process releases the fiend that lies dormant within everyone, for he is strong and ruthless and his power is far beyond the bounds of human frailty. 'Learn to love fear' the article urges, 'love is to learn fear . . . the reconciliation of the Lamb and the Goat in the Final Judgement.'

The Process Church, with its swastika-style emblem, was formed in the early sixties by Robert DeGrimston Moore, an old boy of Winchester, and formerly a member of the Church of Scientology and self-styled pupil of its founder L. Ron Hubbard. Moore's Church initially veered towards the teaching of scientology, but as the sixties' permissiveness gathered pace Moore, in the tradition of many famous occultists, changed his name and announced that in future he would be called Robert DeGrimston – or 'Grim' as he was more popularly known – and began preaching freedom of choice in line with modern thinking in the world of hippies and drop-outs. He did not, however, entertain the drop-outs of the lower regions of society. He pitched his new order to the youth of the wealthy upper classes who were invited to give him their total commitment, and donations.

By 1967, the Process Church had moved from its first head-quarters in Fitzroy Street to a large mansion in the West End of London, not far from the Sanders' home, from where he and his two dozen resident aides published a magazine called *The Process* and a book entitled *As It Is*.

The magazine still has a reputation and apparently an enthusiastic audience in the occult world. As recently as 1992, a magazine entitled *Nox* was advertising collected excerpts from early editions of *The Process*, from an address in Mexborough, South Yorks, at £2 a time, through the columns of one of the foremost of Britain's satanic magazines, the *Dark Lily* – official organ of the clandestine Society of the Dark Lily, which bills itself variously as 'the voice of satanism' and 'the reality of the left-hand path' and is available only by contact through an anonymous post office box in London.

By the spring of 1968, the brotherhood of DeGrimston had set up shop in Los Angeles itself, recruiting young volunteers from the hippie community, who themselves then went out on the streets of LA and San Francisco to recruit more disciples.

Meanwhile, Manson and the family had turned to satanic worship, linked with drugs, LSD and sex – and they too moved to Los Angeles. Manson's following grew and he boasted that he had fifteen women to wait upon him and join him in midnight orgiastic sex rites while male members of the family sat around taking drugs. When Manson gave the signal they all joined in the communal sexual rites he had dreamed up, using what one of his women described as witchy things.

The murders of Sharon Tate, hairdresser Jay Sebring, Roman Polanski's friends Wojiciech Frykowksi and the Folger coffee heiress Abigail Anne Folger, along with a student, eighteen-year-old Steven Parent, shocked the world in their brutality. What struck the police investigators immediately was the way in which the bodies had been arranged as if they had been playing a part in some kind of ancient death ritual – only they were the sacrificial victims. The word pig was scrawled in blood. Tate, in the final month of pregnancy, was ritually murdered with a massive stab wound through the stomach which also killed her baby.

The killings were committed by 'family' members, as were the murders of another wealthy Los Angeles couple two days later. *Time* magazine, then unaware of the satanic background, prophetically recorded, 'It was a scene as grisly as anything depicted in Polanski's film explorations of the dark and melancholy corners of human character.'

The detail of how it was done was chillingly described in court later by two of the girls, Susan Atkins and Linda Kasabian, who both said that they were all under a hypnotic trance induced by Manson, and thus though he was not present at the scene of the crime, he was adjudged equally guilty.

For once, the charge of death by sorcery that had been brought against witches and magicians in centuries past suddenly seemed feasible. There was also more to the case than came out in the trial. Actor-director Dennis Hopper, fresh from his success with Jack Nicholson in *Easy Rider*, was invited to a discussion with Manson when the trial ended, for talks about filming his life story. Hopper was intrigued but backed off when he heard all the details; he could see even then he would never raise the finance for such a venture. And he has always maintained that evidence was held back at the trial. He said, 'The people in the Tate house were killed because they were into some bad shit. What goes around comes around. The people at the Tate house were victims of themselves because they had fallen into sadism and masochism and recorded it all on videotape. The LA police told me this. And Jay Sebring, one of those killed, was an old friend of mine. I know that three days before they were killed twenty-five people were invited to that house for the mass whipping of a dealer from Sunset Strip who'd given them some bad dope.'

Meanwhile, DeGrimston decamped to New York, where he still lives, and his Church retreated to England where it went into reclusion, but not total inactivity. Sub-groups of The Process continued to operate in the United States believing, as the article in Chris Bray's magazine noted in 1988, that Manson 'spoke for a generation and was deserving of the cult following that his infamy had secured for him.'

The reformed Process Church was advertising for new recruits, and Bray was not averse to publicizing this fact through the columns of *Lamp of Thoth*. The article claimed that Manson was right when he said he was a scapegoat, that he had natural talent for seeing 'prevalent social themes' and knowing the right time for action, even if this action was murder. That Manson, however, went astray where others in The Process have succeeded and *got caught*. 'A pity really,' the article commented. And so two decades after Sharon Tate's murder, remnants of the Process Church are alive and well, and living in Yorkshire, England.

But Robert DeGrimston cannot claim the credit for importing satanism into America in the sixties. It was already a thriving industry and, in fact, *Newsweek* hinted at the dark secrets of some Hollywood stars when reporting the Sharon Tate murders: 'Almost as enchanting as the mystery [over the deaths] was the glimpse the murders yielded into the surprising Hollywood subculture in which the cast of characters played. All week long, the Hollywood gossip about this case was of drugs, mysticism and off-beat sex and for once there is more truth than fantasy in the flashy talk of the town.'

In that summer of 1969, Anton Szandor LaVey had already established the First Church of Satan at the heart of American flamboyance in California where he courted the rich and famous, matching the Hollywood razzmatazz in showbiz-style dress and shaven head; seekers of excitement away from the regular mould of the social life of the glitterati began joining his notorious soirées.

He had long been known around Los Angeles as the Black Magician. Marilyn Monroe dallied briefly with him as she was on the cusp of starlet to fame. And, just as Alex and Maxine Sanders had been called in to advise on Sharon Tate's film *The Eye of the Devil*, Roman Polanski recruited LaVey as consultant for his production of *Rosemary's Baby* – and gave him a walk-on part as the devil. By then, LaVey had laid the foundations for what he termed a totally new religion. Under American laws he was able to have it legally established as such, with all the available tax benefits, and would eventually export his brand of satanic worship back into Britain – and onwards into Canada, France, Australia and anywhere there was a lively occult interest.

In truth, LaVey was laughing at authority, scowling at Christianity and staging a public demonstration of blasphemy of a nature previously unheard of, especially in America. If his aim was to shock then, like Polanski, he succeeded in an instant. Naturally, he gathered a great deal of publicity and attracted the participation of some equally high-profile people in search of the weird and kinky. He opened the doors of his temple to all comers who were prepared to swear allegiance to Satan and openly practise the ritual and black magic – and he made no attempt to disguise it.

The techniques Alex Sanders was using in England to promote witchcraft, LaVey was performing in San Francisco, only on a much grander scale. And when he was able to recruit devotees like Jayne Mansfield to do his bidding and serve as one of his maidens, attention to this outrageous character merely heightened.

Like most of the occult's more colourful stars, his background was neither mundane nor in any way 'normal' and in subsequent biographies even the normal bits were massaged to make them appear nonconformist – because total nonconformity is the basis of his belief. As with Crowley and others before him, he had a stroke of genius in his nature that he employed, some would say, in a warped direction.

Born in 1930 of Russian and Rumanian stock, he was introduced to the mythology of the dark arts by his maternal grandmother, a gypsy from Transylvania who recounted stories of witchcraft and the legends of vampires. Thus Bram Stoker's classic *Dracula* was early reading matter. He neglected his school studies for his own interests, among which was his passion for music. He became second oboist with the San Francisco Symphony Orchestra at the age of fifteen but quickly became bored with the formality of the life and ran off to join the Clyde Beatty Circus as assistant to the lion tamer.

When the organ player accompanying the acts fell drunk one night, LaVey took over – and remained in the job for a year or more, accompanying such circus stars as the Great Wallendas, the high wire act and Hugo Zachini, the human cannonball. He moved to the other side of the footlights himself when he became an assistant to a magician in a carnival and learned hypnosis and other tricks; the techniques of showbiz were to prove useful later in his career.

He temporarily ventured into the conformity of suburbia, when he married at the age of twenty-one, rented a house and got a job as a photographer with the San Francisco Police Department – a turning point, he said later, in the confirmation in his own mind that he would finally turn to satanism. 'I saw the vilest side of nature,' he said in an interview. 'People shot, women and children killed by hit-and-run drivers, drug overdosers in profusion. It was disgusting and depressing and I asked myself "How can there be a God with all this suffering?" And I actually came to detest and abhor the sanctimonious attitude of people who chirped up with the age-old saying about death and disaster being God's will.'

He turned increasingly to the study of the occult, accumulating a vast library on the subject. Although he has since dismissed most occult writings as weak and unimpressive, filled with apology and fraudulent claims, he acknowledges four major influences as he veered towards what he finally saw was the path that had been chosen for him – satanism. First he studied the history and trials of the Knights Templar, disregarding the theory some historians have tried to prove that the Templars could never be described as satanic and that the charges that brought their mass executions were politically motivated and exaggerated.

LaVey seemed to accept the stories of the Templars' blasphemy, which suited his new religion very well. On the wall behind the altar of his own Temple, he displayed the insignia of the Baphomet, its design identical to that used by the Knights. Similarly, Sir Francis Dashwood is one of his heroes. He says the Englishman has been much maligned by those who attempted to 'minimize' his activities, by suggesting his group was made up of pleasure-seeking fops and dandies. Benjamin Franklin joined Dashwood's Hell-Fire Club during his first five-year stay in London between 1757 and 1762. He thereafter went on to help draw up the Declaration of Independence, and subsequently the constitution of the United States, and LaVey has made grandiose claims that Dashwood's influence is an underlying aspect of both those historical documents. 'If people knew the role the Hell-Fire Club played in Benjamin Franklin's structuring of America,' he said, 'it might more easily accept the idea of "One Nation Under Satan" or "United Satanic America".'

He reckons that the 'Do What Thou Wilt' key to the writings of Aleister Crowley was first invented by Dashwood for his activities at Medmenham Hall. Crowley's theories on magic were another source of inspiration for LaVey and, though Crowley followers dispute that their idol was ever a practising satanist, he clearly provided a mine of material that LaVey could and would adopt.

The fourth major influence was his study of the notorious Black Order which originated from one of Crowley's OTO lodges in Germany, and in which both Heinrich Himmler and Hitler had taken an interest. All of this he put together with his own view of life gleaned from his experiences in the circus and carnival sideshows, and later as a police photographer.

He told his biographer Burton H. Wolfe that on Saturday nights, he would see men lusting after half-naked girls dancing at the carnival and on Sunday morning when he was playing the organ for tent-show evangelists, he would see the same men sitting in the pews with their wives and children, asking God to forgive them and purge them of their carnal desires. This made him believe the Christian Church thrived on hypocrisy and that man's carnal nature will out no matter how much it is purged or scourged by any white-light religion.

The date he chose for the launch of his new religion, the Church of Satan and the Age of Fire, was the night of 30 April 1966, the day witches and demonic worshippers the world over celebrate the spring equinox, which incidentally was also the anniversary of Hitler's suicide in 1945. He began preparing rituals which, by any stretch of the imagination, were deep in the realms of black magic. He ritually shaved his head, following the tradition he had read of the Yezidi devil worshippers who decreed it necessary for any emerging adept to leave 'the world of the descendants of Adam behind him'.

He declared 1966 as *Anno Satanas* – the first year of the reign of Satan – and thus began his open worship and rituals with his assembled group of 'like-minded individuals whose purpose was to use their combined forces in energy and magic to call up the dark force in nature that is called Satan.'

In order to have his organization accepted as a legitimately registered 'Church', LaVey worked to a formula which was based upon nine parts social acceptance and one part outrage; the latter attracted a very great deal of media attention, and little wonder. LaVey's new temple in an old Victorian house in San Francisco was devoted to smashing the whole concept of what a church should be; it was a temple of indulgence, defying all forms of abstinence. As his biographer Blanche Barton described it, the Church of Satan was outwardly offering a new religion but behind the closed and guarded doors of the temple itself, the shock factor was high: 'The rituals for the first year were largely intended as cathartic blasphemies against Christianity. Many of the elements were consistent with reports of satanic worship taken from the famous writings of diabolists.' For instance, a nude female altar was always used, accompanying music was a series of corruptions of church hymns, the cross was turned upside down, the Lord's prayer was recited backwards, mock holy wafers were consecrated by insertion (with a phallus) into a naked woman's vagina, holy water was substituted with seminal fluid in milk, the names of infernal deities were invoked instead of the Christian God. For some it was all too much.

Just as Alex Sanders courted publicity for his brand of witchcraft in England, Anton LaVey allowed limited coverage of his activities, and in 1967 a photograph of a naked girl lying on an altar covered with a leopard skin went around the world – as did LaVey's own fame. Very soon, he was opening up grottos (his term for covens) in many other countries and his fame was further enhanced by the first public baptism in the new Church of Satan – that of his own three-year-old daughter Zeena, a child who might otherwise be termed as angelic, with her long blonde hair and cherub-like face. She was baptized on the formal living altar of a naked woman from LaVey's community. Zeena herself was dressed in a blood-red hooded robe and sat seemingly unconcerned as her father conducted the entire ceremony wearing his now familiar demonic black head-gear that had two minature horns, giving the very appearance of being the devil himself. And as his daughter sat on the living altar her father performed the rites of baptism in the name of Satan.

But who was Satan? LaVey's early rituals conjured up all the colourful descriptions of the past and it would never be difficult for any of his disciples to imagine the imminent arrival of a horned monster, with glistening green eyes and blood and smoke exuding from his nostrils and fanged mouth. Even LaVey himself, with his black hood and mock horns, looked on occasion like the devil incarnate.

Later, however, LaVey decided that demons and devils and manifestations were old hat – the product of tired occult writings which had no bearing on his own philosophy. He began to say that, to him, the devil was not that stereotyped figure but rather a dark force of nature that humans could barely comprehend; it was a force to be called down by his ritual and he would show the way. It was a more believable concept, and one that oddly enough falls more into line with modern thinking in the Christian Church – that the devil is the means to an end, an unreal entity which is the personification of all thought and deed that is contrary to Christian belief.

LaVey claimed he could call upon that dark force for the enactment of satanic magic and for his speciality, the ritual satanic curse, a blood curdling epic of incantation. The most startling example of this supposed power concerns the death of the Hollywood star Jayne Mansfield who was among the early members of LaVey's Church. At the time, she was being groomed for major stardom by her studio and her lawyer Sam Brody made it known to LaVey that he would do all in his power to extricate his client from LaVey's group, since he was convinced that sooner or later she would be involved in damaging publicity.

LaVey told Brody he would see him dead within one year and went through a ritual satanic curse, conjuring up all the forces to destroy him. LaVey also told Jayne that Brody was under a dark cloud and that it was foolish for her to be with him. He urged her not to get into a car with Brody and never to be alone with him. He said, 'I made it clear what would happen . . .'

Some months later, all that LaVey had promised came to pass. Jayne and Sam Brody were driving in San Francisco on 29 July 1967 when their car was in a bad smash with a lorry. It was a particularly horrific scene. Mansfield was decapitated. Unlike the case of Charles Manson two years later, the San Francisco police showed no interest in pursuing an inquiry of murder by proxy and they could never have proved it, even given LaVey's admission that he had cursed Brody.

He went on, gaining ground and gathering a massive following estimated to be approaching 18,000 by the end of the decade. By then, his book *The Satanic Bible* had been published, oddly enough by the Hearst Corporation's Avon imprint, whose newspaper colleagues had been giving him large amounts of dubious coverage that took him into the realms of infamy.

The Satanic Bible is a ranting, but remarkable work, if only in that it was ever published at all. It is readily available today from occult bookshops and widely advertised in occult magazines. Little has changed in the book that became the blueprint for copy-cat satanic sects the world over. The opening section, which he entitled 'The Book of Satan: The Infernal Diatribe', set the tone of his preaching: when he declared that the 'pulpit pounders' of the past had been free to define good and evil as they saw fit and had gladly smashed into oblivion any who disagreed with their lies, unlike the Prince of Darkness who has 'remained a gentleman at all times . . . he has decided it is time for him to receive his due!'

LaVey spells out the nine satanic statements which are his equivalent of the Ten Commandments:

1] Satan represents indulgence instead of abstinence!

2] Satan represents vital existence instead of spiritual pipe dreams!

3] Satan represents undefiled wisdom, instead of hypocritical self-deceit!

4] Satan represents kindness to those who deserve it instead of love wasted on ingrates!

5] Satan represents vengeance instead of turning the other cheek!

6] Satan represents responsibility to the responsible instead of concern for the psychic vampires!

7] Satan represents man as just another animal, sometimes better, more often worse than those that walk on all fours . . . who because of his divine spiritual and intellectual development has become the most vicious animal of all!

8] Satan represents all of the so-called sins as they all lead to physical, mental or emotional gratification!

9] Satan has been the best friend the Church has ever had, as he has kept it in business . . .

These statements are mild compared with the remaining contents of *The Satanic Bible* in which LaVey gathered pace and diabolism as his work proceeded. His description of the three main rituals represented the basis for all satanic worship and the strength of the words seemed to be intended both to shock his opponents and inspire his ardent followers. On the subject of sex or lust, he exhorts his followers to take full advantage of spells. A man should plunge his 'erect member into her with lascivious delight', a woman should 'open wide her loins in lewd anticipation'. Concerning destruction, he advises his readers to be certain they do not care if their intended victim lives or dies before they throw their curse and having caused their victim's destruction, revel rather than feel remorse. The point he continued to make was that satanism was powerful medicine – psychologically and magically. He repeatedly lectured that it was dangerous to dabble on the fringes because satanism required total commitment; it was impossible to adopt 'liberation without responsibility' and he pointed regularly to some of the most powerful men and women in history who had worshipped the devil, quite unsuspected, and their wealth and happiness had increased beyond reckoning.

This was the heady mixture, then, of ritual sex, power, lust, excitement, wealth and alleged happiness – an all-purpose lure that attracted people by the thousand, first across America and then in London and Paris, the two secondary centres. By the mid-seventies, LaVey reckoned his brand of satanism had spread to such a degree that it was barely controllable in small groups, covens or grottos.

A carefully planned but clandestine move into the pop business was admitted in Blanche Barton's 1990 publication, *The Church of Satan*. LaVey decided that he needed auditoriums and stadiums to spread the word through what he described as Black Metal concerts, developed almost on the lines of religious experience.

Much has been written and reported about heavy metal rock groups who are said to include subliminal satanic messages on their discs which began appearing around the time LaVey was making his switch. The effectiveness of these messages on a subliminal basis has been largely discredited. Most pyschologists agree that it is virtually impossible for the human brain to comprehend backward-spoken words, let alone subliminally introduced backward-spoken words.

But the very fact that several groups have performed this operation on their discs and received publicity for it, had the desired effect. It meant that satanism was being discussed in high-profile media programmes on television and reported in the newspapers – exactly as LaVey intended. The knowledge of a rock group's satanic links was sufficient, in his quite cool and cynical view, to turn the vast audience in a rock concert auditorium into mass worship.

Why else would young cultists be spray-painting the names of their pop heroes on every hoarding? He reckoned the appeal to young people was 'astronomical' and now believes that satanism will become the protest movement of the 1990s. He points to young people adopting the salute of two thumbs, signifying two horns which was 'now more popular than the Masons' handshake'.

By the late seventies, he had deliberately disbanded the tightly controlled grotto (or coven) system of grouping – which is still the basis for white witchcraft. He said that the only way for satanism to spread was to make it open; he wanted it pushed out into society. The effect was remarkable. Copy-cat groups began to form all over the world, and especially in Britain and America. Devoid of LaVey's central control dozens of new secret satanic societies sprang up, some adopting his principles while others went utterly for the shock effect, employing the worst of the blood and sex extravagances and none of what LaVey called their balancing counterpoints, whatever they were.

And just as he had turned to the Knights Templar, the French satanic scandals and Sir Francis Dashwood for inspiration, the new satanic movements gathered up copies of *The Satanic Bible* and other extrovert writings of Anton LaVey, and subsequently others, to copy and expand upon the rituals he recommended.

One puzzling factor remained, however, for those seeking the truth of the blood rites; LaVey dealt with the question somewhat ambiguously in *The Satanic Bible* under a section headed 'On the Choice of Human Sacrifice'. He conceded that the supposed purpose of the ritual sacrifice was to throw energy provided by the blood of a freshly slaughtered victim into the atmosphere of magical workings, to intensify the magician's chances of success. He said the white magician, wary of the consequences of killing a human being, usually resorted to sacrifices of birds or animals. This sacrifice was necessary, according to ritual magic, to release in the atmosphere the energy from the death throes of a living creature which many erstwhile magicians had achieved by cutting the throat of a goat or a chicken. He had also heard of magicians who had acquired foetuses from abortion clinics from which all blood would be drawn.

He insisted however that no 'self-respecting satanist' would sacrifice an animal or a baby, for the simple reason that they considered the purest form of carnal existence 'reposes in the bodies of animals and human children who have not grown old enough to deny themselves their natural desires.' It seemed an odd concept but one which he adamantly maintains is sacred in satanic belief. He raised the question of who then would be considered a fit and proper human sacrifice, and how is one qualified to pass judgement on such a person?

The next passage might well have been taken from the annals of the Third Reich. The ideal people suited for sacrifice, in his view, were those who were emotionally insecure who 'might cause severe damage to your tranquillity or reputation . . . [through] mental illness, maladjustment, anxiety neurosis'. Therefore, he concluded, the satanist had every right (symbolically) to destroy them and if their curse provoked actual annihilation, they should rejoice that they had been instrumental in ridding the world of a pest.

All of this is nonsense, of course, if the reader does not accept the basic premise that the diabolical curses of satanists actually work.

In fact, it was unimportant whether the curse was a success or not. It was the whole satanic attitude, as recommended by the modern creators of it, simultaneously the Church of Process and LaVey's Church of Satan, and available for consumption by all who wished to follow, which contained a disturbing content in unsafe and inexperienced hands . . .

CHAPTER FIFTEEN

DIABOLICAL DISCIPLES

Devil worship mushroomed and brought instant repercussions in Britain, where it quickly became a substitute for the more traditional forms of black magic. The new published guidelines for rituals 'as performed in the Church of Satan' travelled quickly and there was a rash of groups and individuals working alone who were anxious to try them out. More than that, Anton LaVey had taken the whole devil business into a razzmatazz world of showbiz, pop, magazines and media. He had given satanism some kind of dubiously attractive appeal, almost mass appeal, in an age of protest. The demonstrations of his curses, the talk of assassination by proxy and the publicity over his sex rituals held a peculiar fascination for those who sought escape and excitement, or wanted deliberately to turn their backs on family-taught religions and values.

A dozen or more copy-cat groups sprouted on both sides of the Atlantic and we will examine a number of these movements as they operate today. First, there was one in particular that came out of the Church of Satan, born of a group disillusioned with the popular appeal and increasingly mega-star attitudes of their leader, not to mention some of the eccentric rituals he had prepared and published either in *The Satanic Bible* or in separate pamphlets and journals. All were remarkably similar in style and alleged to originate with some of the eighteenth- and nineteenth-century satanists, though apparently without the element of a sacrificial altar. Sex in a coffin to awaken a 'dead' man, with some heavy scourging with a cat o'nine tails, were all part of the ritual. For what purpose? The mystery remains . . .

Michael Aquino, one of the early administrators of the Church of Satan and among the more intellectual of its members, left to form a new movement. He and five other leading priests decided to break away in 1975 to form the Temple of Set, a more serious and secretive organization, and perhaps even more committed to the sinister fundamentals of satanic worship than LaVey himself; its underlying principles were of a far more intellectual nature. The development was important to the whole organization of satanism throughout the world and he wrote a book entitled *The Book of Coming Forth by Night* which explained his philosophy and set out the scriptures for the Temple of Set – a work which he believed was as important to satanism as Aleister Crowley's *Book of Law* was to the Thelemic tradition.

Aquino is a strange and curiously powerful figure to head up a new 'religious institution' as he called it. He is a cool and deep man and a former serving soldier, a major in the US Army with a considerable record of achievement. His wife Lilith is a sharp and naturally aggressive woman who gives no quarter to opponents or interviewers; she brushes aside the obvious question of whether Lilith was her given name or whether she herself adopted it, after the legendary Lilith, first wife of Adam, who changed into a demon after the creation of Eve. Lewis Spence describes the mythical Lilith as 'the princess who presided over the succubi (sex spirits who attacked males in their sleep) and sought to destroy new-born infants. For this reason, the Jews wrote a formula on the four corners of the birth chamber to drive Lilith away.'

In 1983, when Virginian county police were asked to make an inquiry into the leaders of the Temple of Set, they came up with some surprising facts. Aquino was an expert in the techniques of psychological warfare – a skill that was to prove useful to him in more ways than one – and held high-level security clearance on account of his service with the World Affairs Council and had been on secondment to NATO. But another interesting statistic also emerged from the Virginian inquiry – that twelve other leading lights in the Temple of Set organization throughout the US were members of Army Intelligence; the question that the Virginian police were unable to answer was whether or not the Intelligence men were members because of a personal commitment to Aquino's satanic religion, or whether they were simply working under cover to keep an eye on his membership and activities.

The Army, in fact, may well have wanted to dispose of Aquino's services as soon as the top brass discovered that he was *the* leading light in a satanic organization. By then, he had registered the Temple of Set as a religious organization, recognized by the United States government and, according to ToS literature 'consecrated by the Prince of Darkness in his name'.

He pleaded that the rights of any man to follow a religion of his choosing should not be affected by his position, even if he was a senior reservist officer in the US Army, and drawing a salary from the Pentagon. Were not Jews, Catholics, Protestants, Muslims and any other of the mainstream religions all accommodated in Army regulations – why not satanism?

Aquino's brand of satanism was more formal than LaVey's flamboyant methods, but the underlying principles and rituals were much the same. The choice of Set as the figure of mythology around which his organization would be based was important.

Set was the evil god of Egyptian mythology, the twin brother of Osiris, the king. Set tried to become ruler of ancient Egypt by murdering his brother – tricking Osiris to climb into a jewelled chest which became his coffin. Set and his helpers quickly nailed down the lid and threw the box into the Nile. Osiris's wife Isis went in search of the box and found it embedded in a tree at Byblos in Syria and brought the body back to Egypt. When Set discovered this, he stole the body and had it cut into fourteen portions which he scattered throughout Egypt. Isis, outraged, tracked down thirteen pieces but the last, his penis, was never found. She had a replica of his member cast in gold and buried it as Mendes in a temple dedicated to the goat god. And thus, at this shrine, strange rituals with naked priests and priestesses were performed over the golden penis of Osiris and in medieval times the devil himself became known as the Goat of Mendes. This finally brings us to Aquino's point; that Satan was Set and he predated Christianity by three thousand years.

Aquino built Egyptian mythology into his satanic worship specifically to include some of the individuality of thought expressed by Aleister Crowley in his *Book of Law*, allegedly inspired by Osiris's son, Horus. Aquino explained that he believed the worship of Set was the worship of individualism. In the Church of Satan this was taken to mean indulgence in all desires of the body and ego. The Temple of Set was determined to preserve the principle of individualism and add to it the 'higher self' aspirations of Aleister Crowley. The glorification of the ego was not enough, it was the complete psyche, the entire self or soul which must be recognized.

However, Aquino was careful to state that he recognized that participation in the Black Arts could be highly dangerous and most emphatically *not* a field for the unstable, immature or otherwise emotionally or intellectually weak-minded people. Those whose criminal or degenerate attitudes surfaced would be expelled. Those who aligned themselves to the 'simple-minded synthesis of Christian propagandas and Hollywood horror movies' were not the sort who could enjoy the 'colourful legacy of the Black Arts and the many forms of historical imagery [we use] for our stimulation and pleasure.'

In his quest for this colourful legacy, Aquino also sought other European content in the establishment of his new order by making additional studies of the Black Order which operated in Germany before the Second World War. In 1980 he made a study visit to Wewelsburg Castle in northern Germany, which was once used by Heinrich Himmler.

Himmler, and later Hitler himself, took a great interest in both the Order of New Templars, a German offshoot of the OTO, and the Thule Society which recruited Nazi thugs from the streets of Berlin during the rise of Fascism. In the very year Hitler appointed himself leader of the Third Reich, Himmler was involved in Thule Society rituals at the castle where he established a temple, called the Hall of the Dead. It was to this castle that Aquino travelled in October 1983 – exactly fifty years later – to perform ritualistic workings which he described as being part of his 'search for the key principles of the true Powers of Darkness'.

That he had chosen to visit the very epicentre of the cults embraced by Himmler and Hitler, whose heroes shared the Nazi intolerance of the weak and non-Ayrans gave some indication of the thinking of the man who had founded a new satanic route which was gathering strength in both America and Europe. These Nazi cults were his acknowledged source of a new and darker satanism which he believed would 'energize' his workings. He explained in an essay on his rites there that because the castle was conceived by Heinrich Himmler to be the *Mittelpunkt der Welt* (centre of the world) and as the focus of the Hall of the Dead was to be the gate of that centre, his purpose was to summon the Powers of Darkness at their most powerful focus.

Back in America, the Temple of Set continued to flourish, adding new members and embracing almost every walk of life, but especially the white collar professions. At the same time Aquino himself remained under the tentative observation of the military police, and quite probably the CIA too, though it was never a close watch. His organization was also the subject of an Army investigation concerning a rumour that a human sacrifice had been performed by members of the Temple of Set. In the hysteria of alleged satanic crime that began in the mid-eighties in the American pre-school care community – and eventually spread to Britain – the military would not take a stance that might be construed as harassment.

However, in the early summer of 1987 the military authorities began to take a deeper interest in Aquino. Earlier that year, the FBI had arrested Gary Willard Hambright, aged thirty-two, a Southern Baptist minister who had worked at the child day-care centre at the US Army Presidio Base in San Francisco. He was charged with sodomy, oral sex and other lewd and lascivious assaults on a three-year-old boy who had been in his care at the base.

In the ensuing investigation, the FBI took statements from more than fifty other children, many of whom talked of being abused, and in October 1987 Hambright was indicted by a Federal Grand Jury on twelve charges of offences against children, not one of whom was over the age of four.

During the investigations, one of the children, the daughter of a US Army chaplain, mentioned another man, 'Mikey', as having taken part in ritualistic abuse. She was taken in a car with FBI officers to a house which she said she could identify as being the place where Mikey lived. It turned out to be 2430 Leavenworth,

Russian Hill, San Francisco. The owner was Michael Aquino. The child said that she was taken into the house, and then into a room which was painted black and which had a cross painted on the ceiling.

Later that day, San Francisco police obtained a court warrant to search the house. The police team, led by Inspector Glenn Pamfiloff, removed tapes, photographs and computer records and noted that the lounge was painted black. Aquino protested strongly. He knew nothing of the child abuse scandal, he said, and furthermore it was totally against the principles of the Temple of Set. He described as total fabrication the evidence of the children whose statements had accused both 'Mickey and his wife' of ritual and sexual abuse.

As the months passed, the police case grew gradually more fragile. Many parents had seen the effects of questioning – however gentle – on their children and were anxious not to involve them in the trauma of official testimony. The children's stories were all similar and involved many of the acts of defilement that featured in the British scare over satanic ritual abuse which followed soon afterwards. The whole investigation became shrouded with difficulty and doubt. No charges were made against Aquino or his wife. The police decided they could not proceed after the judge in the case ruled that the children's evidence was not specific enough in terms of time and place, or even in the identity of the alleged abusers. Aquino claimed he had been 'set up'.

In November 1988, the Presidio Criminal Investigation Command of the Sixth Army appointed a team of investigators under a judge advocate-general to look further into the abuse allegations, and specifically at the possibility of Aquino's involvement. The investigation was proceeding as Aquino appeared on several American chat shows, including Oprah Winfrey's, which resulted in dozens of false accusations against him. A year later, the US Army inquiry was halted and again no charges were brought.

In the midst of these troubles, Aquino's Temple of Set had moved into Britain and established its first High Priest, a man named David Austen. Issue number eight of the *Dark Lily*, the official magazine of the British satanic order the Society of the Dark Lily, founded in the early eighties, carried an advertisement for the Temple of Set which they were now seeking to introduce to 'sincere and mature devotees of the left-hand path in many other nations . . .'

Incidentally, below that self-same advertisement was the one for *Nox*, the selected excerpts from *The Process*, the magazine of the original satanic order that spawned the American counterparts, along with some assistance from the writings of Denis Wheatley. The latter was recognized in a hands-across-the-sea article promoting the Temple of Set which appeared in Chris Bray's *Lamp of Thoth* in the summer of 1988, written by Aquino before he became immersed in defensive action over the allegations of child abuse. He wrote that the two principal American satanic movements, the Temple of Set and the Church of Satan, both inherited key components of their symbolism and ritual practices from British occult predecessors. Contemporary America's first taste of satanism, he said, came from Britain after the US publication in the 1960s of three of Denis Wheatley's satanic novels. His satanists were elegant, powerful, mysterious and insidiously successful in whatever they wanted to do. This was a powerful aphrodisiac for certain American occultists who were impatient with 'parlour' esoteria.

In May 1989, Aquino's hopes of establishing a formal British order under which to marshal the groups who wished to operate under the umbrella of the Temple of Set became a reality. He appointed the chef from Kent, David Austen, then thirty-two as the first High Priest. Austen quickly established a retinue of between forty and fifty initiates who were to become the nucleus of the new organization; they included people from all walks of life, including a tax inspector and a prison officer.

Like his American boss, he was quite happy to expound upon satanism to the media and especially upon its central theme of self-indulgence. In view of Aquino's then current difficulties with investigations concerning child abuse, Austen was also remarkably frank about the satanic stance on sex and paedophilia.

He admitted that the sexual (and bi-sexual) rites of the satanic order could be construed by some as indecent, but that was a matter of opinion. Sex was a means to an end in true satanism, and strictly for consenting adults. He agreed there were many people who claimed to be satanists who were abusing children. He had also heard of cases of human sacrifice though he had never seen one, in spite of having been credited with having witnessed a sacrifical ritual by the *Sunday People*.

There were many other groups which followed in the wake of the two main satanic Churches in America, and some sought allies and membership from Europe. They were a varied bunch whose activities ranged from the so-called orthodoxy of the Church of Satan through to the extremes of ritualistic endeavour that match anything a novel writer could imagine. They included: The Church of Satanic Brotherhood, the Order of the Black Ram, The Church of S.A.T.A.N., The Church of Satanic Liberation, The Universal Mission of SATAN, The Black Hand and Ordo Templi Satanas. Some are now defunct, others remain with fluctuating memberships, some running into thousands.

More recently in Britain, the leading groups with over 1000 members include the Society of the Dark Lily, the Order of the Black Chalice, the Antichrist Society, with members in various parts of the country; the Fraternity and Children of Lucifer, operating in London and Edinburgh, the Order of Lebana Yareah (White Moon) in Northamptonshire, in London and the south – to mention a mere selection from what is a very long list.

Membership is drawn from all walks of life; the range of groups is vast and entry is not necessarily a foregone conclusion for would-be joiners, especially in some of the more secretive or orthodox orders, as is best demonstrated by an appeal for members in the magazine of the Society of the Dark Lily which advised that a limited number of places had been created. Applicants should preferably be aged twenty-five or over as below that age they were unlikely to have had sufficient experience of life to know enough about themselves or anything else. However, younger people would be considered provided they could demonstrate a mature outlook. They were looking for candidates from a professional background, self-confident, adaptable, of flexible thinking, yet dedicated, single-minded, perhaps even ruthless. They must be aware that the way to achievement is not 'purely by melodramatic ritual and magickal formulae'. Applications from suitable couples were also invited. The Society of the Dark Lily believed that their methods, though not a new concept in occultism, were unheard of in the mainstream of occult systems, whose adherents would not have sufficient will-power and determination to benefit by membership.

Clearly, the Society of the Dark Lily is seeking new members of a high intelligence, preferably academics. It is *not* a group for the simple-minded or perverted.

At the other end of the scale are orders headed by committed satanists who run what are generally termed pseudo-satanic groups and who deliberately recruit from the lower regions of society. The reason for this will become clearer as this chapter proceeds. In a nutshell, those with lesser will-power or resistance are deliberately sought by groups who indulge in the worst kind of satanic ritual; women who are prepared to become pregnant for the cause, men who readily indulge in sado-masochism and perverted sex, and those who will permit children to be included in the group's rituals.

The cry of 'It's not us . . .' has become the familiar response of most of the established satanic organizations both in Britain and America. Virtually every magazine and every piece of literature I have obtained from over two dozen organizations which consider themselves to be 'real occultists', as opposed to the pseudo groups, makes the point that it is against all satanic codes to indulge in sexual depravity with children, and certainly they would not entertain the sacrifical rites of babies or even foetuses.

Nor do these mainstream groups seem to believe it is their responsibility if some renegades pick up a book containing the satanic rituals devised by Anton LaVey, add to them the sacrificial descriptions pertaining to eighteenth-century satanism in France, spice them up with the theory and practice of magic, as devised by Aleister Crowley – and end up with a dastardly combination of headless chickens, dead babies and drinking a concoction of unspeakable ingredients so horrible that it does not bear description.

But there is a paradox frequently to be observed in occult magazines whose editors on the one hand decry Christian fundamentalists for accusing occultists of all kinds of despicable deeds, yet on the other publish texts relating to rituals which can only be described as titillating to its readership and may perhaps be compared with the photographs and descriptions in a pornographic magazine.

Let me give a case in point. *Chaos International* is a smart and authoritative occult magazine costing £2.70, published by Temple Misanthropy, London Pact of the Illuminates of Thanateros and devoted to a mix of intelligent, often complicated articles on various occult traditions combined with science, theories and esoteric thought – on the basis that out of chaos comes order. It carries the disclaimer that the views expressed in *Chaos International* are not necessarily in accord with the beliefs of its editor, Ian Read. In its issue for the autumn of 1991, Read berates the Christian fundamentalists for continually wasting police time and money by having them chase what 'was after all only a canard'.

A few pages further into this issue, Read published the second in a series of articles describing the roots of the Black Mass, under the headline 'The Great Satanist Scandal', a translation of extracts from *La-Bas*, a French novel which first appeared in 1891. These extracts are published and republished in graphic detail, providing descriptions of black ritual as, for example, when a priest in the novel was said to have descended the altar steps backwards, knelt, and in a quavering high pitched voice declaimed, 'Lord of Evil, Thou dost reward sins and heinous vices, Satan it is Thou whom we adore ... Thou dost save the honour of families aborting wombs fertilized in the forgetfulness of orgasm ... Thou dost suggest to the mother the hastening of untimely birth and Thou art midwife to the stillborn, sparing them the agony of growth of the original sin ...'

The extract goes on to describe a torrent of blasphemies and abuse and foul profanity by the priest before the servers to this Black Mass rang little bells. It was a signal for the women in the satanic congregation to fall to the floor. One was said to have clucked like a hen, and then fell dumb, while another with her pupils dilated, lolled her head back on her shoulders, then stiffened in a spasm, ripping at her breasts with her nails. Yet another, sprawling on her back, undid her skirts revealing a huge and swollen belly, her face twisted in a monstrous rictus and her tongue drawn back until it touched her palate. The priest, the passage continued, spewed forth more frightful insults while acolytes knelt in front of him; then instead of kneeling after the consecration he faced the congregation with an erect penis, haggard, dripping with sweat. He staggered to the edge of the altar steps where the acolytes raised his chasuble to display his nakedness upon which the acolytes sprinkled holy water.

There was more, much more, horrific description of a Black Mass. The extracts are from a novel, and though certain events and descriptions are said to be based upon fact, the settings are imaginary and there is no proof that any of the incidents ever took place. However, these passages have been frequently republished and are available for all those who wish to copy the rituals. I would pose two questions: is the interest of these so-called intellectual groups who publish and read this material purely one of historical inquiry? Who is to blame for the extrovert groups who have appeared with remarkable productivity throughout the world, and especially in Britain? They *do* exist, performing all the rites and bloody, sexual activity that – as I suggested at the beginning of this chapter – might come straight off the pages of Denis Wheatley who in turn researched nineteenth-century novels, as above.

To answer this point, I took the view of a satanic master who agreed to speak to me on the understanding that I did not publish his name. He is an intellectual occultist of many years' standing who yawns wearily at the descriptions of the naked girl on the altar. His is a quieter, more contemplative form of satanism largely devoid of blood and sex and the derivative ritual of LaVey and Aquino. He explained:

Satanism has for years been misrepresented by everyone from Wheatley to Hollywood so it is inevitable that there are misunderstandings from new recruits as to the true principles. I am not going to say that the more lurid Black Masses and living altars are wrong . . . they just do not necessarily have a place in modern satanism, and those who use them are really play-acting. They are not getting on to the higher levels of inspiration and thought,

examining life, gaining the knowledge to cross the abyss, because
that is the true power – knowledge. Not some spurious energy
allegedly acquired from an orgasm on a black altar at the very
point of the death throes of a sacrificial killing. Yes, we have all
heard about that. The people who perform such ceremonies and
rituals are using us – they are hiding behind the cloak of satanism
for their own disreputable purposes, be they paedophilic, homosexual, sado-masochistic or just profiteers. And, yes I know what
you are going to say – how do I justify people who indulge in the
despicable, and even the actions of some so-called intellectual
satanists I know who do go in for dark ritual for the simple
pleasure of it? Actually, I don't have to justify it, because it is
not my problem. It is the sickness in society. Now that is a cliché
and a cop-out, but does the Christian Church ever attempt to
justify some of the very cruel things that have been done in its
name in the past? Does the Christian Church ever attempt to
explain or excuse the actions of some of its own ministers and
priests who have, in great number over the years, been accused
of many crimes, not least abusing children? It is our aim as
satanists to free ourselves from the dogmatic and puritanical
philosphy that Christians have been trying to ram down the
throats of society in general for the past 2000 years. So please, let
us not argue on doctrine – we can at least learn that message
from the Christians.

For myself, my principle beliefs are that Satan is my Lord
and Master, my protector and my guide. Those who, like myself,
dedicate themselves to the Master, are the chosen of his Church.
And he who believes in Satan creates him, because satanism is
the keyword of positive psychology.

That is why the pseudo-satanists, who are the cause of our
problems today, try to justify their actions by throwing in your
face the Crowley addage of 'Do what thou wilt'. It is an outdated
law of anarchy and the cowboys don't know it yet. How can they
possibly understand that what they do is merely converting the
old ways of satanism to satisfy their own anarchy and personal
egos, through sexual and other indulgences? All I can say is that
I hope, some day . . . they will realize that the freedom they seek

is already inside one's own subconscious. It is much more difficult to find, but it is an essential discovery.

That is the case for the defence, sold as the quest for knowledge which is achieved by work, experimentation and thought. And yet even the mainstream of satanic worship is filled with double standards, double talk and, within the larger organizations, a mixture of commericalism aimed at the base instincts of would-be practitioners. In the end, it becomes very difficult indeed, try as one might, to dismiss the underlying threat of malevolence.

The Church of Satan, for example, advertises strongly in most of the satanic magazines distributed in Britain, and its own magazine *The Black Flame* – 'a forum for satanic thought exploring the philosophy of creative alienation attracting a new generation of iconoclasts' – has a growing subscription of British followers.

When I contacted the Church of Satan at its headquarters in San Francisco in November 1991, I was given a membership package outlining its aims and objects, giving quotations from Anton LaVey explaining why I should enroll as a member, and send a fee of $100. It also provides an excellent portrait of how the world of Satan, and the organization behind the whole network of satanic worship, builds and operates. On completion of this preliminary entrance requirement, I would receive a questionnaire which would be reviewed by the CoS to assess my eligibility for further involvement. I would be 'processed' through their very strict degrees of initiation. It was suggested I should follow the directions in *The Satanic Bible* and further the cause by forming my own group or grotto. I was informed that if I wished to pursue group activities using the Church of Satan as an identity, I was legally required to be a registered member of the Church. If I represented myself as affiliated with the Church or acting as its spokesman, I was legally required to register with them.

With this package came a list of books and videos which are suggested for purchase, including books by LaVey and others, an album entitled 'Hymn of the Satanic Empire' written and per-formed by LaVey and a video entitled *Death Scenes* described by the hand-out as an extremely graphic videodocumentary of Hollywood crime scenes including suicides, murders, sex crimes, never-before-seen morgue photos and fascinating histories of stars' deaths. The narration and on-camera introduction was by Anton Szandor LaVey. To order, I had to send $39.95.

Ironically, with it came another pamphlet, entitled 'The Satanic Bunco Sheet' bearing a health warning about the dangers of joining pseudo-satanic groups. Potential initiates could be led into bad habits by cults offering sex orgies and drugs, or killing animals in the name of Satan. These are not part of satanic practices, the pamphlet stresses, and the initiates should not let someone take advantage of them for his or her own perversity.

This in itself constitutes an admission that there are many perverse groups around. The writer goes on to warn against those who claim to have a direct line of communication with Satan since selling that kind of mysticism is 'exactly how Christianity has kept people enslaved in ignorance for centuries' ... The initiate must look out for jargon and secrets that only the initiated can be privy to and be warned, there are unethical individuals out there who will prey on them.

Money often comes into the satanic equation, as Canon Dominic Walker, vicar of Brighton and Church of England special-ist on occult affairs has discovered. Canon Walker is not a man either to exaggerate or give away secrets about those who consult him when in difficulties. I have already made the point that unlike some counterparts in Christian evangelism, he shuns publicity and somewhat reluctantly imparted scant detail of some of his case histories when I interviewed him in the summer of 1991.

One was the case of a wife who had come to see him about her husband, who had joined a satanic group and had been paying money to the High Priest, or the Master. The fee had reached £200 a week, and the man had, unbeknown to his wife, taken out a second mortgage on their house to finance the contributions, thereby going into overdraft at the bank. He was scared and felt he could not leave; husband and wife went to see Canon Walker who advised him on how to escape from the group, a move which was subsequently successful. Another case in which Canon Walk-er's help was sought concerned a family in Sussex whose life had been virtually taken over by a New Age occult philosopher who had actually moved into their home, and had established a remarkable hold over husband and wife, controlling all that they did, down to how they spent their money. This woman refused to leave the house, warning of dire consequences for all if they did not remain under her tutelage.

This is not an unusual occurrence, as is confirmed in issue number nine of the magazine *Dark Lily*, when a reader wrote in to say that she was trapped by a phoney adept. She had given him all her savings and he now took all the money that she earned. Although he had never been physically violent to her he constantly criticized everything she did and refused to teach her any more about the occult. She ends, 'But I am too scared to leave. What can I do?'

The *Dark Lily*'s adept replied in a manner which would instantly disqualify him from the title of a satanic Claire Rayner: by suggesting that if the writer is so easily parted from her money, it is probably better that someone else is looking after it for her. Constant criticism, the adept continued, could be a method of teaching. Why was she so scared to leave a non-violent man? Because he might have magical powers and might put a spell on her? No need to worry on this point; if he had power he would not use it for such a trivial purpose; if he had no power, the adept reasoned there was no problem. He admitted that leaving one's place of residence was not a simple matter, particularly without money. But if she really wanted to go she would have gone. His response to her question 'What can I do?' was that the best way to improve her life if she had the ability to follow his advice is to *stop whining*!

But the Adept of the *Dark Lily* must also know that it is often not that easy to escape some of the more virulent groups. Violence was mentioned in this case, though not applicable. In other instances it is certainly a constant threat.

The Order of the Black Chalice is a satanic group with a strong membership in Britain. Like most orders, it is obsessively secretive about its activities and the identities of its members. All who join are warned in advance – and must sign a statement of acknowledgement – that they will not be allowed to leave; merely to retire. I cannot relate what transpired at group meeting or the tone of the rituals because the escapee from the Order of the Black Chalice was afraid for his life.

On acceptance into the order, he had to put his signature to a document which confirmed his agreement that if at any time he tried to leave the order, he would be subjected to a code of retribution which moved through three definite stages. First, any satanic pupil wishing to leave after having completed the initiation and acceptance into the order would be visited by senior members and encouraged by means of conversation and friendship to withdraw his intention to depart.

If this failed, he would be visited again and subjected to more severe forms of persuasion, i.e. violence, and thirdly, if all else failed, the wayward initiate would be reminded of the final stage of retribution – death itself. And the departing satanic pupil of the Order of the Black Chalice who told this story had, at the point of giving this testimony, experienced the first two stages, and lived in fear of the third.

Claims, therefore, that it is only the pseudo-satanic groups which cause the problems are not always borne out by the facts.

Further evidence of this can again be drawn from the columns of the *Dark Lily*. In issue number six, there appeared an advertisement, under the exchange advertising scheme, for a new occult quarterly . . . which will feature material on alchemy, androgyny, Chaos magic, Crowley, gnosticism, Holy Grail, Luciferianism, phallism, Qabalah, satanism etc.

However, in issue number eight of the *Dark Lily*, there appeared a second announcement from *DL*'s own editor stating that they had had to discontinue their exchange advertising with this new quarterly in view of 'their editors' support for the criminal activity known as paedophilia'. The *DL*'s editor denied that he was being placed in the uncomfortable position of arbiter of sexual morals and stressed that paedophilia was not only illegal but it had nothing to do with occultism and could actually impede one's development in satanism.

And so, here was the first published evidence – revealed in an influential occult magazine – that supporters of the internationally outlawed paedophilia movement were using satanism and other branches of the occult as a cover for their activities. It must therefore be a source of supreme agitation to investigators on both sides of the Atlantic that there has been, over the past decade, a large-scale invasion of the occult by sexual deviants, especially those who get their pleasures from the abuse of children.

From the above, it may be seen that there are two levels of operation in satanic orders – one for those who treat it as seriously as the devotees of any religious order and who claim that their rituals exclude sacrificial elements, and one for those whose motives are simply tied to the debauchery and blood-lust of satanic history.

There is a dividing line between the two, but where it actually falls is difficult to pinpoint. What is clear, as I have already indicated, is that notwithstanding the denials of leading satanists about depravity within their own groups, there is plenty of it about; and below that line of division the depths to which the worst of the satanic covens will plunge seems to have no bounds.

There are small groups who come and go like ships in the night and whose importance to the occult scene is negligible – except for the damage they may cause to gravestones, skeletons and the chicken and cat population of the countryside. These people have always been there, though many believe that these do-it-yourself occultists would not know a Baphomet from a pentangle. Occasionally, they slaughter a goat, or a donkey. Occasionally, a village churchyard will suffer an outbreak of body snatching. But these instances tend to come and go, and the groups responsible lose interest when they discover that after all that bother, they have done nothing to get excited about, except perhaps to give themselves a new ejaculatory experience.

It is the serious groups who are the most difficult to locate and contact. They may operate in any sphere of society, in council flats or country houses. The darkest secrets of satanic activity are always closely guarded. I have, however, been able to draw on case histories of people who have first-hand experience of ritualistic worship, and from other sources. I compiled numerous descriptions from men, women and young adults who have become involved with satanic groups and taken part in sadistic, bloody rituals.

The stories are remarkably similar, not only in themselves – comparing one experience with another – but also in relation to the historical rituals I have detailed elsewhere. I have made the point repeatedly that the occult relies on history and draws upon the graphic descriptions of satanic rituals, whether taken from the reported facts of an eighteenth-century trial in France, or from the writings of an imaginative novelist.

Renegade groups act out these rituals almost to the letter as if they were performing a passion play, except that the whole scenario is one of real-life sadistic horror. The stories of the virtual torture of young women on the black altars have become increasingly familiar, as more seem prepared to reveal their experiences. Psychiatrists believe that it was always fear, and self-disgust that enabled satanic groups to remain undiscovered for years.

In reviewing the interviews and statements of a number of former practitioners, the repetitiveness of the detail stands out, and thus I do not feel there is much to be gained from giving anything but a brief account. Basically, they are stories of women who have been badly abused, some over a long period of time, in repeated satanic rituals.

Sylvia, now in her forties, was mistress to a satanic Grand Master who travelled Europe to administer and supervise Black Masses and general orgiastic rituals, mostly in the private houses of wealthy people:

> He believed that the more evil he could perform, the better it would be for him in the after life; he truly believed this. Not only that, as Grand Master he was paid handsomely for conducting these rituals. Local girls were usually brought in; sometimes, especially in Holland, they were plain prostitutes though he did not like that at all. He wanted supple young women, preferably virgins but of course, it is difficult to get those these days.
>
> You don't want me to go through it again, do you? It was the usual; it was always the usual – the black altar with black fur draped across and girls, and sometimes boys if it was a homosexual or bisexual crowd. He would dress as a Roman Catholic priest to read the rituals and the Enochian keys that sound like gibberish but they are not – they each have a meaning. He stands

with the knife, cuts the girl's arm, or marks her breast perhaps, and allows blood to drip into the chalice. The chalice may have other concoctions, all the usual things – a mixture of herbs and alcohol. Some of these men went the whole hog, if you'll excuse the expression, and ejected semen and urine. It was foul – too foul to describe.

As mistress to this man, I have stayed in some country houses and in France, and elsewhere on the continent. It never fails to surprise me the sort of people we are dealing with – often rich, though I have never met anyone famous. The girls? It's not just girls. It's youths who are brought in for the whipping ceremonies, or for them to be smeared with unction, blood and a horrible mixture; and handled and mauled while making love. The sexual orgies – because blood and sex are the keys to satanic power, always – go on for hours and hours sometimes. I have been told about children being present, I have never seen any; I have been told of human sacrifice but I've never seen that either. But they will stop at nothing; they hold nothing sacred. That is the truth.

Frank Smyth, author of *Modern Witchcraft*, quotes this description of a typical altar scene from Serge Kordiev, who describes exactly what he witnessed:

The atmosphere was unbearably repulsive and, at the same time, weakening. One felt immediately light-headed on entering the room. The black candles seemed to contain pitch and stank abominably. Their smell was partly masked by a brazier of incense which stood to the left of the altar and which I suspect also contained hashish. Over these odours was the hot reek of sweating naked bodies; everyone left his or her clothes outside the room and apart from the black facial masks all were entirely nude. The priest was a heavily built man with red hair; he walked down the aisle formed by the congregation until he stood between the legs of the girl lying on the altar. Slipping out of the heavy cloak he was wearing, he handed it to one of the two acolytes, one a man and the other a woman, who knelt at either side of him. He kissed the girl on the altar three times and proceeded to say a Mass in which Satan was substituted for Christ. At the consecration, the priest pulled her slightly towards him and proceeded to have sexual intercourse. To my horror she started to scream and moan and blood ran down her legs. I am certain he was wearing some sort of spiked ring around his penis which lacerated the woman as he entered. One of the congregation was a doctor, who later attended to her.

Ursula, twenty-seven, joined what she thought was a' pagan witch coven; she was seeking alternatives in her life and friendships. Unwittingly, she had become involved with a lesbian satanic grotto and did not discover the fact until she was blindfolded and tied for the ritual that was described to her as the normal initiation for witchcraft. It was neither pagan, nor Wiccan but a painful black ceremony. The atmosphere was lively; they had been smoking marijuana beforehand which was handed round to get them all in the mood. Ursula had no idea what the initiation was all about but she was told it was 'all good fun'. She was laid naked across the altar while her new colleagues made their incantations. She began to get scared when the woman who was the leader began strapping her arms and legs in leather and buckles, so tight that she could not move. Her legs were wide apart. The woman spoke soothing words to begin with, telling her not to be afraid, then her voice changed in an instant and she began the most loud chanting, over the sound of taped organ music in the background. The woman High Priest, unknown then to Ursula, had strapped on a hard rubber phallus, mounted the living altar and pushed it inside with such force that she let out a loud scream, and then fainted. When she awoke, she had been taken off the altar and laid on the cold floor; blood was pouring from her vagina, and she had suffered internal wounds. She got up and could barely walk. She dressed and ran from the house, never to return. Nor did she tell the police. Some months after the event, she was still in therapy.

No one can now investigate the case of Caroline, who was twenty-three when she died of a drugs overdose in Blackburn Royal Infirmary. The coroner recorded an open verdict in February 1990 in view of a 200-page diary she had left, describing in horrific detail her involvement with a satanic sect which so horrified her father that he could not believe such events could occur, nor that any human could be capable of them, let alone his daughter; he still barely believes it. The girl wrote that she became involved with the group some years ago, when a teenager, after she began a relationship with a boy whose parents were practising satanists. She became pregnant and her references to 'death of innocence' suggested that the baby was aborted and the foetus used in a sacrificial ritual by the group. She had a second baby some years later and, according to the diary, this too appears to have been taken at birth and possibly killed. Caroline is no longer here; she was apparently unable to cope with the mental trauma caused by all that she had been through.

Jane was twenty-one and was forced to take part in satanic rituals for fourteen years; like Caroline, she was of low intelligence and exactly the type of girl who is being sought and used in pseudo-satanic ceremonial. There were a large number of people present from a regular ring of about a hundred, many of whom she knew to be professional people. She was just five years old when she was first taken to the group by her mother and father. At twenty-one, medical examination confirmed she had been physically and sexually abused over a long period of time. She had one child who she says was taken from her by the group; she had the second child adopted. Her story has all the usual ingredients which once made these accounts of satanic abuse suspect; I personally believe that this adds confirmation simply because of their similarity. She says:

Wherever we met, whether in a cellar, attic or hastily converted living room . . . in one corner there was a pile of stones. This was the altar. A table is very rare, in the belief that natural things hold power because they are of the ground. In Black Masses, which are a series of rituals involving the sacrifices of animals or sexually related rites, the naked back of a woman is used as the altar. Marked on the floor was what I came to know as the circle of Agrippa. The circle has three further circles inside it. In the middle is the five-pointed star. Three men stood around the top of the circle. I learned that one of them was called the Grand Master who is the head. He is usually invited to a Black Mass and performs Philtres, spells inciting love, usually at a child's first sexual experience. In my case I was five. Women danced around the circle. I felt sick and hot and the voices were deafening . . . I began to scream and scream. That was the worst thing to do, because the fear became too much and I didn't know what to do. I was held and I was burned with heated skewers. I felt so guilty, because everything they did, they said, was for me . . .'

CHAPTER SIXTEEN

A QUESTION OF
BELIEF

From the foregoing chapters it will be seen that with sufficient
research, investigation and documentation of the state of witchcraft, occultism and satanism as world movements, no exaggeration, overstatement or silly claims were necessary. The facts speak
for themselves. It exists. It is growing. And certain aspects are
indeed very, very ugly and disturbing.

And yet . . .

In the stirrings of fundamentalism as the world heads towards
the last years of the second millennium, which Christian evangelists believe will be marked by the Second Coming, we are seeing
the resurgence of a Holy War that has existed since the beginning
of the first year after the death of Christ. The battleground as
always is the views held by non-believers and more especially the
opposers of Christ, the dreaded worshippers of Satan, Lucifer and
other leading lights of the Underworld.

And battle commenced in earnest in the spring of 1986 when
400 leaders of evangelist movements from around the world met in
California to begin the formalization of their campaign to convert
twenty million people to Christianity by the year 2000. It was part
of the worldwide Christian Decade of Evangelism which was to
begin in 1990, to which the satanic movement replied instantly
with its own Decade of Vengeance, in which it was rapidly joined
by most other groups in the left-hand side of the occult movement.
Punch and counterpunch began to be delivered almost immediately. I can quote from this sample, sent to me in one of the satanic
magazines I acquired for research:

Decade of Evangelism, or Decade of Vandalism . . . these people mean business . . . nobody is safe . . . they are cunning and clever. These powerful politico-evangelical groups, emanating from the USA, have one aim in mind: total world domination via an iron grip on theocracy . . . these wicked people have subverted institutions and famous charities everywhere and are setting cultures against each other with their fanaticism . . .

The pamphlet was filled with anti-Christian vitriol and was widely circulated, albeit only to occultists, and similar attacks on the evangelist movements have been printed in pretty well every occult magazine I have seen in the past eighteen months – hundreds in number. Meanwhile, in Britain, an organization calling itself the Evangelical Alliance was formed to fight the devil and his disciples and can be seen to have promoted a massive campaign which highlighted many alleged incidences of child abuse, sacrificial rites and terrible cases of sadistic torture during Black Mass ceremonies.

Elsewhere, powerful, cash-rich Christian groups in America began their own extensive lobbying and the weight of the Roman Catholic Church was added to the international campaign when, in 1987, the Holy See began preparing its own review of Satan past and present, inspiring debates and conventions on the theological issues surrounding the Prince of Darkness. This followed a message sent by the Pope to the Archbishop of Canterbury, Dr Robert Runcie, stating that he believed the devil's hand was behind today's increasingly hedonistic values. 'It is not a myth that the devil has appeared to St Anthony,' Pope John Paul II told a Polish friend. 'I too have seen his evil grin.'

But perhaps the most crucial development, highlighted by individual members of the Evangelical Alliance, had surfaced even before that organization was officially formed.

Until the middle of 1987, very few people in Britain had even heard the phrase satanical ritual abuse of children. In my thirty years in journalism, which included several years of local court reporting, work in several other countries of the world, and finally a senior editorial position in national newspapers, I can honestly say I had never previously encountered a single case involving it.

Yet suddenly, out of the blue, the media were being deluged

with stories of terrible things being perpetrated by satanists and witches. And in various parts of the country, social workers began rounding up children and arbitrarily spiriting them away to safe havens, out of the clutches of their seemingly abusing parents – an allegation for which the foundation of 'evidence' was controversial in the extreme.

The publicity was enormous, as one story followed another, culminating in widespread allegations of a worldwide occult network of vile and bloodthirsty people who were breeding and killing thousands of unbaptized babies each year for ritual purposes, who were abusing children in similar numbers and who were putting young men and women through terrifying ordeals of sexual torture and sometimes death.

The hysteria, for that is what it became, only began to assume some kind of perspective in Britain on 12 August 1990 when Rosie Waterhouse, a young journalist then employed by the *Independent on Sunday* wrote an article under the headline 'The Making of a Satanic Myth' that asked the simple question: Where is the evidence? 'Investigations have produced no bodies, no bones . . . no bloodstains. Nothing.'

That last sentence was music to the ears of occultists everywhere. It was reproduced, to my knowledge, in a dozen underground magazines in this country and was reprinted abroad. The enthusiasm of the general non-tabloid media for the satanic horror stories was suddenly replaced by scepticism and disbelief.

Until then, and for almost three years, these tales of satanic slavery had reached incredible proportions and the general public had been asked to accept without challenge that Britain and America were riddled with highly organized and perverted groups of degenerates, who had formed an occult alliance stretching from local group level to higher international orders, with its tentacles established far and wide through society, into the judiciary, politics and the police.

It was claimed to be basically occult, largely satanical and allied to the remnants of the old Paedophile Exchange network and the surviving vast industry of paedophilic pornography and snuff videos. Various 'survivors' of occult sects went public to tell of their experiences, but at the heart of the matter were the children involved in alleged satanic ritual abuse (or SCA – satanic child abuse, as it is also known).

Between 1987 and 1991, 211 children in six British centres were taken into care during investigations of child abuse (I have not included single cases which occurred elsewhere). Of that total, 121 were involved in the notorious and discredited Cleveland investigation in which there was never any hint of satanic ritual abuse, although there were similarities in the procedures social workers used for establishing the indications of abuse shown by the children. Cleveland became the subject of a wide ranging government-sponsored inquiry which resulted in new and stringent guidelines being published.

In Nottingham, twenty-seven children were involved in investigations relating to a ring of abusers who were eventually gaoled; again no evidence linking the abuse to satanic ritual was offered in court, although it had been examined in the investigations of police and social workers. The remaining sixty-three children were all said to have been associated with satanic ritual abuse and there were many incredible claims of the terrible acts to which the children had been subjected. But once again, no firm evidence was offered, not a single prosecution resulted and most of the children were returned to their homes.

No bodies, no bones . . . no bloodstains. Nothing.

When that one line was published in the *Independent on Sunday* article after the Rochdale children had been taken from their homes in a dawn raid, the media and other commentators began to challenge the very existence of ritual abuse. Social workers and child charity organizations had inspired much of the original publicity by repeating theories contained in imported material supplied by certain evangelist organizations, and were soon to be subjected to the torment of a critical press.

The pendulum swung rapidly in the opposite direction, returning to the status quo – and the theory that none of these things could be true, that the stories of death and torture were largely the inventions of fertile imaginations, or an elaboration of details accidentally planted in young minds by the set-form questioning of social workers. Or, in the case of adults, a combination, perhaps, of childhood memories and a need to quell their own guilt for some past actions (though that brief summary is all too simplistic, and I will elaborate later).

What remained, however, in the minds of most non-occultists – and undoubtedly a good number within the movement itself – who had followed these developments was an underlying doubt: 'What if it is true . . .?'

This prospect suddenly took on real meaning when, in February 1991, another seventeen children were taken from their homes by social workers in the Orkneys on the basis of inquiries being made into another massive outbreak of ritual abuse committed by a ring which, by implication, included some parents. Again, it was based upon unprovable descriptions from the children . . .

No bodies, no bones . . . no bloodstains. Nothing.

Confusion and doubt remain, even as I write, to the extent of occultism itself. I have seen one newspaper report that even challenged the very existence of satanism in 1992, and the same article dismissed witchcraft as the playground of cranks and old crones whose activities were not even worthy of discussion. I think I have already disproved that ridiculous theory but it is one of the extreme examples – while we are discussing extremes – that illustrate how, through fear and ignorance, many people are prepared to dismiss the occult world as insignificant and ignore the possibility that there could well be an element of truth in certain of the allegations.

Personally, after two years of continuous investigation and interviews, I believe the latter to be the case but it has been overshadowed almost to the point of elimination by the massive media reaction to the welter of anti-satanic material deliberately pumped out by Christian fundamentalists and originating in the commercially orientated US anti-satanic crime lobby, aided and abetted by some high-flying American therapists and a large number of uninformed but impressionable social workers in Britain.

The evangelists have much to answer for; the over-zealous promotion of their belief that the world was full of satanic perverts has caused anguish and disorder in many a happy family home.

So much of their propaganda was barely believable, as much again was patently untrue, and the whole was so hysterical in its foundations and presentation that important issues about the badness and malevolence and ritual abuse in satanism became wrapped up into a single-issue package that seemed unanswerable and unprovable, and so was swept back to where it had always survived – in the shadows of society.

No bodies, no bones . . . no blood. Nothing.

True, but the lack of them proved nothing, either, and this is the point of this foregoing preamble to what is my final chapter. The constant reiteration of that phrase in all quarters where there is disbelief or disinformation regarding occult badness – and which I have deliberately repeated for this purpose in the previous paragraphs here – itself caused a false view to become established. Just as there is no basis for the grossly exaggerated claims of one side of the divide, neither is there any reason to dismiss them, just because no one has found any bodies, bones or bloodstains.

Evil exists and it is practised in the name of satanism.

But it is being covered and lost in the Holy War and in the cause of self-interest by a multitude of people – the children became pawns and victims. Their plight must also be viewed separately from the gory accounts of so-called satanic 'survivors' whose stories began flooding the pages of the Sunday tabloids from the mid-1980s onwards because there are so many additional complications caused by the self-interests of other groups – including the paedophiles, the therapists and criminologists who climbed aboard a fast-moving bandwagon and have made a living this last decade out of this work; the social workers and child charity organizers who were swept into the network and finally the propagandists from the two sides of the religious war, the fundamentalists and the satanists. They all had an axe to grind – the whole damn lot of them.

Let me now try to bring some reason and sense into this issue and put some dates to the emergence of an international scandal.

Until the early 1980s, the existence of satanism as a specific threat to society in terms of media perception – which is where most of the public discussion is centred – was focused on the actuality of its ritual and ceremony, founded as they are on principles which are a complete reversal of Christian values. Anton LaVey and Michael Aquino were distant high-profile figures. Equally distant were the incidental outbreaks of defilement propagated by satanic groups in Britain. Thus publicity centred largely around the leaders and around outbreaks of nastiness by outlaw groups who were merged and confused in press terms with the activities of black magicians and black witches, thrown in without much discernment for truth. The result was headlines about the killing of goats, cats or chickens for sacrificial purposes, spiced with the description of naked ceremonies performed by covens of witches and the desecration of churches and graveyards.

Talk of human sacrifice and cannibalism was vague and infrequent. In fact, as early as 1975, Maxine Sanders talked of having 'heard' of babies being killed by a particularly disreputable group who followed a form of Druidism but she had no first-hand knowledge of such events. This revelation received absolutely no publicity at all, presumably because it was unbelievable.

In the sixties and seventies, the devil was more likely to have been discovered living in the bodies of pre-pubescent children and thus highly melodramatic tales of exorcism surfaced with regularity. That was until a succession of mass murderers like the Yorkshire Ripper, Peter Sutcliffe, and the American serial killer, Richard Ramirez, known as the Night Stalker, were said to have been guided by the voice of the devil.

There were deeper implications, too. Ramirez had a pentagram tattooed on the palm of his hand and shouted 'Hail Satan!' when he left court. Other mass killers in America claimed membership of satanic groups, and the British-originated Process Church was often mentioned as being the provider of a belief-system which appeared to give permission for murder, since Satan existed as the executioner and the administrator of the final judgement.

One other famous case was that of David Berkowitz, who became known as The Son of Sam Killer, responsible for six murders and six attempts. Long after his conviction and imprisonment in 1977, he revealed in letters to a Californian priest that he had been a member of an occult group which pursued 'a mixture of satanic practices which included the teachings of Aleister Crowley'. He eventually identified the group as an offshoot of the

Process Church of the Final Judgement, based in New York. Berkowitz's prolific letter-writing began to warn against satanism in general: 'These people cannot be taken lightly. Please try to understand their philosophy of life and society. They have no fear of man-made laws or the laws of God . . . to them murder comes easy . . . these people will stop at nothing . . .'

How often have I heard that warning? Time and time again. And it was interesting that the last line of Berkowitz's letter – this one written to a lawyer in October 1979 – stated that these 'are not a careless group who are apt to make mistakes. But they are secretive and bonded together by a common need and a desire to mete out havoc on society. It was Aleister Crowley who said, "I want blasphemy, murder, rape, revolution, anything bad . . ." Surely you will agree that death follows Crowley's footsteps.'

As these cases began to increase, criminologists in America came to a fairly widely accepted conclusion that satanic practices were the root cause of a number of mass-killings, especially those involving cannibalism.

It was possible, they theorized, for a killer to pick and choose beliefs from the writings of the various groups and end up with a way of life in which every kind of corruption and evil could be condoned – and this was certainly borne out by the proliferation of particularly brutal murders in which the victims were often eviscerated and dismembered and body parts used and consumed in rituals to Satan. This was proved and admitted in several known cases, and is beyond doubt. Satanic and occult related crime was a definite fact, indisputable and irrefutable and worthy of a more detailed examination than can be given here.

Alongside the mounting files of ritual murders, a satanic crime industry began to emerge, whereby specialist detectives and investigators made themselves available for their knowledge on satanic activities.

This activity and the satan-linked killings were largely unique to America. The only other mass killer of recent times in Britain, Denis Neilsen, who killed fifteen people and cut up their bodies, does not appear to have indulged in either cannibalism or satanic ritual, although some writers have attempted to link him to the devil community. In fact, neither he nor Sutcliffe could be remotely identified with true satanic crime.

However, mass killers and other brutal crimes with pseudo-satanic links saw the emergence of the anti-satanic crime lobby in the American judiciary in the early eighties, and to this was added a growth industry inspired by another totally unexpected source . . .

In the late seventies a woman named Michelle Smith (née Proby) began regular sessions with a psychotherapist called Dr Lawrence Pazder at the Royal Medical Centre in the Canadian suburban town of Victoria, British Columbia. She began to talk of being abused during childhood and, according to Dr Pazder, her recollections became more incredible and more bizarre at each session.

Lying there on her therapist's couch, she described how she had been offered to Satan at the age of five by her mother. She told how she had witnessed scenes of awful debauchery, had been locked in a cage with snakes, made to eat a soup of worms, seen kittens and other animals bloodily killed, babies sacrificed and how she was made to drink an awful mixture of blood and other foul substances, all at the altar of Satan. Dr Pazder claimed he brought these memories to the surface during two years and 200 hours of therapy.

Subsequently they wrote a book based upon their therapy sessions, entitled *Michelle Remembers*, published in America in 1980. In the meantime, Michelle left her husband and Dr Pazder left his wife and four children. They both eventually divorced and doctor and patient became husband and wife. Their book became a best seller and Michelle and her doctor were invited to the Vatican to give a first-hand account of how satanic groups were infiltrating society.

Hollywood inquired about the screenplay and suddenly, the world was awakened to the deeds of satanists. At the same time, Michelle's father, Jack Proby, still living in the suburbs of Victoria, had been to see his lawyers concerning his daughter's allegations against her mother – describing them as the worst pack of lies a girl could ever make up; he could not think what had made her say such things and denied, point by point, that anything she 'remembered' had ever taken place. His lawyers confirmed that, because Mrs Proby had died some years earlier, there could be no action for defamation. However, Proby filed an action for Notice of Intent against the publishers which effectively stifled the film deal.

The Roman Catholic Bishop Remi de Roo listened to the therapist's tapes and arranged for doctor and patient to be received at the Vatican, where they were met by Cardinal Sergio Pignedoli, then head of the secretariat for non-Christians. The bishop also wrote a preface to *Michelle Remembers* in which he said, 'I do not question that for Michelle the experience was real. In time, we will know how much of it can be validated. It will require prolonged and careful study. In such mysterious matters hasty conclusions would prove unwise.'

The bishop was right to be cautious but his caution went largely unheeded. Pazder began lecturing on the subject of satanic abuse – claiming that Michelle had become the spokesperson for those who, until then, dare not tell their story because it was locked away in the subconscious, forced back into the shadows of the mind through a mixture of fear, shame and guilt. And if Dr Pazder is to be believed, there were many people young and old who were waiting to be released. *Michelle Remembers* was followed by a dramatic upsurge in cases of ritual abuse, virtually unheard of until then. Not one case had ever been recorded by the Royal Canadian Police Force prior to the publication of her book.

In America, it coincided with another phenomena, and suddenly all the things that Michelle had called to mind were being repeated by children in pre-school day centres where allegations of sexual abuse were being investigated.

In 1983, child-care specialists and police became aware of a growing number of abuse cases relating to children, often under the age of four, attending the pre-school centres. The figures began to mount to such astronomical proportions that study groups were set up to monitor them, and it must be said that the allegations were made under conditions of counselling. By February 1985, there was such widespread concern that America's first conference on Day-Care Centre and Satanic Cult Sexual Exploitation of

Children was staged at the FBI Academy in Quantico, Virginia. Ken Lanning, of the FBI's Behavioral Science Unit, signalled the difficulties that lay ahead in getting to the truth of this mass of allegation when he said: 'The lack of first-hand confirmation of bizarre child sexual abuse has made investigating reports of such activity very difficult ... the many unanswered questions about satanic cult exploitation of children illustrate the complexities of the issue in this new area of investigation.'

Less than two years later, another conference was arranged by the Affirming Children's Truth (ACT) at Hermosa Beach, California, on 4 May 1987. The conference demonstrated how far the problem had expanded when it was claimed that in southern California, eight different children's day-care centres had been visited and investigators had found that a combined total of 870 children had been victims of ritual abuse. A further fifty had allegedly been abused at a day-care centre at the Presidio Army Base in northern California.

A specially commissioned and confidential document in my possession entitled 'A Report to the President', was prepared for President Reagan and submitted in 1987. It noted that the 'United States has seen the emergence of child abuse cases called satanic or ritualistic abuse ...' In a successive report, published in 1988 by a team of child specialists from the Family Research Laboratory at the University of New Hampshire, it was claimed that in a careful analysis of 270 day-care child abuse cases, 13 per cent, or thirty-five cases, included allegations of ritual abuse.

By then, these cases were attracting the nationwide attention of child psychologists and social workers who began networking their information. Paper after paper – almost two dozen in a three-year period – were published and circulated through the professions linked to child care and numerous organizations and universities began studying the phenomena. I could now relate the contents of a dozen or more theses on the subject, but there would be little point. None was able to state conclusively that they could confirm absolutely the existence of satanic ritual abuse.

However, a heavy anti-satanic movement was under way and a number of leading child-care specialists were already on the lecture circuit giving hints and guidelines on how to identify ritual abuse – as opposed to ordinary sexual abuse – among children. One team of specialists recorded a series of videos, commercially produced by a company called Cavalcade Productions of Ukiah, California, starting at $195 for a thirty-minute tape. Among the Californian specialists were Catherine Gould, a clinical psychologist from Los Angeles, and Pamela Hudson, a qualified professional from Mendocino, California. They were among eight nationally recognized specialists in the field of child pyschology, multi-personality trauma, and other problems relating to mental and physical behavioural problems.

Catherine Gould's video, priced at $225 a copy (or available for rental at $60 a time) was entitled 'Identification of the Ritually Abused Child' and proclaimed 'overwhelming intimidation by the perpetrators makes identification of ritual abuse a challenging task. This video programme highlights some of the subtle indicators that point to possible cult victimization. Clinicians utilize a variety of play therapy techniques, including sand-trays, projective art and The Snow Man Games . . . a wide range of figures and toys help the children re-enact their trauma experiences.'

Pamela Hudson, whose video was for sale at $195 (in 1989) was discussing the 'mind control techniques employed by cult members which leave the young victims fearful, confused and deeply traumatized.' Finally, a Ritual Child Abuse Professional Overview, with a discussion by eight clinicians, was advertised on the basis that leading professionals shared their insights from hundreds of case histories, with topics including mind control, victim credibility, day care safety, ritual molestation and cult homicides.

Catherine Gould in her video and in the papers she subsequently presented to numerous conferences and conventions on the subject, provided her audiences with a list of key indicators which were designed to prove that the child had been subject to satanic ritual abuse. I have a copy of Catherine Gould's original paper on the subject, first published in May 1986.

She listed thirty-three separate indicators for discovering symptoms characterizing satanic ritual abuse and sexual abuse in children, ranging from bedwetting, fear of the dark and nightmares to identifying specific stains in children's underwear. Even then, these specialists realized the difficulties in establishing a believable result from the questioning of children.

In a later paper, entitled 'Therapy with Children who have been Ritualistically Abused', Pamela Hudson quoted Freud's seduction theory in which he said a patient's hysteria originated from violent infantile sexual experiences which had a damaging and lasting effect. His words were: rape, abuse, seduction, attack and trauma. Seven years later, Freud completely reversed his views and said the scenes described by these hysterical patients were fantasies. This followed his experience with one specific case, that of Emma Eckstein who described scenes of devil worship – remarkably similar to Michelle Smith's – of being circumcised and having blood sucked from her. Freud refused to believe that these descriptions were real and, though accepting that the Sabbats and ritualized ceremonies were real events, decided that there was no scientific proof of Emma's claims and he therefore judged them to be the product of her imagination. In 1989, Pamela Hudson wrote that ninety-three years after Freud's landmark paper was presented in Vienna, psychologists were back to the startling decision that their patients were telling the truth. They were raped and traumatized and the lasting effect was chronic post-trauma stress syndrome, not hysteria. She went on, 'by sharing our work, we can develop guidelines which are effective in the treatment of ritualistically abused victims.'

Before proceeding any further, it is perhaps worth noting that in spite of all the great volume of activity throughout America, police and prosecuting authorities found great difficulty in actually bringing cases to court. Case after case collapsed through lack of corroboration of the children's stories, or because parents became increasingly unwilling to allow their children to be put through the trauma of hours of questioning as laid down in the process of checking off the satanic indicators.

One particularly famous case involved the McMartin Day Center in Los Angeles, where a hundred pre-school children were enrolled. Allegations of child molestation first surfaced in 1983 and the Los Angeles Police Department began what became a marathon investigation – the longest such investigation in modern times – fraught with all the problems of establishing confirmation of the children's stories. Seven years later, and at a cost of almost $14 million, charges against the owner and staff at the school were finally thrown out or scrapped.

One of the key defendants, Ray Buckley, who faced eighty-two charges, spent five years in gaol awaiting trial and in the final outcome, he walked free, commenting: 'It was Salem revisited.'

Inevitably in a case of this nature there remained some unanswered questions. One mystery especially puzzled parents of children who claimed they had been taken into a secret tunnel where they had seen naked people cavorting before them and had witnessed devil worship, and had foreign objects inserted into their bodies. Underground tunnels were a feature of many such cases, and it is a known practice of many occultists to seek deep and dark caverns underground which are said to provide spiritual energy for rituals.

In 1991, a McMartin parent financed an excavation at the school by a leading archaeologist, Dr Gary Stickel. He discovered a forty-five-foot cavern under the school, entered through a nine-foot-wide entrance under the west wall of a classroom.

The Los Angeles police discovered, at great cost to the public purse, the difficulty of establishing a provable case, as is shown by the statistic I quoted at the beginning of this book: during the five years when academic debate on satanic ritual abuse was at its height – between 1985 and 1990 – there were only three recorded prosecutions for abuse where the evidence confirmed ritualistic content.

This was in spite of literally hundreds of potential child victims being interviewed and put through the child psychiatry ritualistic indicators tests. The one remarkable factor in all cases was the similarity of every story told by the children; in fact it became so much like an imprinted recitation that opposers of these ritual indicators claimed the children were being brainwashed by the questions.

This very same description would soon be applied by Professor John Newson, of Nottingham University's child development research unit, to the techniques adopted in Britain by some child-care specialists. Hostility towards the child-care experts' views on satanic ritual abuse was already mounting in the United States but in Britain, the children had yet to go through the pain barrier . . .

Alerted by Christian groups of psychiatrists and fundamentalists, the videos, theses and papers containing lists of abuse indicators were soon to become available in Britain and, in fact, were being heavily circulated among the British social services community by 1987, the year the Cleveland scandal broke.

In Cleveland, 121 children were diagnosed as having been sexually abused. Ritual abuse was not mentioned. The children were taken into care and later released without charges being laid against parents, and in an inquiry conducted by Lord Justice Butler-Sloss, the social workers and paediatricians involved were criticized. The case also brought the issue of child abuse into the public forum.

The first – and only – major British prosecution was already under investigation by then. It involved an appalling catalogue of the perverse and sadistic abuse of twenty-seven children, not one over the age of eight, by a ring of nine adults, mostly relatives.

In February 1989, months after the ending of the trial, the accused men and women were given prison sentences totalling forty-three years. The main feature of this case, though, was the fact that no mention of ritualistic abuse was made in the evidence. It was prosecuted on the basis of standard offences, mostly of incest, which accounted for fifty-three charges.

After the case, a dispute broke out between the police and social workers who comprised the investigating unit known as Team Four, over the fact that there were signs of ritual abuse and certain elements of the evidence taken from the children, of which I have seen extracts, were not revealed at the trial. This related to descriptions of sexual abuse within this low-life family group and the children also talked of family members giving birth to babies who were slaughtered and cooked in microwave ovens. There was also mention of rituals conducted in tunnels, later indentified as catacombs beneath Nottingham Rock Cemetery.

However, the local Chief Constable and head of social services for Nottingham agreed to set up a joint inquiry team to examine these allegations for their own purposes, not connected with the court hearing, to try to establish grounds for believing in ritualistic abuse. It was to be made up of six men and women who had not previously been involved in the case. For the next eighteen months, police and social services became embroiled in a secret battle interviewing social workers, foster parents, children and even one of the gaoled perpetrators of the abuse.

The Joint Enquiry Team (JET) produced a massive 500-page report in which it rejected the presence of satanic ritual abuse. This concurred with the statement of Professor John Newson of the Child Development Research Unit of Nottingham University who advised the inquiry team.

The Nottingham experience was networked to other social services departments. One of the city's social workers admitted, 'We had many telephone calls from other social workers seeking help. I told them that at first we did not believe what the children were telling us, and then by sheer force of numbers we began to take them seriously.'

The list of 'satanic indicators' brought over from America by Pamela Klein was also used in what was then thought to be Britain's first true case of alleged satanic ritual abuse, in Kent in 1988. A two-year-old boy showed signs of disturbed behaviour, laughed hysterically and talked of 'funny drinks'. Thereafter the Kent social services department was involved in nine cases of ritual abuse, involving seventeen adults and a total of seventy-five children. These cases have been shrouded in secrecy ever since, and many of the interviews were conducted by social workers from outside the area. No charges were ever brought and the fate of the children was never made public.

Next, in Manchester in the late summer of 1989, two sisters aged four and seven were taken into care. Three months into the investigation, they began to talk of witches and gave descriptions of what sounded like satanic rituals. A further eleven children were taken into care, and they gave much more detailed and alarming descriptions of child sacrifice, blood-drinking and animal killings. Eight of the cases were eventually dropped and the local authorities were criticized about their methods when the High Court was asked to make all thirteen children wards of court.

In November 1989, a six-year-old boy was found hiding in a school cupboard by his headmaster in Rochdale and sparked off the largest ritual abuse scare in Britain yet. Although the boy was dyslexic and retarded, the two social workers who were assigned the case decided that the boy was telling the truth when he spoke of ghosts and devils, and how he saw 'big babies and little babies' being stabbed to death.

Four more children in the same family were taken into care almost immediately; an eleven-year-old girl talked of being abused in her dreams. As a result of what she told them, twelve more children were taken from their homes in a series of dawn raids on 14 June; another child was taken in the same month, and three more from another family on 7 September – all resulting from the first case.

Gordon Littlemore, Rochdale's head of social services who had attended a seminar on satanic abuse, made no mention of it when he explained, 'We are dealing with allegations of emotional abuse, degradation, humiliation, drugs and exposure to acts of violence which would not necessarily result in physical injury.'

Three days later, on 13 September, James Anderton, Chief Constable of Manchester, announced that his inquiry team had been working on the Rochdale case for three months and had been unable to accumulate enough evidence to sustain a criminal prosecution.

Meanwhile, the Rochdale social services received prompt support from various organized groups, including the newly formed Ritual Abuse Information Network which claimed that month to have investigated eighteen cases of ritual abuse involving thirty-three children.

For the first time in any such case, the Rochdale parents got together and took the local authority to court. In March 1991, ten of the remaining fourteen children were ordered to be returned home after a forty-seven-day hearing in the High Court. Mr Justice Brown severely censured the social services department for failing to read the Butler-Sloss report. Gordon Littlemore resigned.

One more – and possibly the last – case of mass evacuation of children after allegations of ritual abuse came in the spring of 1991, incredibly just a month after the Rochdale case had been thrown out. Seventeen children from families on the island of South Ronaldsay in the Orkneys were taken to places of safety after the daughter of a local family, later described as disturbed because of a family crisis, began to talk of ceremonies, of dancing and chanting by people wearing robes, and of sex being performed by adults on children. Before long, several of the children were producing what had become standard replies to the controversial therapy sessions which had been introduced into the social workers' routine.

Even local Presbyterian Minister Morris McKenzie, aged sixty-eight, was implicated in the children's evidence and when police visited his house, along with the homes of parents and others, they took away his academic robes. The social workers' questioning of the children seemed to uncover the allegation that people in dark robes had taken part in lewd and libidinous activities in night-time ceremonies between June and November that year.

Locals began to ridicule the claims but two appeals to have the children released back to their parents' custody were rejected by the island's children's panel. However, on 4 April 1991 Kirkwall Sheriff David Kelbie adjudged the social workers' case to be fundamentally flawed and the dawn removal of the children was judged illegal. He ordered their return forthwith and thereafter the government promised an inquiry into the whole satanic abuse scandal.

There were other damaging effects from the ritual abuse scare as it was being fostered and promoted by some Christian groups. It was they who helped draw the attention of the existence of ritualistic abuse to senior officers of the National Society for the Prevention of Cruelty to Children. In fact, the NSPCC can now be seen to have played a crucial role in the exposition of most of the ritual scare.

In spite of the mounting suspicion that hysteria was developing in these cases, the NSPCC called a press conference in March 1990 which attracted a very great deal of media attention – massive front-page reports, including the whole of the front page of the *Daily Mirror* under the headline 'Kids Forced Into Satan Orgies: Sex slaves' ordeal exposed by NSPCC'. The influential children's charity was claiming that children as young as five were being forced into devil-worship and suffering sexual and physical abuse, and if anything, the scale of the problem had been underestimated.

Mr Jim Harding, the society's director of child care said, 'We believe the children's accounts. They are obviously talking about very painful experiences that it would have been impossible to make up. We work closely with the police; the problem is securing a conviction.' The tabloid press grasped willingly at his statement – seemingly confirmed by one of the nation's leading child-care officials – that children were made to eat part of a human heart and one baby was microwaved and another was kept in a deep freeze for future use.

Before long, the NSPCC had seven of its sixty-six child protection teams working on suspected cases of ritual abuse. Material released to the press was almost identical in its formation to much of the material emanating from America and being circulated through the social work system. Among those in contact with the NSPCC were the Reverend Kevin Logan, a leading member of the Evangelical Alliance, who had sent a dossier on satanic crime to NSPCC officials. Logan and his associates had also obtained much of the American literature, thus the same material was going around the country, just as it had done in America.

With full knowledge of all the facts, seen against a background of the promotion of disclosure therapy by the self-interest of various groups, the ritual abuse scare can now be seen for what it was – a serious problem, hyped out of all proportion so that, in the end, the basic underlying cause was discredited.

For a calmer and more accurate perspective, I turned to Canon Dominic Walker at Brighton who has more experience than almost anyone in this country in dealing consistently with cases of occult abuse, and certainly over a lot longer period of time. He pretty well dismissed the idea of widespread ritualistic abuse of children. There was child abuse and ritualistic abuse. His own Church of England group has come across five or six cases a year of abuse which might have been linked to occult ritual, but there was certainly no pattern or evidence of a nationwide conspiracy or anything to support the theory that it was becoming a national scandal.

But the pressure did not cease, even as the warnings by other child specialists began to be sounded, telling of the dangers of hysteria. It could be *The Crucible* all over again. There was a surprising degree of sympathy for this view. And by now it was becoming increasingly difficult for anyone to interest prosecuting authorities in any case of alleged ritual activity.

CHAPTER SEVENTEEN

DIVERTED
ATTENTIONS

The undoubted good intent of those who sought to enliven public awareness to satanic practices can hardly be questioned. But it can now be shown that their attempts at media manipulation, inspired by their initial success in that field, led activists towards a damaging over-hype that in the end turned their campaign in on themselves. More importantly, the true heart of the matter – the well-being of children – actually became a side issue, totally overshadowed by the self-interests of religion, politics and head-lines that sold newspapers.

These outbreaks of media hype were easily distinguishable and simple to track. Interspersed between the allegations of child abuse were regularly placed stories involving adult survivors of occult activity, whose remembrances were far more horrific than anything the children had dreamed up. In almost every publicized case in Britain, these revelations could be traced back to a specific source – to members of the Evangelical Alliance. It is interesting to examine some of their contributions to media exposés in turn because they appeared in the press under huge banner headlines at times, coincidentally (or was it?) when interest in the child abuse scare was beginning to flag.

Dianne Core, forty-six years old in 1992, was a central figure in revealing many ritual abuse cases in the north of England and introduced the subject to Humberside social services department which – like most other similar offices through the country – had little or no knowledge of it before 1986/87. When it was being discussed at a national level, therefore, these departments were glad to get hold of any material they could and several Christian groups, such as the Evangelical Alliance, became willing suppliers.

Core was a devoted child-care worker who had been state trained and employed; she had also been sexually abused as a child and thus had the background to continue something of a crusade. In 1984, she formed Childwatch, a Hull-based organization which she ran from her home. Its aim was to counsel and help children and families who were being abused. Her work brought her into contact with the media, and she appeared frequently in television and radio programmes and in newspaper articles; she also met the Revd Kevin Logan.

By 1987, while continuing the work in the conventional sense, she began increasingly to become involved in the satanic abuse lobby and publicly announced that Childwatch was taking a special interest in the subject and cases were being invited and referred to her. Her campaign became more concerted as the months went by, and she appeared to make no distinction between witchcraft, black magic or satanism – she merely lumped them all together as a whole menacing package.

She continued to press parents and victims of abuse with whom she came into contact for details, and made copious notes, snatching at snippets of information and then repeating them to the press apparently without serious verification. Because this information came from Childwatch, a respected children's help line, it was intitially accepted at face value. The publicity surrounding her became such that her relationship with the Humberside police and the social services department became strained, she being dubbed a busybody and a crank by some, while the authority was labelled the heavy hand of officialdom by her.

In October 1988, she figured in an 'exclusive' exposé in the *Sunday Mirror* which gave the case history of former black witch, an American woman who claimed she had been sexually tortured and used as a child breeder by satanists. She said she gave birth to twins after being raped by a friend of her father's at the age of twelve. One of the children was a boy, who was allowed to live. 'The other was a girl. She was placed upon a table and my head was turned so that I could watch, and they drove an upside-down cross through her heart.' Further, she alleged seeing other people tortured to death by satanists and one was nailed upside-down so that all the blood drained from the body.

Dianne Core's contribution to the story went as follows: 'Women are being used as brood mares. They are made pregnant at occult ceremonies and then their babies are used as sacrifices.'

The result: a massive headline, reading BABIES ARE SACRIFICED TO SATAN.

At the end of 1988, Core was approached by the American magazine *New Federalist*, sponsored by the arch right-winger Lyndon LaRouche, to join a lecture tour around the United States on the subject of ritual abuse. She willingly accepted and there came into contact, first-hand, with the heartland of American theorists who believed in a worldwide satanic conspiracy. She did not limit her brief to satanism in her speaking tour. Witchcraft, she proclaimed, was equally as dangerous and she was certain that the British educational system had long been infiltrated by witches who teach the history of paganism.

She added the startling allegation that some teachers inspired after-school recruitment activities by casual discussions about ouija board, tarot cards and other curiosities which relate to witchcraft and lambasted heavy metal rock groups for their subliminal messages. Her speeches were videotaped and were later made available to any social services department or social workers who wished to have them.

On her return, she was soon back in the newspapers again, and giving help to *Daily Mirror* reporter Fred Harrison in his 'exclusive' series exposing the fact that 'satanists are weaving a web of evil across Britain. Children are their prey – and cash, drugs and sex are weapons used to trap them. Today we begin the harrowing story . . .'

Meanwhile, a similarly committed woman was working away in the unofficial Intelligence department of the Evangelical Alliance, running an offshoot of that organization called the Reachout Trust. It was set up on behalf of the EA in October 1988 and run by Maureen Davis from her small semi-detached in Rhyll, North Wales, and was mainly concerned with rescuing survivors from bad occult experiences. Anxious to promote her organization, she initially became a regular source and contact for newspaper reporters seeking the latest revelations of occult badness.

In October 1988, for example, she appeared in the *Independent* newspaper, quoted in one of her earliest interviews as co-ordinator of Reachout, alleging that occultists were currently carrying out an extensive recruitment campaign and schoolchildren were among the targets. She said that in her experience children first started dabbling in the occult as a form of rebellion. She estimated there were 80,000 witches in Britain who belong to official covens and many others operating as individual satanists. She attributed the rise in the number of occultists to fantasy books and computer games like Dungeons and Dragons.

Within six months, Maureen Davies was dishing out stronger meat. In another '*Sunday Mirror* Investigation' published on 21 May 1989, she was the source of a story concerning an occult survivor named Penny, then twenty-three, who had been a satanic breeder, having had five pregnancies terminated by her coven so that the foetuses could be sacrificed. Mrs Davies told the *Mirror*: 'Penny's life is at risk. If the satanists knew she was going to spill the beans, they would stop at nothing to shut her up. There is no record of the abortions because they were performed by a doctor who was a member of the coven.' The police were never involved. They were, however, called in to investigate the case of a girl then aged fifteen, who said she had been involved in a satanic group since she was eleven. She said she was repeatedly raped and had eight forced abortions.

When her mother learned of one of the abortions and that she had buried one of the foetuses in the garden, she called the police. An eighteen-month investigation resulted in the girl's grandmother being charged with procuring an abortion, and accused five men with rape. The case got no further than the Crown Prosecution Service. It was decided that there was insufficient evidence to sustain a conviction, since the case rested entirely on the evidence of the girl.

That year, Mrs Davies went on the Roger Cook television programme discussing satanism and said that these cases were by no means isolated. The horrors of satanic cult worship were spreading through Britain like wildfire. Eventually, Mrs Davies broke away from Reachout to form her own counselling group, but she also suffered personally, working herself into a serious illness.

*

Another of the most active publicity seekers for the Evangelical Alliance campaign against Satan throughout this period, and one who has faced similar criticism to that suffered by Core and Davies, was the Reverend Kevin Logan, a parish vicar from Blackburn. A former journalist, he has written books on the threat of the occult and has been a long-time campaigner against the likes of Chris Bray and witch covens, appearing on northern television programmes and claiming that the north of England harbours a hotbed of occult activity – and in that he is absolutely right. It does.

On 25 March 1990, he was involved in another remarkable satanic horror story when a young girl came to him for help, saying she wanted to get away from a group of satanists who had threatened to kill her. She confessed to him that she had murdered her own baby in 'frenzied ritual'. Logan befriended the girl, twenty-three-year-old Caroline (whom I have mentioned in an earlier chapter), and gave her temporary lodgings.

Logan said in melodramatic terms, 'She kept telling me she couldn't stand hearing the screams of her children inside her head.' And on 5 March, Caroline died of a drugs overdose and a post-mortem examination revealed eleven scars and burns on her body which Logan said tended to support her claims of having been involved in satanic ritual.

Further, Caroline left a 200-page diary in which she said she had been involved with a satanic group since she was thirteen and her writings went on to make incredible claims. She described how she went to coven meetings with a boy named Danny whom she met while living in a children's home. The boy's mother was a High Priestess and his father was The Master – a known satanic term for the leading member of the group. She described other practices which are known to be common in satanic altar initiations – that of having her armed pricked and blood drained into a chalice from which it is drunk.

'Much sexual perversion went on that night . . . later I learned more of Satan and practised my arts calling on the power of darkness. Satan had become my Lord and Master.' Later she described how she aborted a baby she was expecting by Danny then made the claim that Danny himself was sacrificed by his own father in retribution, and how she was forced to watch as he was hung upside down. She claimed to have seen other sacrifices of many newborn babies, stabbing them at orgies in which drugs were taken heavily. She also appeared to have had another child of her own which was also offered up for sacrifice.

At her inquest on 14 March, the coroner recorded an open verdict after the pathologist noted that Caroline's body had signs which confirmed she had given birth at least once, and had been subject to sexual abuse. The police took up the case, but no charges were brought and the investigation was closed without further action.

But if all of the above was found to be more than enough to inspire the most lurid of headline writers, more than enough to test the credibility of all who were proffering these dramatic and barely believable accounts of satanic abuse and more than enough to attract the interest of social workers all over Britain, more seemingly authentic allegations were to come from a series of conferences organized by other Christian groups. The first at Reading ran under the title, Not One More Child. Delegates from medical and social services sat open-mouthed as Detective Gerry Simandl of the Chicago Police Department told of the terrible happenings that had confronted investigators in America. He had come over with Pamela Klein, the Chicago social worker who related her own experiences. Maureen Davies made sure that delegates and newspaper people were aware of her dossiers and several more case histories from her files were filtered out into the media. Everything these people said was being taken as gospel by press and social workers alike because the allegations were coming from the mouths of so-called experts.

Even more surprising were the allegations made at a later conference, organized by a Christian group of therapists and staged over three days at a hospital in Harrow. There, Su Hutchinson, herself a satanic 'survivor' and now operations director for another counselling service called SAFE, made the horrifying claim that children were hung up by their feet in satanic ritual, and suffered all forms of sexual abuse, including rape, buggery and bestiality.

She said she had personally counselled fifty women who were suffering from the after-effects of cannibalism and was seeing on average ten occult survivors a week. Vera Diamond, a Harley Street specialist who co-organized the conference, said she knew of several cases where children had been killed.

In 1992, she said she was continuing to treat patients who were coming out of occult experiences.

Then there was the speech of a psychotherapist who came up with the astounding claim that 10,000 babies were being bred each year in America especially for satanic sacrifices. The figure is even more astounding when set against another statistic which he did not have available at that time: up to March 1991, the number of cases of alleged ritual abuse against children in the United States amounted to just over 10,000; there had been only three known prosecutions for ritual crime. Maureen Davies worked out that there were probably 3,000 sacrifical babies born in Britain each year. And the newspapers printed these statements without reservation – because the conferences were organized by senior medical people, it was assumed they knew what they were talking about.

Gradually, however, one or two saner voices began to appear, like Ken Lanning, the FBI's expert from the Center for the Analysis of Violent Crime. By October 1990, he was making it clear that the law enforcement agencies 'cannot ignore the lack of physical evidence. Until hard evidence is obtained and corroborated, people should not be frightened into believing that babies are being bred and eaten. Satanic crime has become a growth industry . . . speaking engagements, books, videos, television and radio appearances. You name it . . . and name the fee . . .'

By the beginning of 1992, the hysteria surrounding satanic ritual abuse of children had all but collapsed, and with it went all the stories of blood and gore, and dead babies and cannibalism.

No bodies, no bones . . . no bloodstains. Nothing.

And so Kevin Logan, Dianne Core and Co. retired hurt. Chris Bray and Co. continued to defend the position of occultists everywhere. The pagans stayed hidden behind their box numbers. The police dived for cover every time someone mentioned satanic ritual abuse. And gradually the topic virtually disappeared from the news pages – until the next time. Because there will be a next time; this piece of history has been repeating itself for two thousand years and more; the Holy War will continue and while the Christian activists drew worldwide attention to the march of occultism and some of its badness as the Decade of Evangelism got under way, they also caused a very great deal of apprehension and even derision.

And there never was any need to exaggerate, either.

Certain sections of the occult were damning themselves by their own actions and any perpetrators of the despicable might well have been brought to trial, eventually, just as they were in Nottingham. Instead, those who cried 'Wolf!' too loud and too often might well have allowed the guilty to go free because to say that it did not exist is just as wrong; moreover the satanic ritual abuse hysteria and the outrageous claims of so many babies being bred for blood-lust, actually diverted attention away from what many anti-occultists believe should be the main thrust of their battle – the continued flourishing of *all* occult practices.

If there had been such widespread abuse on the scale claimed by those with vested interests for revealing it, Canon Dominic Walker at Brighton would undoubtedly have been aware of it, since he has been dealing with the occult and the paranormal for most of his professional working life.

The cases he deals with are disturbing enough, but they do not occupy his entire life. What he finds especially interesting is that over the years the emphasis has moved from seeing people who have been scared or in some way affected by poltergeists and ghosts, to dealing with casualties from the occult.

This has been an obvious development; long gone are the scenes of deliverance where the local Methodist minister in the Welsh valleys was to be found in some television documentary ridding an unfortunate child of the evil spirits which possessed her body. That, once, was a common enough sight. It, too, like the plethora of ghosts, poltergeists and green men, has all but disappeared from view.

It was far easier to believe Dominic Walker, a gentle, softly spoken and handsome man who, without a dog-collar, could be imagined in a far more glamorous profession, when he said that there was very little satanic abuse of children in Britain in 1991 (I interviewed him in the summer of that year) nor had there been in recent years. And when I invited him to describe his view and understanding of Satan, or the devil, he was honest enough to give the impression that he is prefixing his remarks with, 'Well . . . I would say that wouldn't I . . .' His answer was not a bible-thumping castigation, but a more logical approach, providing me with reference points in the Bible which I might examine to make up my own mind.

Returning to the issue, he pointed out that ritual abuse had always been present, but it was only in recent years that victims had been persuaded to come out and talk about it. To link every case to satanism or the occult in general was wrong, said Walker, and there have been those who have accused even him of being a devil's disciple in disguise for refusing to say otherwise. Ritualized abuse was undoubtedly a fact of life. He was equally certain that some cases were satanic in origin; but to say that it was widespread, to encourage the belief that the world was in the grip of a satanic conspiracy, laced with horrendous practices, was merely to slip into the jargon of the excitable Christian activists and the born-again brigade.

A proper perspective had to be achieved and maintained, otherwise the whole question, the whole Christian challenge to bad occultism and devil worship, would merely become denigrated and discredited so that in the end the clergy at large, social workers, child carers and the police would simply become too scared even to contemplate that a case of satanic ritual abuse existed within their province. This state of affairs, I suggested, was reached in 1991. He nodded agreement.

There were casualties enough, said Walker; extravagant claims were not necessary and in spite of my prodding he steadfastly refused to give other than the briefest outline of cases he had dealt with, mainly through fear of disturbing 'clients' who were receiving his guidance and support, and secondly because years of practice has taught him that the very mention of the word devil by a Church of England priest invariably invoked headlines and the sensationalist publicity that he deliberately avoided.

He will continue to warn against the occult, guide people out of the maze, although not necessarily back into the Christian fold; it is his stated intent to rescue anyone from the clutches of sinister groups who seek to take control of people's minds, thoughts and deeds and I can understand that the latter prospect is also no exaggeration. He has counselled and aided many who felt that their involvement with occult groups had ruined their lives, either psychologically and mentally, or in their home life and financially. They were victims of occult leaders who sought power by various means to hold sway over their lives – almost an identical description, it will be recalled, given to me and warned against by some occultists.

This aim was usually achieved by the psychological hold the leaders of these groups have on their members, to the point that they feel totally subjugated to their will, either by manipulation through fear, drugs, hypnosis or purely and simply by threats against them. The professional family man whose case was mentioned earlier, and who was almost ruined by his membership of such a group, was not untypical of those seeking Walker's help.

This type of casualty, he said, tended to come from involvement in some of the darker practices of the occult, and quite often those who became involved did not know what they are joining. They may have shown some kind of interest towards paganism and old religions or they were inclined to experiment with witchcraft, joining one of the fairly harmless groups or covens who practise skyclad rituals, herbal medicines and casting spells – all seemingly pretty innocuous.

He believed – and perhaps this is well borne out by some of the glimpses of the occult in earlier pages – that involvement at this level could ultimately lead them down a more dangerous path. 'I suppose the analogy is that of a drug-taker who experiments with soft drugs initially and is eventually pulled towards an addiction to hard drugs,' said Walker. 'Many people have thought, for instance, that they were joining a white magic group whose only aim was to do good. White witches are sworn to "harm none" – but then when you challenge a white witch and say, "Have you ever hexed anyone?" they would reply, "Yes, but it was for his own good." New initiates can quite often find that they have moved into a sort of "grey" magic area which borders on the more dubious practices of black magic, and eventually they may be pulled towards the full ritual of black magic practices – even satanism itself – and find that because of the vows they must take, they cannot escape.

'Once the secrets of these groups become known to a member, they are warned that they cannot leave and must adhere to a strict code. It is scary stuff. There are many who dabble in witchcraft and black magic and a lesser number are involved in more dangerous and devil-linked pursuits. It would be an exaggeration to say that it represents a great threat to society; of course it does not; but it is bad enough. There *is* a growth of interest in the occult that is worrying. It has to be watched . . .'

In the cool, calm atmosphere of the front room of a Brighton vicarage, sipping our afternoon tea, Dominic Walker seemed to me to be a master of the understatement.

If any further proof was required that witchcraft, occultism and satanic worship are all very much alive and recovering from the ritual abuse scare, it arrived as this book went to press. The edition of the London-based magazine *Chaos International*, published in October 1992, might be called in tabloid terms 'an action-packed issue'. For one thing, my eyes fell upon an item in the review section. Among the recommended recent releases of tapes and CDs was a compilation by a group called Neither/Neither World and the title track, Dismember Them, was 'a tribute to Jeffrey Dahmer, the cannibal serial killer'. But overall, the magazine contained a number of pointers to the future, including a long article by Diana Vera, international coordinator of the History of Satanism and Correspondence Network in which she states the case for a 'political alliance' between satanists and neo-pagans. Meanwhile, a rousing editorial reports that the organization was going from strength to strength which was pleasing because 'the only way we are going to drag this world screaming into the 5th Aeon is by better communication . . . our conspiracy demands this. We need to be tapped into every computer mailbox in the world to be in the forefront of power when it comes . . .'

Power? It sounds ambitious, even ridiculous but also menacing . . .

THE OCCULT UNDERGROUND

As will have become apparent in the text of this book, there is no hierarchy overall in the organization of the occult. Witch covens and small secret societies sprout up in towns and cities all over the country without any specific national affiliation. There is, however, a fairly effective, if haphazard, worldwide networking system and though the tiny local witches' covens or small mystical societies working pretty much on their own are unlikely to be part of any international concern, there are, as we have seen, larger international groups such as the Ordo Templi Orientis which has affiliated lodges throughout the world, as do a number of international satanic orders, notably the Church of Satan, the Temple of Set and Embassat (the Embassy of S.A.T.A.N.). And whatever the status of the group, large or small, there exists a broad spectrum of contact and exchange of information, ideas and action through which there is a considerable level of activity, covering every aspect of the occult.

The author does not believe that there is any sophisticated international conspiracy operating among occult or satanic groups; far from it. But as discussed in Chapter 12, the existence of an élitist organization which acts as a world supervisory body cannot be discounted. The machinery is certainly in place and available whenever required and contact between seriously committed occultists really knows no boundaries.

It is a relatively simple matter, through the information exchange system now operating, to instigate debate, to encourage contact between groups, to promote a particular cause, to isolate a special interest for inter-group action or to whip up support for a campaign, as was done in 1990 to try to counteract the widespread claims of satanic ritual abuse. Each specific group, such as witches and pagans, Ordo Templi Orientis, Crowleyana and Thelema, Qabalists or satanists each have an active media with overlapping contact. Some are the official organs of particular groups, like the *Wiccan* for the Pagan Federation of Great Britain or the *Black Flame*, published by The Church of Satan, and there are literally dozens of magazines and newsletters dealing with witchcraft and the occult being pumped out around the world. It is through these publications that a very substantial measure of underground contact is maintained.

I use the word underground, because virtually none of the occult media is available through normal channels and more often than not, it can only be bought through specialist occult retail outlets or, more generally, by subscription through post office box numbers. It is a simple matter, however, to obtain copies. There are a couple of dozen fairly well known writers in the occult generally, otherwise editors and contributors may often prefer to remain anonymous.

Indeed, the following list of publications represents not merely a fairly typical cross-section of the published material available at the time of writing but also gives a fairly good guide to the diversity of organizations that are sufficiently well established to offer regular magazines or newsletters to their followers, and now operating in Britain or who are in contact with British enthusiasts. These publications come and go, although some have been running for years. They range from expensive glossies aimed at the occult intelligentsia to amateurish home produced desktop publications. Most have a fairly lively following.

WITCHCRAFT

There are three central bodies, the Pagan Federation, PaganLink and the Green Circle which encompass membership by most of Britain's most senior witches. They are active on all fronts of witchcraft and on the whole consist of responsible leaders who are intent on trying to ensure a better public image for paganism, and especially witchcraft, and offer advice and ready contact through a strong and diverse media of magazines. They have no overall control, of course, of any witch coven but they run helplines and advice through confidential telephone numbers. Witches who run into trouble spiritually or with their rituals or spells or who are unable, for example, to disperse malevolent spirits lingering in their magic circles, may telephone for assitance. Witch covens may be set up anywhere without reference to any governing body, so long as the founder is an initiated witch. Groups who specialize in black witchcraft, or other corruptions which lean towards a higher sexual activity than is normally practised, are unlikely to be in touch with the main advisory groupings.

British and American elders of witchcraft are fairly high profile characters within their sphere, often found attending lectures, discussions and festivals throughout these countries. Their levels of activity range from passive pagans more interested in ecology and nature through to the most serious of witches who meet to practise intense ritual, either in their own homes or in some secluded spot in the countryside.

The witch media at the beginning of 1992 included: *The Wiccan*, official organ of the Pagan Federation; *Ace of Rods*, a Pagan contact magazine and listings of events, lectures and news published by Seldiy Bate and Nigel Bourne, in London; *The Cauldron*, journal of the old religions and one of the longest established and published by well-known pagan author Michael Howard from Wales; *Circle and Network News*, pagan views and craft newspaper imported from America; *The Deosil Dance*, for New Age paganism, crystals and clairvoyance from Wales; *O Fortuna*, spiritual and ecological topics with a children's pull-out section published by Seldiy Bate; *Greenleaf*, a magazine for ecological pagans and travellers; *Der Hain*, European nature religions, published in Germany and available in England; *Isian News*, journal of the Fellowship of Isis, an association for mass pagan worship; *Open Path*, journal of the Open University Occult Society; *ORCRO*, published as an Occult Response to the Christian Response to the Occult, London PO Box; *Pagana*, newsletter of MENSA occultists, from the US; *Pagan Funeral Trust*, published for senior citizens and the unwaged,

Oxford; *Pagan News*, newsletter dealing with all aspects of witch-craft and the occult, from Leeds; *Pangryria*, journal of pagan happenings in the Pacific North-West, from Washington; *Pipes of Pan*, pagans for world peace; *Quest*, journal of magic, paganism and witchcraft edited by Marian Green, head of the Green Circle; *Shadowplay*, witchcraft and paganism published in Australia circulated worldwide; *Sirius*, monthly goddess-orientated magazine, published by the Centre of Vesta, Clywd; *Starlight*, pagan voice of Finland, circulated in Britain; *The Vigil*, journal of witchcraft and earth religions, Omaha, Nebraska; *The Web of Wyrd*, The Children of Sekhmet, international witchcraft magazine, published London; *Gates of Annwn*, contact and discussion on witchcraft, published by Beth Thompson, London; *Wiccan Gateway*, witchcraft magazine from Shrewsbury; *Touchwood*, magazine of shamanism, totemism, earth magic 'and kids' bits' published in Tyne and Wear; *Pagan Prattle*, published by a Leeds witchcraft group; *The Open Gate*, published in Bristol; *The Unicorn*, quarterly pagan topics and write-ins, from Hessle, East Yorks; *Silvermoon*, pagan response and views, from London; *Hobgoblin*, pagan arts, from Thorgoland, Yorks.

GENERAL OCCULTISM

The following magazines were from a selection available in England by applications to box number addresses in January 1992. They cover a vast range of lodges and magic groups: *Mercian Mysteries*, occult folklore from Nottingham; *3rd Eye Horror Film Fanzine*, advertised as 'nice yucky photos and vagal inhibiting text' published from Radford, Nottingham; *Lunch*, journal of conscious evolution and forum of new ideas, from Manchester; *Wild Places*, all-round occult magazine produced by Kevin McClure, Austell, Cornwall; *Jezebel*, described as 'a no-holds-barred occult fun and tumble', from Humberstone, South Humberside; *Horus Video*, mouthpiece for amateur/underground film and video producers, from Newcastle; *Wolf's Head*, occult fanzine, from Tewkesbury, Glos; *Peace and Freedom*, New Age magazine from Hartlepool; *Dalriada*, pagan Celtic quarterly, from Brodick, Isle of Arran;

I-Was, journal of 'Arcadian Disturbance', from London; *Revelation*,
New Age occultism, from New Brighton, Wirral; *New Moon*,
Scottish Celtic Norse and Zen interests, published from Glasgow;
Mythos, sci-fi occult fantasy, Bournemouth; *Dark Cycle*, bi-monthly
for occult poets, astrologers, witches and mediums, from Australia;
Earth, bi-monthly paganism and mysticism, from Bradford; *Katherina's Insight*, described as 'compelling read, full of shamanistic
magic, sex etc.' from Doncaster; *the Manifold Path*, general occultism, from Wolverhampton; *Chaos International*, published in London
by the Temple Misanthropy, London Pact of Illuminates, contains
strong and diverse occult material from Qabalah to satanism;
Lightning Flash, Kabbalistic magazine, published from a London
PO box; *Ryder*, 'original and exclusive stories of sado-masochism
and related erotic', from London; *Lamp of Thoth*, self-styled as 'The
UK's most influential occult magazine', from Leeds; *Abraxas*,
published under the auspices of the American Gnostic Church and
its subsidiary the occult fraternal order Ordo Templi Baphe-Metis
(Temple Order of the Knights of Baphomet), from Corpus Christi,
Texas, but deleted from the list of recommended reading by the
editor of a British satanic magazine because its own editor failed
to give assurances regarding content; *Anubis*, German language
occult magazine, imported from Munich; *Aquarian Arrow*, glossy-
covered magazine which often contains material for students of
Thelema, published by The Neopantheist Society of Great Britain,
from a post office box in London; *Aurora*, newsletter of the Arcanum
Camp of Ordo Templi Orientis, Jacksonville, Florida; *Aurora
Borealia*, newsletter of the Nepthys Lodge of the OTO, Edmonton,
Alberta, Canada, but billed as of special interest to students of
other areas of Thelema; *Bahlasti Papers*, Kali Lodge, OTO, New
Orleans; *Baphomet Breeze*, Hermes Camp, OTO, Glendale, California; *Ben Ben*, Bennu Camp, OTO, Maribor, Yugoslavia; *Blado*,
magazine on Western Mysteries and Magick imported from the
Netherlands; *Caduceus*, Babalon Zavidovici, OTO, Yugoslavia;
Journal of Ceremonial Magic from Cincinnati, Ohio; *Critical Mass*,
Athexa Camp, OTO, Morriston, New Jersey; *Electric Fireflies*, 'art
dream-machines and more' from Southport, Lancs; *El Khouariki*,
montage 'magazine of occult and poetic terrorism' published in
Birmingham; *The Equinox*, glossy British Journal of Thelema,

Batcombe, Dorset; *Gnosis*, glossy and expensive imported American magazine published by the Lumen Foundation, 'a journal of the Western Inner traditions'; *Gnostic News*, Gnostic Catholic Church newsletter; *Golden Dawn Supplement*, containing rituals and discussion on this magical order, published by an Oxford group; *Hermetic Journal*, also from Oxford; *In the Continuum*, imported from California and boasts unpublished Crowley items and other Thelemic material; *Ignator*, Derby based New Age magazine of contemporary culture; *Organ*, newsletter of Tahuti Lodge, OTO, New York; *Khabs*, official news magazine of the Typhonian OTO, published in Leeds; *Lashtal*, Evlis Lodge, OTO, Atlanta, distributed by an OTO group in Nottingham; *Mezia*, 'an heretical Journal of the OTO' imported from Spencer, New York; *NW – Northwestern News*, from OTO, Springfield, Oregon; O–2, Ordo Templi Orientis, O–2 lodge OTO, Aachen, Germany; *Oyez*, Heru Ratla Lodge, OTO, Newport Beach, CA; *Pyramid*, Pyramid Lodge, OTO, Lenmore, New York; *Snowflakes Through Strain*, described as 'distinguished by imaginative artwork' published by Doncaster group; *Starfire*, a large and classily produced magazine dealing with the OTO and Thelema, from London, used by OTO hierarchy for international contact; *Starry Wisdom*, newsletter of Esoteric Order of Dagon, London; *Tahuti*, occultism and OTO, from Montmorency, France; *Thelema*, Lodge Newsletter, from Berkely, California; *Waratah Blossoms*, Crowleyana from Glasgow; *Weirdglow*, billed as 'essential reading for those interested in the Nath Community' published in Oxford.

SATANISM AND BLACK MAGIC

Dark Lily, influential and sternly authoritative magazine described as the 'reality of the Left-hand Path' and the 'voice of satanism' published by the Society of the Dark Lily, London box number; *The Black Flame*, official journal of The Church of Satan, published in San Francisco, widely available in England through contact groups and by subscription; *Trident*, official magazine of the Embassy of S.A.T.A.N., which describes itself as 'an alternative choice to the sinister isolationism adopted by pseudo-satanic religions', imported from Panna, USA headquarters of Embasat; *Cry of the Raven*, satanic fanzine and black magic course, imported by subscription from Meredosia, USA; *Fenrir*, 'journal of satanism and the sinister, not for the squeamish', published from Shropshire; *Brimstone*, 'keeps the hellfires burning – we are seeking true initiates who are not too frightened to explore the dark side of nature', Malden, USA; *Daisy Papers*, from the Coven of Daisy, satanic witch organization, based in Columbus, Ohio; *Black Candles*, magazine of the New Temple of Bast, imported from the US; *Nox* No 6, includes selected excerpts from the defunct satanic magazine of the Church of the Final Judgement, *Process* (which some are attempting to revive), from Mexborough, South Yorks.

SELECT BIBLIOGRAPHY

Barton, Blanche, *The Church of Satan*, Hell Kitchen Productions Inc, New York, 1990.

Beyerl, Paul V., *A Wiccan Bardo*, Prism Unity, Bridport, 1989.

Bourne, Lois, *Conversations With A Witch*, Robert Hale, London, 1989.

Cavendish, Richard, *A History of Magic*, Arkana Penguin, London, 1990.

Crowley, Aleister, *The Confessions of Aleister Crowley*, edited by John Symonds and Kenneth Grant, Arkana Penguin, London 1989.

Crowley, Aleister, *Magick in Theory and Practice*, Castle, New York, 1969.

Crowley, Vivianne, *Wicca, The Old Religion in a New Age*, Aquarian, London, 1989.

Farrar, Stewart and Jane, *The Witches' Way*, Robert Hale, London, 1984.

Farrar, Stewart and Jane, *The Witches' God*, Robert Hale, London, 1989.

Gardner, Gerald B., *Witchcraft Today*, Rider, London, 1954.

Gardner, Gerald B., *High Magic's Aid*, Michael Houghton, 1949.

Graves, Robert, *The White Goddess*, Faber and Faber, London, 1946.

King, Francis, *Techniques of High Magic*, Sphere Books, London, 1977.

King, Francis, *Modern Ritual Magic*, Prism Press, Bridport, 1989.

Howard, Michael, *The Occult Conspiracy*, Rider, London, 1989.

Howard, Michael, *Earth Mysteries*, Robert Hale, London, 1990.

LaVey, Anton Szandor, *The Satanic Bible*, Avon Books, New York, 1969.

LaVey, Anton Szandor, *The Satanic Witch*, Feral House, Los Angeles, 1989.

Leland, Charles Godfrey, *Aradia: Or The Gospel of the Witches*, Samuel Weiser, New York, 1974.

Martin, B. W., *The Dictionary of the Occult*, Rider, London, 1979.

Murray, Margaret A., *The Witch Cult in Western Europe*, Oxford University Press, Oxford, 1921.

Sanders, Alex, *The Alex Sanders Lectures*, Magickal Childe Publishing, New York, 1984.

Sanders, Maxine, *The Witch Queen*, Star Books, London, 1974.

Smyth, Frank, *Modern Witchcraft*, Macdonald, London, 1970.

Spence, Lewis, *The Encyclopaedia of the Occult*, Bracken Books, London, 1988.

Suster, Gerald, *Crowley's Apprentice*, Rider, London, 1989.

Valiente, Doreen, *ABC of Witchcraft*, Robert Hale, London, 1984.

Valiente, Doreen, *The Rebirth of Witchcraft*, Robert Hale, London, 1989.

Valiente, Doreen with Jones, Evan John, *Witchcraft, a Tradition Renewed*, Robert Hale, London, 1990.

Wilson, Colin, *The Occult*, Grafton Books, London, 1979.

INDEX